AFTER
THE
STORM

AFTER THE STORM

HOW THE GAA FOUND NEW HOPE

DAMIAN LAWLOR

BLACK & WHITE PUBLISHING

First published in the UK in 2022
This edition first published in 2023 by
Black & White Publishing Ltd
Nautical House, 104 Commercial Street, Edinburgh, EH6 6NF

A division of Bonnier Books UK
4th Floor, Victoria House, Bloomsbury Square, London, WC1B 4DA
Owned by Bonnier Books
Sveavägen 56, Stockholm, Sweden

The publisher has made every reasonable effort to contact copyright holders
of images in the picture section. Any errors are inadvertent and anyone who
for any reason has not been contacted is invited to write to the publisher so
that a full acknowledgement can be made in subsequent editions of this work.

This book is a work of non-fiction, based on interviews about the lives,
experiences and recollections of its contributors. The author has stated to the
publishers that the contents of this book are true to the best of their
knowledge.

A CIP catalogue record for this book is available from the British Library.

ISBN (PBK): 978 1 78530 466 8

1 3 5 7 9 10 8 6 4 2

Typeset by Data Connection
Printed and bound in Great Britain by Clays Ltd, Elcograf S.p.A.

www.blackandwhitepublishing.com

To every GAA man, woman and child who found it tough going during covid. I hope you all found a way back. And that returning to Gaelic Games helped.

In memory of Fr Jimmy Doyle PP, one of life's gentlemen, an accomplished Carlow hurler and footballer and among the greatest GAA stalwarts of them all. Jimmy, who served in Kildare for decades after his ordination, passed away suddenly in October 2020 and we are all the poorer without him.

To the late Ger Gavin from Nenagh, Co. Tipperary, who also passed suddenly in May 2021. He was unwavering in his unshakable commitment to our games. These men left some legacy.

CONTENTS

PROLOGUE

People

The country was living on scraps of hope.

In the darkest of covid times, on the night before she started treatment for Grade 3 Hodgkin's Lymphoma, Marianne Walsh heard a knock at the door. Outside were her friends from the Mooncoin camogie team.

'They pitched together a few bob to buy materials I would need during chemo,' Walsh says. 'A lovely gesture. I didn't know when we would next see each other, with all the restrictions, but I badly wanted to play with those girls again.'

That was the target she set. Marianne started chemo on 12 January 2021 and finished on 15 June. The treatment was gruelling from the first day to the last. Just five months later, however, Mooncoin were crowned county champions and Walsh was voted Kilkenny junior player of the year. They inspired each other. Bravery remained. Even in times of crisis and misfortune.

The pandemic showed Domhnall Nugent that human decency was as powerful as any vaccine. When Antrim won the 2020 Joe McDonagh Cup final, Nugent wrapped his manager, Darren

Gleeson, in a tight embrace and wrestled him to the ground. As a teenager, Nugent excelled in several sports and had the world at his feet before finding himself homeless for a period. He wasn't long out of rehab for drug and alcohol addiction when the virus struck. Counsellors advised him to stay around those who could help, but instead a series of restrictions and boundaries left him facing the terrifying prospect of bearing lockdowns alone with his thoughts. The mind is its own island and can take you to heaven or hell. But Nugent wasn't isolated.

'During the lockdowns Darren was on the blower all the time. On the evening of the final, for instance, he gave me the keys of his car so I could stay away from temptation. When the boys did their thing, I took his car, got a pizza and a coffee. He went all out to ensure I would be okay. Others did the same.'

Covid's storm threatened mass wreckage. People fought to get off ventilators, they lost jobs, the elderly and vulnerable were lonely. Everyone had their own struggles. Indeed, some of the greatest battles were fought within the silent chambers of the soul. But society rallied, too. Just one act of kindness seemed to throw out roots in all different directions. In the toughest of times, it was the power of people that would prevail.

Pandemonium

It was a television show that didn't know when to end. Three very long seasons with unlikely plotlines curving in every direction.

The pandemic killed almost seven million people as it swept across the world, twisting and mutating all the time.

Wuhan, a city of eleven million, was the epicentre of the plague's start. On New Year's Eve 2019, a Chinese government website confirmed the discovery of a 'pneumonia of unknown cause' in a seafood and poultry market there.

The outbreak was rapid and deadly. Over the next three months the coronavirus grew through human transmission, savaged economies, halted international travel and confined people to their homes. It had many faces, which made it harder to limit. We were taken off our tracks and thrust into a time of stillness. The world shut down.

On 29 February, the Limerick hurlers flew back to Dublin airport after a five-day training camp in Portugal. They entered the arrivals hall just as the country was hurtling head-first into the storm. The moment they touched down, Tom Condon, one of their most experienced players, had a dawning realisation that things had changed.

'The first case of covid-19 was found in Ireland on the same day we flew back. Our medics gave us masks and gloves for the airport, although we were the only ones wearing them inside. A group of lads standing around in shorts and GAA gear with masks on – people were looking at us wondering, "What are these lads at?" But in a very short space of time everyone was wearing them. Everything stopped.'

And no entity or business, sporting or otherwise, would remain untouched.

Politics

On 17 March 2020, Taoiseach Leo Varadkar spoke to the Irish nation from a state visit to the White House and confirmed the country was grinding to a halt. Many fresh hells followed in the next three years, including five waves and four lockdowns up there with the most restrictive in Europe.

Varadkar was warned that Irish hospitals could resemble battlefields if he didn't act quickly. In northern Italy images of infirmaries being overrun, bodies being stacked in morgues and exhausted medics being engulfed were captured. Beds were occupied with people in terrifying distress. They gasped for air, clasped at their chests, grasped tubes pumping oxygen into their lungs.

Ireland was desperate to avoid that scenario and it did. But from 2020 to 2022, as the virus recurred in different forms and variants and moved to its own timeline, the country was greatly curtailed.

John Horan was leader of the GAA when covid-19 gripped the nation and there was no presidential playbook to follow. Things evolved rapidly, often in a matter of hours. The association he fronted, like everything else, shut down until it was safe to resume.

With Gaelic Games gone, the rhythm of the Irish summer was broken and there was little clarity on when the tempo would rise again. Deprived of the outlet of sport, a great anxiety prevailed among lots of Irish people.

Within the GAA, there was massive concern too. Finances were in total freefall. The organisation headed for a €34 million loss for the year and its Croke Park staff took a series of wage cuts.

Club games eventually returned in the summer in front of small crowds, but there were insufficient funds to self-finance the 2020 inter-county championships, the jewel in their crown. The Croke Park administration risked sinking into a deep financial crisis, unprecedented in its near 140-year history, if they tried to proceed.

The GAA, the largest cultural and amateur sporting organisation in the world, was at a crossroads and the consequences of not having a championship were complex. No All-Ireland series had failed to be completed since 1888, and 1926 was the last time the football championship was not completed in its calendar year. But many of the organisation's 600,000 members wanted the season to be shelved. With people sick and dying, and hundreds of thousands drawing welfare benefits, life was thrust upside down. Sport was of secondary concern.

The government hinted it would help stage the championships, but with Christmas only fourteen weeks away there was still no firm indication of funding. It all came down to a Central Council meeting on Saturday, 12 September at Croke Park. Horan's phone buzzed in his pocket. It was the Minister of State for Sport, Jack Chambers. The fate of the 2020 All-Irelands hinged on the call.

'D-Day,' Horan admits. 'If we didn't have their financial help, the whole thing was over. The damage we would have inflicted on ourselves in trying to self-finance the championships would have been considerable.'

Chambers confirmed that the government had committed to financial aid. In fact, Micheál Martin, who replaced Varadkar as Taoiseach in June 2020, wanted the GAA to play a significant role in Ireland's fight against covid. He put his money where his mouth was and €15 million was granted to run the competitions.

'I wanted Gaelic Games to stand as a symbol of resilience against the pandemic,' the Taoiseach explains. 'The nation was bowed down because of the virus. We needed to lift people's spirits. They wouldn't be able to attend games, but they could watch on TV. I didn't want 2020 to go down as the year we had no championships. I didn't want that history. In my heart I was saying, "This has to happen." It was almost as if we had caved into this thing if we couldn't have an All-Ireland.'

They didn't cave in.

Instead, the GAA and its players provided welcome distraction, drama and entertainment when the country needed it most. A shaft of light to break the shade.

The virus raged with a furious gust at times, but, like willow trees bending in strong wind, people adapted to every strain it carried. They helped each other. Small acts of humanity shining like sapphires in the dark.

Here are their stories.

1

THE VIRUS AND THE VENTILATOR

NIALL MURPHY AND THE FIGHT OF HIS LIFE

24 April 2020, Belfast

Niall Murphy rolled his head to look sideways and all he could see were guardian angels. Frontline heroes. Nurses, doctors, cleaners and consultants. All gave him a guard of honour as he emerged from a sixteen-day coma. They clapped as he passed in his hospital trolley, and that's when it hit him hard. 'Jesus Christ, it should be the other way around,' he thought. 'I should be clapping them.'

Tears welled in his eyes. He tried to unleash the emotion but couldn't thank anyone because he wasn't able to talk. He had a stab at trying to punch the air, though he didn't have the energy for that either. It took all his strength to raise a thumbs-up to the staff and medics as he wheeled by.

They lined both sides of the corridors at Antrim Area Hospital and cheered heartily. This was a good news story. Early proof the virus could be fought from the brink.

Murphy, a Gaelic Games devotee and chairman of Club Aontroma, the county's official supporters' group, was only forty-three when admitted. He was a son, a husband and a father of three children aged twelve, eleven and seven. But he was also a propelling force for good. A solicitor who had devoted his life to seeking social justice for others. And he had come through the fight of his own life.

That uplifting image of the staff applauding him became an iconic one. It was splashed on several media outlets, as Ireland struggled with the first onslaught of covid, his thumbs-up the embodiment of defiance.

He laughs that the procession from the Intensive Care Unit (ICU) back to the general hospital wards took place on the night of Good Friday of all nights, the anniversary of the historic agreement between the British and Irish administrations on how the north should be governed. As someone entrenched in high-profile criminal trials and civil court cases, often representing victims of the Troubles, the families of the bereaved or the injured, and the loyalist community, the significance of the date simply couldn't be lost.

'Ironic all right.' He smiles. 'But I would have taken it on any day. It was just great to get back to a ward.'

Murphy's release from ICU was both life-affirming and poignant.

'The doctors said it was touch-and-go as to whether I would make it,' he states. 'Obviously I was out of it, totally unconscious, but on 30 March my wife, Marie, received a call from the doctors.' His voice trails off momentarily, as he grapples with the gravity of it all. 'They said: "Marie, your husband may not make it through the night." That was about as shocking a call as anyone could get.'

Symptoms first developed when Murphy, a human-rights activist partner in KRW Law in Belfast, returned from a trip

8

to New York in mid-March 2020. He was there to speak at the Brehon Law Society's annual St Patrick's Day dinner on Tuesday, 10 March and, never a man to take on one job when he could take on three, he had lined up further engagements whilst in the States. One of those was representing Ireland's Future, a group to examine the possibility and viability of a new constitutional united Ireland. Next, there was a trip to Glasgow. He reckons he could have contracted the virus at any time in transit.

Danger didn't strike immediately. He had been looking forward to a huge celebration to mark his club St Enda's success in the Ulster intermediate hurling final, planned for the day after he landed home, but that was shelved due to rising virus concerns.

Instead, hours of consultations and court sittings lay ahead and kept him busy right until Friday evening, when he finally left the office. On the way home he stopped to get a Chinese takeaway for dinner and it was only that evening around 8 p.m. that he began to feel weak. Upon awakening the next morning, he registered a temperature of over 40 degrees and immediately self-isolated, putting twelve days down just grazing on fruit with an appetite for little else.

He drifted in and out of consciousness and recalled his temperature being 'uncontrollable' on several occasions. He didn't receive an assessment, as testing was restricted at that time, but he hardly needed further evidence of having contracted the virus. On 25 March, he plummeted and fell critically ill.

'I felt as though I was drowning. I couldn't breathe. I asked Marie to get me to the hospital as quickly as she could.'

The alarm on the nurse's face when she tested his oxygen levels is something Marie will never forget. He was put on a ventilator minutes after being admitted and became totally incapacitated. That was a severe jolt for his family, but nothing compared to the suffering they would endure over the next two weeks, as they faced up to perhaps the greatest terror of the lot – the unknown. Murphy went into an induced coma, as doctors updated Marie on how perilous the situation was. She looked on. Helpless.

Meanwhile, her husband, blessed with a disposition for unstoppable slugging, proceeded to fight the battle of his life.

As he did, Gerard McNamara, another partner at KRW Law, got working on the concept of 'A letter to Niall'. It involved compiling good wishes and sending them to the Murphy family. McNamara was floored by the responses that poured in from all over the world.

Aside from candles being lit across Ireland, more than five thousand messages were received from the US, Canada, Australia, Europe and Britain. They ranged from ordinary Joe Soaps to renowned public figures such as Tom DiNapoli, the New York State Comptroller, former Senator Edward Kennedy and Trina Vargo, President of the US-Ireland Alliance.

Murphy's friends say he would never differentiate between any of the above and that's what sets him apart. Significantly, both sides of the political divide in the north were represented in the well-wishes, including families that Murphy had previously worked with.

The testimonials gathered played out like a show reel from the tail end of *It's a Wonderful Life*. People supporting a man who had given so much to them and their communities. Murphy feels the prayers worked.

As Easter arrived, with its natural new life and blooming buds, hope filled the air and maybe his lungs too. He found the will to come back from the verge. During Easter week his condition improved, so the doctors turned him from lying on his chest to resting on his back and waited to see if it would help.

It did.

He slowly came out of the coma, improving sufficiently to be taken off the ventilator. It took a while to get his bearings, make sense of what had happened and, when he was finally brought up to speed, he couldn't help but think of his mother, Brigid, and her strong faith. His mam had spent two weeks praying that his bed would be guarded by angels.

'It was too,' he insists. 'Those angels were the doctors, nurses, physios and staff of the National Health Service. Their care helped me survive.'

Others were not so lucky.

Once he began to recover, Murphy let it be known how furious he was with government health officials, berating them for putting frontline workers in the line of fire without sufficient personal protective equipment (PPE), voicing his disgust that nurses had to strike the previous winter for pay parity, that the government had voted against pay rises for NHS employees. He called for an immediate rise and sustainable pay structure to be established and called on the wealthy to pay more tax to fund it. It was one of the first signs that this GAA stalwart, human-rights lawyer, a whirlwind of his local community, was on the road back.

Murphy lives in Glengormley, north Belfast, where he was born in 1977 to parents who were both primary school teachers. The Troubles didn't directly affect them but had a severe impact on their club, St Enda's, or Naomh Éanna, as it is known in the native tongue.

From the late 1960s to the late 1990s, the club was an easy target. Located in a remote spot at the time, in a largely Protestant area, club members were easily identifiable as Catholics. Supporters were encouraged not to walk alone, nor to hold a hurl in their hands. Donning club colours was a complete no-no.

They stuck to themselves but nonetheless suffered greatly with bomb attacks and shootings. Five club members were killed and the club was burnt down thirteen times in the 1970s and 1980s. At a memorial stone to the side of the club's premises, members still place a bunch of yellow flowers each summer to honour those lives lost.

The club's anguish began in 1981 when nineteen-year-old Liam Canning was gunned down by an off-duty Ulster Defence Regiment (UDR) officer. In the early 1990s, sectarian troubles saw a horrific upsurge in violence and, in 1991, the horrific murder of sixteen-year-old Colin Lundy was another tragedy to deal with.

The onslaught continued. In 1992, a gun attack on a packed club was aborted, leaving a car pierced by thirteen bullets. Later that year the clubhouse was burnt to the ground.

Members regrouped and rebuilt it, only for it to be burnt down again in July 1993, with a minibus also set ablaze. In October of that year the club's president, Sean Fox, was murdered by the Ulster Volunteer Force (UVF) in his own home.

In 1995, a booby trap bomb was discovered at the front gate. And in 1997 another club legend, Gerry Devlin, was murdered by the Loyalist Volunteer Force (LVF) at the gates of their premises. Gerry was murdered on the last night of the 'old' club. The first function at the 'new' club was his funeral. At his graveside, friends urged each other to keep the club open. It was what Gerry would have wanted.

They did, but the attacks were relentless. In 2002, the Ulster Defence Association (UDA) murdered another St Enda's member, nineteen-year-old Gerard Lawlor, who was identified as a Catholic by his Glasgow Celtic shirt. But still the club refused to yield. They just wanted to play their native games.

For long periods during 2020 and 2021 that was again denied them, this time because of the pandemic. But when Murphy emerged from hospital and set on the long road to full health, it was a club thriving in all aspects that awaited him. One that caters for a thousand members and recently boasted the mantle of being Ulster intermediate champions in hurling and football.

In the summer of 2021, then GAA president Larry McCarthy officially opened their state-of-the-art indoor facility, Halla Éanna, as well as re-dedicating the Gerry Devlin Park. It was a momentous day. They now have three grass pitches and a £1.8 million hall with no debt – the official endorsement by the president was another seismic moment in their history.

'One of the first things I looked for when I woke up from the coma was how the club was doing,' Murphy, their vice-chairman, says. 'How did we fare without games and interaction during the initial lockdown and restrictions? I need not have worried. They were catering for the community. Delivering groceries, visiting the vulnerable, checking in on others. Keeping the locality going.

'And when games returned and restrictions eased, we couldn't wait to welcome everyone back. We're a four-code club and whereas once we had to call upon under-10 players to help make up an under-16 team, we are now the largest outfit in Antrim, with 998 members. People like Ciaran McCavana,

Dara Woods, JJ Lawell, Stevie Jennings, Kevin Curran and others made that happen.'

Murphy started an Irish language primary school in Glengormley, with just seven pupils. Gaelscoil Éanna now has 230 children and is preparing to extend, with a new £4 million development.

'Every single pupil at the Gaelscoil wears our club colours, bearing our club crest,' he adds. 'Their most formative and fond memories will be on our site. There has been an overwhelming crossover of children at the Gaelscoil to our club and a whole new generation will grow with us, all through the medium of the Irish language.

'All I feel is intense warmth, pride and identity. We have had our past troubles. They tried to burn us down, but we kept rebuilding. We have never lost those who were taken from us and how we looked after our own during the pandemic matters more than any cup or trophy. The moment I was taken off the ventilator I asked for my family. Then I asked for my club.'

The virus took an awful lot out of him. A bear of a man, Murphy lost over two stone during his time in hospital. The medics were concerned enough not to allow him home until he put weight back on. He was specifically put on an intake of junk food.

'See when I was in hospital? Most of that two stone I lost was in body mass and muscle while I was in the coma. I lost a huge amount around my legs and shoulders, and the doctors felt it was a very unhealthy loss. I wasn't getting home until I put weight back on. In the recovery ward they fed me ice cream every morning! On top of that, people were sending me banana bread and cheesecake, and sure I was laid out and couldn't do any exercise, so the weight came back fairly quickly again.' He chuckles.

When he was eventually released back to the homestead, there was plenty to ponder. Contracting the disease totally changed the way he approached life.

'I gained a whole new outlook. From when I contracted covid-19 in 2020 to 2022, I managed to healthily lose three stone in weight. I lost two initially with the sickness, put it all back on with the lack of exercise and rich food I was fed, and probably put on more besides.

'When it all calmed down a little, I knew I had to turn things around. I needed a proper diet and a wee bit more cardio to improve my lung capacity.'

He set to work. His lung capacity went from eighty-four to one hundred per cent. Three times a day, and no more, he sat down to eat. 'I was biblical about it. No snacks, no chocolate, no fizzy drinks, no chips and no shite.'

Instead, his days began with 50 grams of porridge, peppered with some flax seed, strawberries and blueberries. The old lunch was a monster sandwich. The new regimen was the produce of a local fresh food company, a 350-calorie diet of chicken pasta or baby boiled potatoes and green beans.

Dinner was at 6 p.m. and could involve brown rice, chicken or minute steak. For ten weeks, he went at it hammer and tongs on a diet of only 850 kcal per day.

'Our hurling manager, Mickey McCambridge, asked me to join his backroom in 2021. Sure, I couldn't be shouting at lads to run faster if I was carrying timber myself. That was my motivation, and since I lost the weight and got back involved with the team I'm feeling a bit younger too.'

The only obvious reminder of the virus is a numbness in his thigh. Mentally, there was no lingering anxiety from his close brush with death.

'I am a glass half-full sort anyway, but my outlook has been, "Fuck, you have dodged a bullet, you are lucky." I certainly didn't feel, "Why me?" I have four of five female friends who are dealing with breast cancer and those people deserve my support more. I rationalised what happened to me; I know I'm lucky, and I avoided long covid too, which by all accounts is a nightmare. I don't dwell on it. I'm just thankful.'

There are knock-on effects, however, that Murphy does consider. 'Societally, I think there was some collegiality formed during the pandemic, albeit in a socially distanced manner,' he says. 'It makes me think of those great Irish lyrics – "*Ar scáth a chéile*", meaning "united we are strong".

'But there were political missteps, too. Things were not done fast or early enough, and I would apply that more so in the north. Both jurisdictions [the northern and southern Irish governments] didn't cooperate, collaborate or adapt the joint approach that a small island should have taken – just like New Zealand. We should have been able to endure a much less serious pandemic experience, like they did.

'Politically, we were not sufficiently joined up in our approach and I feel the reasons for that were more ideological rather than biological. In my view, the DUP [Democratic Unionist Party] stuck to a Tory ideology, where the strong would survive and let it rip through the herd. That inhibited cross-border communication. There were also times when the southern government didn't apprise Stormont as to their intentions. So neither jurisdiction got it right. That was as much out of political interest as showing an overall genuine concern for the situation on the whole of the island.'

Murphy is also one of the main voices calling for a border poll through Ireland's Future movement. The organisation has the support of high-profile stars such as *Line of Duty* actor Adrian Dunbar, singer Christy Moore and international footballer James McClean.

Ideally, he would like a citizens' assembly to consider what the protocols of a united Ireland would look like, but he maintains that society is well into its first movements towards unification.

'That's down to the economic flow that has happened since Brexit,' he says. 'Stats show that cross-border trade, from north to south and south to north, is up by billions. And capitalism shows that the mercantile class is like a river – it always finds its way, independent of constitutional governance.

'Money finds a way to flow, and we can see plainly that it is flowing on an all-island basis. I believe things will flow constitutionally too. It's inevitable.

'Managing that means we will have to look after every entity: the new Irish, the northern unionists, everyone needs to feel that this is their country. And that identity must be cherished and protected. It might be difficult, but this is what is ahead of us. We will be serious fodder for future historians. I believe the researchers of the twenty-second century will pour over our lives as a revolutionary period and will be enthralled looking at the lives we have led.

'Ireland will be the only primarily English-speaking nation in the EU, and we will be a bridge between North America and the EU. We bear a huge responsibility to manage this safety, but the debate on a united Ireland is a fast-moving one. The trade statistics show that, and I am happy to let those show the way. The constitutional stuff will come in time.'

The virus flattened Niall Murphy. But he rallied, regrouped and went back at full pelt again. His voice, never destined for a backing chorus, was more powerful than ever.

2

STATE OF EMERGENCY

THE GAA – BUT NOT AS
WE KNOW IT

The days didn't matter anymore. They were all the same.

One evening we came home after working. The next morning we were working from home. Shirts, blouses and jackets for the camera – shorts and tracksuit bottoms beneath its glare. In virtual meetings we clicked on mute and forgot to unmute ourselves. We baked banana bread and took virtual quizzes with the family. Walked a lot. Home-schooled. Then sought ways to alleviate the stress of home-schooling. We lost a stone. Or put one on. Or both. Some cherished the chance to leave the rat-race for a while, to stay at home with the family, to get off rush-hour motorways. Others struggled. The virus not only led to an economic shutdown and closed schools, but it resulted in lost livelihoods, lonely hospital deaths, drive-by funerals and depression. For some, idleness was a danger.

The sports sector had its own challenges to contend with. The GAA, normally a mainstay of community and participation, saw its people kept apart. Immaculate pitches lay out of commission behind locked gates swathed in black and amber covid warning signage.

19

In twenty-one years as a full-time administrator, Feargal McGill thought he had seen it all, but there was no comprehending this. The Leitrim man began his career working in the Croke Park media department, advancing to a current role as director of player, club and games administration. That vast range of experience would stand to him as the association navigated its way through some of its most difficult times.

'I remember sitting down in mid-March 2020 in the first lockdown and I still felt that everything would be fine,' McGill recalls. 'The country would respond well, there was no need to pull championship fixtures at that point. By May and June we might be back playing. But as time went on it became more apparent the 2020 season might not get up and running, never mind finished.'

He watched closely as a ripple of concern rolled into a great wave of anxiety.

It was 132 years since the GAA had failed to complete the championships, and that long and proud legacy was one that they wanted to maintain. During the Second World War rationing and fuel shortages had led to the national leagues being suspended from 1941 until 1945. The next significant disruption to the GAA calendar was in 2001, when an outbreak of foot and mouth disease led to a five-week suspension of the league from 25 February to 1 April.

Even with the Easter Rising, the 1916 All-Irelands were played the following year. It took the Civil War to inflict real damage on the association's games, but that was at a time when families were split, never mind clubs and counties.

Now history loomed large again. How could they plan to stage a series of games in 2020 when looking into the future was a futile exercise? It would be a leap into the unknown.

'The pandemic was a black swan event,' acknowledges Croke Park stadium and commercial director Peter McKenna. 'Go back a few years and there had been bird flu, various strains of influenza and SARS. There were a lot of viruses floating, but they didn't travel. But the key date was 12 March, when the World Health Organisation [WHO] announced the pandemic. Suddenly, there was a new language about. The penny dropped for me when Leo Varadkar made his White House address. It was real then.

'It instantly affected the whole country. The health service. Our way of life. For us at Croke Park it was also catastrophic. We're an organisation that distributes all the money it takes in, so there is no point in saying otherwise – fear was the first thing we felt in the early days of covid. Fear that you might get the virus, that your health could suffer badly, and that the country, economy and GAA would lose games, receipts and revenues. That we would be plunged head-first into a colossal recession.'

The GAA's director of communications, Alan Milton, says they stood on the cusp of the unknown. 'A games organisation with no games,' he states. 'This was a scenario touched on during foot and mouth but realistically not experienced on this scale since the Emergency and, before that, the civil strife in Ireland that accompanied the War of Independence and the Civil War.'

McGill feels the GAA's early response to the pandemic was compromised by the fact that no one knew what was coming. 'Science was leading the fight and any move out of lockdown depended on the science,' he states. 'Would we be without activity for one month or two? The consensus was that no one had a clue. Very quickly the thing grew from a worry for the world to being a pandemic. We realised this virus would have a longer impact on us than we hoped. There was a slow dawning of that reality.'

Everything chugged to a halt after St Patrick's Day 2020. League fixtures for early March were postponed. Around that time McGill joined the association's president John Horan and director-general Tom Ryan on a conference call and remembers urging patience before they decided to pull any more scheduled games.

'I wondered if we should wait another few days before making a move. But the lads were decisive on it. My head at that time was still focused on a games programme that I needed to finish. Ultimately, we made the decision to pull those fixtures and there wasn't a ball kicked or a sliotar hit until July.'

The knock-on effect was instant. The organisation's 2019 accounts had made for rosy reading, with record income of €73.9 million, a sixteen per cent increase on 2018's €63.5 million total. Gate receipts rose from €29.6 million to €36.1 million. An additional €20 million was earned in commercial returns, with the Croke Park stadium company also delivering an exceptionally strong performance, bringing in €10.5 million in total revenue, a thirty-one per cent increase on the previous year.

Things were going swimmingly. Crowds were flocking to matches in droves; the league, championship and club series were all proving hugely popular with supporters. Companies and corporate firms were keen to either link up or stay involved with the organisation. Concerts were booked into HQ and, with 84 cents in every euro earned ploughed back into grassroots and other branches of the organisation, every unit could benefit.

'I would say that 2019 was probably our strongest year ever,' McKenna agrees. 'We had great results and there was huge positivity about.'

And then from boom to bust.

Instantly, the organisation's finances were decimated.

At the end of 2020 gate receipts for that year would stand at just €3.6 million, €33 million less than the previous year. Commercial income was reduced to €8.7 million. A 2020 deficit of €34 million was registered, the worst results on record. To add perspective on that, Croke Park stadium lost €10.2 million just one year after it had provided a dividend of €10.5 million to HQ.

That's just the numbers game. The GAA is all about games and members. But play stopped and people remained at home. The cornerstone of the organisation was under attack from all angles.

'Incredible really,' McGill reflects. 'If you told me in the early days of March what was ahead, I would have said it was not possible for the GAA to go through it all and still be the GAA.

'Suspending activity was a seminal moment. Everything stopped. Matches, office work, club committees, training, the whole lot. From ploughing ahead at 100mph to reaching zero, it happened overnight.'

Activity in the association can mean a lot. Like training and games. It also incorporates identity, selling Lotto tickets, fundraising to sustain the club, committee meetings and cups of tea among friends in clubhouses. For many, the social side is vital for their well-being and wellness, essential for strengthening a person's connection to their place.

It was snatched away in a shot.

23

All eyes turned to the top table. As a key figure across many departments and committees, McGill was stationed at the epicentre of their fight against the virus.

It wasn't life or death, but he was thrust into the teeth of a crisis at the same time.

3

GETTING TO GRIPS

THE DOC AND THE GAA'S
FIRST RESPONDERS

On 10 December 2019, Dr Con Murphy closed the door on his GP practice in Mardyke Street, Cork, after four decades of service to the community. It was a tough day. One cloaked in sentiment. As he locked the clinic for the last time, former Tipperary hurlers Pat Fox and Joe Hayes, who had driven down from Cashel, were outside to mark the milestone.

'Joe presented me with the jersey he wore against us in the 1991 Munster final,' Con says. 'It was one of the nicest things ever.'

Not long after the surgery closed, almost a thousand others from around Ireland gathered at Cork City Hall to pay their own tributes to Dr Con. He had probably helped most of them somewhere along the way. One of the country's most venerated physicians and sporting personalities, he was medical advisor to and selector for twelve senior All-Ireland-winning teams. For over forty years, as much Cork as the famous blood-red jersey.

'The Doc' stayed working until he was seventy because he loved it. Retiring from a vocation is no easy thing.

'Emotional,' he says, nodding. 'I found it very hard to stop helping all those families and friends. Luckily, my son, Colm, has a GP practice down the street. We were able to hit a button and send patient details directly to him. And ninety-five per cent went straight down to him. That was good for them, and it was good for me as well.'

Down through the years, Con's days were heady and hectic. Just how he liked them. Mornings began with breakfast at the River Lee Hotel before a gentle amble across the road to the surgery for 9.30 a.m. There he'd stay until about 7 p.m. before heading over to training with the Cork teams. This was the routine from 1976 onwards. Purposeful and joyful.

'I loved every bit of interaction, every day of it,' he asserts. 'I'm a people person.'

But covid-19 quelled that contact and the array of exciting retirement plans he had. On 27 March 2020, the country went into its first full lockdown and within weeks Con went from meeting perhaps a couple of hundred people each day to hardly bumping into anyone. For one so sociable, it was difficult.

'I'd spent my life trying to help people and you don't just turn that off. Even though I retired I was still worried about what the shutdown could do to people's mental health. How it might affect my old patients. It affected me too. I did my best, but it took two years before I felt back to myself. The first lockdown, especially, was tough.

'I had friends at the River Lee who I met every day. People who worked or had their meals there. We loved meeting each other. When Ireland reopened from lockdown, many of them never came back. Whether covid got them or they didn't feel comfortable re-emerging into society, I don't know, but it was never the same afterwards.'

By now, Colm and a good friend of Con's, Dr Aidan Kelleher, had assumed primary care of the Cork hurling and football teams, with the Doc remaining as an assistant to both. When it eventually resumed at the end of the year, the inter-county scene of 2020 didn't lend itself to allowing much contact either. It was a sterile set-up, run off in the strictest conditions to get it completed.

'Players arrived in their own cars, already togged out, and ran straight onto the field,' he says. 'For the first time in nearly half a century, there were Cork players that I didn't know because I was nowhere near them. They arrived, trained and went home. There was no craic, no dressing-room banter. That's what you missed the most.'

Still, it was an outlet all the same.

Off the field, backed by forty-three years of service and professional insight, Con needed a focus too.

'In the first lockdown I tried to meet one person outdoors every day to see if I could help – obviously just in terms of advice only. That was a way I could stay engaged. But you were at home most of the time.

'It was important to try, though. No one knew what was coming next. We were in the thick of the unknown and the impact was huge. I could see straight away that the HSE [Health Service Executive] backlogs of people looking for various treatments were massive. I feared people in rural Ireland, where there is a shortage of doctors, would suffer. Or that people would get depressed.

'That's where sport was important. Sport is a way of life and a sort of escapism at the same time, but it was no longer there to distract you.'

He decided to devote much of his time to charity. His first project was as an ambassador for Cork University Hospital's healthy ageing initiative. The programme highlighted studies of global populations who aged well. Con shared his experiences, and his thoughts were well received.

'Having a purpose, exercising, keeping the mind stimulated, walking and stretching. Cooking. Trying more fish. Good sleep. Those are all needed at the best of times. But especially needed over the past few years.'

As restrictions eased, he staged a golf classic at Fota Island to help raise funds for the hospital. The great and good turned up, including Kerry legend Eoin 'Bomber' Liston, whose team won the event, landing even more silverware to add to his seven All-Ireland medals.

'I rang Eoin to congratulate him a day later, but he joked that he didn't have time to chat – he was too busy bringing the new trophy to the schools around Kerry. I enjoyed that.'

As 2020 and 2021 played out, he noticed how many inter-county retirements there had been right across the country.

'Maybe fellas saw there was other stuff to life than devoting all your time to a county team – especially if there was no chance of winning anything.'

And yet both codes delivered joy and distraction for him in that time. When Cork pipped Kerry in the last seconds of the 2020 Munster semi-final with late drama, Con approached the team huddle and thanked the players for what they had done. For him and the county. And for those in dark places.

He also saw the Rebels land three underage All-Ireland titles as the virus started to clasp the country.

'Those were huge releases and great distractions. But we must stay vigilant. We sometimes thought we had a handle on this virus and then it surprised us again. We were learning from it all the time. And we must stay learning.'

* * *

The trick in that first lockdown was to take a leaf out of Con's book and stay as connected as possible. Clubs ran online skills and drills sessions, featuring ball-wall challenges and keepy-uppies from club members near and far. Social media reconnected the diaspora and when all of that played out, 5km virtual runs, walks and Zoom quizzes were in vogue. It was all a bit of a novelty.

RTÉ and TG4 tried to plug the gaping void by replaying games of yore but nothing could beat live action. Absence certainly made the heart grow fonder. The GAA knew they had to work hard to keep hearts and minds engaged and give people something to look forward to, but it wasn't simple.

'Initially, we were very reactive,' McGill suggests. 'That is natural because the whole world was very reactive. We were waiting for word and guidance from the WHO. The response of Nphet [National Public Health Emergency Team] to the disease had not even formed by then. So we were waiting for someone to tell us what was happening next before we could get a plan together. That meant a huge vacuum of information in April, and we couldn't be proactive because there was too much uncertainty.

'Most people understood this was well above the heads of Croke Park. The truth is that we were waiting for answers too. While there was a massive yearning for games, people also knew there was a serious battle ongoing. They soon stopped caring about what would happen without games because they had bigger worries, like their health or the health of loved ones.

'Because of the love of our games, we generally can't see the wood for the trees, but this was one occasion where people knew what was happening was much bigger than any sporting organisation. The early questions about returning to play stopped. People were more worried about when they could leave their house.'

At the end of April 2020, seven weeks into the lockdown, it became apparent that the world couldn't live with such stringent restrictions forever. There was going to have to be a way back at some stage and the GAA had to fix their coordinates on some point down the road.

'With that in mind, John Horan put together an advisory group to assess the information that was coming out from world health sources, advising how people could live through this pandemic,' McGill says, picking up the story. 'With such data emerging, John knew the spotlight would soon be on us. He may even have been ahead of the government at that stage, with his implementation of a review group.'

The first meeting of the GAA's covid-19 advisory group was held in mid-May and featured Horan, McGill, Tom Ryan and representatives of the Camogie Association and the Ladies Gaelic Football Association.

The Ulster Council's Stephen McGeehan was an essential member, as his work was spread across two jurisdictions, north and south, with the north falling under the governance of the Northern Ireland Executive and the south guided by the Irish government.

'It was crucial to have Stephen on it,' McGill says. 'It was fine for the twenty-six counties to work to a GAA guideline, but it had to work in the six counties as well. We also had some of our lead medics who'd helped us over the years, including Dr Pat O'Neill, Dr Kevin Moran and Dr Sean Moffat.'

Their first meeting underlined how, even though they had highly respected health professionals and safety specialists, more expertise was needed, specifically around infectious diseases. That's where Professor Mary Horgan came in. A world-renowned expert in that area, Professor Horgan worked on the covid-19 ward at Cork University Hospital throughout the pandemic and later served on Nphet. Her late father, Declan, was one of the founders of Bord na nÓg in Kerry and the family was steeped in the organisation. When the GAA came calling, she was keen to help.

'The fact that the professor has such a strong connection with us, and eventually ended up on Nphet, meant that she became a significant link for us. No one will mind me saying that she was the key member of our advisory group. She is one of the top infectious disease experts not only in Ireland but in Europe too. Along with the others, she volunteered her time, even though she was so busy with work and other committees. They all freely gave their time and expertise. The strength of our association really is incredible.'

* * *

Whilst the administration got to grips with the dynamic new world, grassroots reverted to doing what they do best – helping others.

The GAA is unique in that it is entrenched in every community in Ireland. Across the first weeks of the disease's spread that network was called upon. Twenty thousand volunteers from 1,600 clubs supported 35,000 people with the delivery of meals, collection of essential goods and other services. An alliance with retail giants SuperValu, a sponsor of the football championship, helped bring food to the vulnerable.

'They wanted to know what they could do to help in a practical manner to service people who were cocooning,' Peter McKenna explains. 'They wanted to especially help old people and the vulnerable, who needed basics like food and medicine delivered.'

The plan was simple but effective. The GAA could hit every corner of the land and local knowledge would detail who most needed help. SuperValu agreed to take payment details from customers over the phone once deliveries were complete.

'I think the association played a leading role in the early stages, with services to vulnerable people,' Alan Milton says. 'That prompted necessary discussions about insurance, vetting and best practice around entering people's homes. Much of this was new territory for our members. We liaised with numerous government agencies that we would rarely encounter and what we saw was an acceptance that the GAA was able to command the attention of a cohort that the government was finding it hard to communicate with.'

In that regard, McKenna contacted the HSE to see how both organisations could combine effectively to help the frontline fight.

'We set out the first drive-in testing centre in the country at Croke Park and I will never forget when it opened. The young nurses and doctors came to Croke Park, had their breakfast and walked out the back of the stadium in their PPE gear. It brought the reality home that we simply had no idea how infectious this virus was.'

Days were spent liaising and exploring other areas where the organisation could offer help.

'Our event management team planned in terms of how we could use the stadium to help. But one of the more chilling parts of the pandemic – and thank God it didn't arise – was that if infections went out of control the HSE would need far more bed capacity.

'We offered the Hogan Stand and other big spaces in the stadium as potential field hospitals,' he reveals. 'It made sense with the space, the number of bathrooms and kitchen areas. It was surreal to have conversations and make plans to turn the stadium into a field hospital, but they were not normal times.

'From there, we moved out to Thurles and Cork, with big clubs across the country also providing test centres. Our grounds are owned by the GAA and 800,000 members nationwide. With Croke Park, it was not my gift to give the stadium over; it was my duty.'

In July 2020, McKenna signed a deal with the Royal College of Surgeons Ireland (RCSI) to enable medical students to continue their education in a safe environment at Croke Park as the pandemic raged. More than 650 students used the facilities to continue their learning at a safe physical distance in smaller learning communities, with students gaining access to study spaces, restaurants and other amenities there beyond teaching hours.

In December 2020, the stadium facilitated the courts service to hear criminal trials, which helped clear backlogs that had developed due to restrictions.

This was the business side of things – practical alliances that could help and keep the stadium ticking over at the same time; but, as McKenna points out, the response was heavily focused around its people.

4

MAKING ALL THE
RIGHT CALLS

DAVID BRADY AND HIS
LOCKDOWN OUTREACH

Seamie is Kerry to the bone. He lives remotely, in an unchanging landscape where it would be rare to have anyone wandering the roads or hills day or night. Soft contours are in scarce supply and instead it's the odd house that breaks up the rugged terrain.

The loop of an empty day is tough going. At night it can constrict you, making a world of difference between solitude and loneliness.

One Friday night late in 2020, in the thick of another yawning lockdown, Seamie heard his phone ringing. It was a number he didn't recognise but he answered it all the same. On the other end of the line, David Brady introduced himself.

'Jaysus, I know the voice,' Seamie replied. 'Who put you in contact with me?'

Seamie's daughter had touched base with Brady on Twitter weeks earlier, wondering if he would mind checking in on her dad, something the kind-hearted former Mayo footballer had taken to doing during the pandemic. Brady replied that it would be no problem, but such was the volume of call requests logged in his diary, it might take a while.

It took a bit longer than expected.

'You probably don't know what happened so,' Seamie carried on. Just two days earlier, with the virus hurting the elderly and vulnerable around the country, his long-time partner had been buried. 'You're calling me now, as I'm sitting down doing a crossword and the pencil in my hand is the only company I've had in the last forty-eight hours,' he said quietly.

For once, words didn't come easy to Brady. 'Here was this man, on his own in the depths of lockdown after suffering a huge loss. The people he loved were protecting him by staying away, trying to contain the spread of the virus. The pencil was all he had. I wasn't the better of that for some time.'

Yet Seamie wasn't feeling sorry for himself. He was quite prepared to use that pencil of his to map out a new future. Once he was given the opportunity.

'It was remarkable how he kept his spirits high,' Brady remarks. 'I can't imagine just how lonely he was, but he didn't let it show. We chatted for ages and as we finished up he said he'd send me "a nice book in the post". One that I could learn something from.'

A week later it arrived. A chunky chronicle too big for the letterbox, centred on the greatest Kerry footballers to ever lace up a pair of boots.

'No shortage of class down there. It was full of stuff about Moynihan, Jacko, the Bomber.'

The 2020 All-Ireland football final between Dublin and Mayo took place soon after. Working in a media capacity, Brady was one of the chosen few to attend the closed-doors decider. He remembered how Seamie loved to collect match programmes and, though the 2020 programmes were a collector's item, as rare as hen's teeth, he managed to nab one and post it south.

A Christmas card arrived from Kerry in response, enquiring about Brady's family. Between them they kept An Post busy. Two strangers who had never met, connecting during the pandemic. Bound by their love of the GAA.

* * *

Brady had wanted to help people during that time, but just didn't know how.

'I was feeling inadequate, to be honest. I work in the pharmaceutical area and saw the pressure my friends on the frontline were under. I wondered if I could do anything at all to help. I was thinking of maybe volunteering for the test-and-trace system. But then one evening it all fell into place.'

Over Easter weekend 2020 Brady checked his Twitter account and found a direct message.

'From a lad called Kevin Byrne. His father, Tom, came from Swinford but had lived in Wicklow for decades. Kevin and his sister were isolating to protect their dad, which meant he was alone. Kevin asked if I would mind ringing Tom for a quick chat about Mayo.'

Asking Brady to talk football is about as taxing as seeking contrition from a priest for a white lie. He instinctively dialled the number in front of him.

Ireland was shut. The national mood was raw and uncertainty was rife. Tom, a sixty-two-year-old farmer, was in self-isolation and not mad about this new normal. After a few rings, he picked up.

'Tom, this is David Brady. I played football for Mayo for fourteen or fifteen years. I hear you're mad into it.'

Silence.

A few more seconds.

And then: 'Is this a skit?'

'Nah, 'tis not a skit,' Brady replied. 'Your son, Kevin, gave me this number and asked if I'd have an oul chat with you.'

Good enough.

Off they went. Along the by-roads of Tom's life and times. Up through highlands of happier times and down through more testing territories. The chat swung any old way. How he ended up in Wicklow, how he became a farmer. How he bought six heifers off a man though he had no field for them.

Brady knew instantly that Tom was a good skin.

'Well, he was out herding cattle for an elderly neighbour when he answered the phone so that was a good sign,' he surmises.

It was a eureka moment. Brady realised this was how he could make a difference. He began making calls every day. By 2022, he was gunning for a small stake in Vodafone, such was the traffic directed through his phone.

'Calls to every corner of Ireland and beyond. Manchester, London, Liverpool, New York, Boston, Minneapolis, Chicago, you name it. The message was always the same. "David Brady here. Used to play for Mayo. How are you keeping? Would you be up to talk a bit of GAA?"'

Half the time football didn't even come into it. Once Brady hears the voice at the other end of the line say 'Wait 'til I tell you', he knows he is sucking diesel.

'The longest call lasted one hour and fifty-two minutes. At the end, the man I was talking to became flustered because we hadn't even mentioned GAA.'

As he worked the phones and listened intently to folk relay their life and times, he ran up a seven-week excess of call requests.

'Mostly, people just wanted someone to talk to. Or someone who would listen. They know me from football, and probably knew that I would talk for Ireland, but I learned to listen too, that was a very important lesson for me. I've had some real emotional and personal chats. Those people transported me back in time. One man brought me to the 1935 All-Ireland final and recounted it blow by blow. Sure, it wasn't about the match at all. He was more animated describing how his dad had brought him to the game. It was just a chance to reminisce about his father. That's the truth of it.'

Others didn't spare him. One assassin had no bullets left by the time he finished peppering Brady over mistakes he had made in the 2004 All-Ireland final – another day when the Promised Land proved to be a mirage for Mayo. The man was eighty but he could still line up a target. Sulphur hung in the air for a while after that call.

A fella in Kiltimagh randomly blurted out Brady's date of birth at the start of their chat because he remembered hearing it on Mid-West Radio previously. One Dublin supporter gave him hell for Mayo's commandeering of Hill 16 in 2006, when the Mayo panel and management marched like soldiers on a mission up to Dublin's spiritual home and started to warm up in front of them, forcing the displaced Dubs out of their natural habitat.

'I got another right doing for that.'

Brady's network of requests grew via Twitter, an unpleasant, knuckle-rapping podium on the finest of days, but sometimes a stage for unparalleled unity too.

At the height of lockdown, the Ballina man, domiciled in Dublin with wife Liza and their two kids, Hannah and Luke, was making over twenty calls a day to people who were cocooning.

'I came off that first phone call with Tom on a pure high. I was doing something small to help others. Meanwhile, Tom was helping his own neighbour with cattle. A sort of a multiplier effect. I got more out of it than anyone. I saw what the GAA was really about. As a Mayo football man, people try to define you, whether you like it or not, by the loss of several All-Ireland finals. But I learned that it's not about what you've won but where you have come from. The GAA is not just the Croke Park administration; it is a local community. I rediscovered how important it is across the world, both from a cultural and holistic point of view. It's not about the game played last week; it's about looking forward to the next one, helping your own people, reinforcing where you are from.

'Without games, there are no conversations or memories. So matches are important. But we are about way more too. Every last person I called, no matter what part of the globe they lived in, their minds rambled back to their own home, village, club. The parish they came from. Their stronghold. What poured out of elderly people when I spoke to them was the power of the local community.'

He tears up slightly as he winds the tape back on those chats. 'Some have since passed on, but if they even got those few minutes to recall their life stories it was all worthwhile.

'Christ, it's mighty. No creed, race, colour or religion matters, from what I can see. You are welcomed. The GAA is not about a game, it's a life story. Every conversation told a life story.'

Brady offers a few more. There was a man from Longford who spoke to him on the 25th anniversary of his wife's passing. 'That man was left with three small kids after his wife was killed off a bike and said he would never forget what the local community did for him. First, they gathered around him, and when time passed, they offered a sense of purpose.

'They brought him down to the club and he started off helping with water for teams. A few years later he was elected club chairman. He told me the GAA saved him.'

Paddy Prendergast passed away at the end of September 2021, aged ninety-five. Paddy played full-back on the last side from Mayo to claim Sam Maguire honours when they beat Meath in Croke Park in 1951. He was high on Brady's list of people to call.

'Paddy was living in Tralee, but the lovely thing is that Aidan O'Mahony, a garda and former Kerry footballer, was already calling to see him. Aidan was some player, but he's an even better man.'

There was a ninety-seven-year-old from Carlow in an old folks' home in Borris. Brady reckons this man knew his football better than any other he spoke to.

'We started our call on FaceTime. I rang the reception of the nursing home and his carers brought the mobile down to him. I'd say technology didn't interest this man one bit because I ended up looking into his eardrum for 40 minutes as we chatted it out. He has sadly passed since.'

The experience taught Brady to be thankful for the good times, learn from the hard ones and take the knocks as they come.

'And they do come. No one I spoke to had plain sailing in life, but they just got on with it. There's a lot to be taken from that.'

A Kildare farmer told how if you looked six fields over to the left and six fields over to the right there was not sight of life nor a household. Those who did live beyond that were not of his acquaintance, although he would have known their families going back decades.

During covid, however, the new generation of dwellers started showing up with groceries and messages, leaving them on the farmer's doorstep, checking to see if he was okay.

Up north, a man recounted how he had been contacted by a local team in the thick of the restrictions. A team with whom he had trained at minor level twenty years previously. They never forgot him.

'The conversation began with how they had thought enough of him to reach out two decades on,' Brady says. 'By the end of it, he was telling me he was gay! Half the time you didn't know where the calls would take you, but I hung on every word of them.'

5

THE IRISH ABROAD

NEW YORK STATE OF MIND

A fair chunk of Brady's requests came from expats in New York.

The Irish have always held a tight connection with the place. After the 1845 famine nearly one million emigrants came through the port there. Irish New Yorkers once accounted for almost one-third of the city's total population and still make up five per cent of its inhabitants. Plenty of them would have made the trip to Gaelic Park in April 2020 for the exiles' clash with Galway in the Connacht senior football championship, a perennial western fixture that has always brought the Irish together, connecting veteran settlers with fresher generations. Much of the time it's an occasion first and a game second, but this long-established ritual paused for 2020 and 2021 as the city ground to a halt.

The undocumented Irish felt the strain more than most in that time.

'Pretty soon after the pandemic began, we started to see the effect it was having on the Irish here,' New York GAA president Joan Henchy remembers. 'So many of our people work in the hospitality business and thrive with their warmth and personality, but they all lost their jobs. Hundreds and thousands more worked as home helps and community aids, but with families now staying at home themselves they were no longer needed. It was absolutely devastating for our people, who are still not over it. We saw extremes. Everything from poverty and loss of income to domestic violence. It was frightening. That's the only word for it.'

Henchy becomes emotional as she recounts how a city that never sleeps suddenly slipped into a slumber.

'Like, it's New York! New York never stops. But the whole city shut down. It's still surreal to think that.'

Along with the GAA board, four other Irish organisations, including the Aisling Irish Centre, Emerald Isle Immigration Center, New York Irish Center and the United Irish Counties, joined forces to form a collective fundraising effort. It was called Sláinte 2020 and its aim was simple: to assist the Irish community in the tri-state area during the crisis.

The machine quickly swung into operation. The New York footballers and team management, led by Galway's All-Ireland-winning hurler, Johnny Glynn, completed a thousand-kilometre run within the allowed radius. They raised $38,890 (just over €35,000).

They helped on the frontline. Team selectors Dermot York and Cormac McCormack prepared and delivered meals to the staff of Lenox Hill Hospital. The meals took hours to assemble but each day nurses were served fine, home-cooked cuisine. York wasn't allowed into the building because of the virus, so instead called ahead, dropped the food outside and went on his way again. He didn't know any of the nurses or staff there; he was just determined they would have one decent meal each day. As the weeks passed, he began enquiring what their favourite dishes were and took orders. It was like a virtual menu service.

With each delivery, York left a hand-written note encouraging them to keep going. He didn't know it at the time, but his kind words fuelled the weary nurses to get to the end of a shift. They were often in tears at his thoughtfulness.

New York football manager Gerry Fox also played a blinder in helping to feed staff in four hospitals between New Jersey and the Bronx. Meanwhile, Rockland GAA arranged a food-drive for those most in need; and New York Celtics brought food to the staff of Lawrence Hospital, their juvenile members designing posters thanking the hospital staff for their work.

But the Sláinte 2020 initiative and the New York GAA project didn't just focus on helping frontliners. They put a huge emphasis on looking after their own too. Sláinte's motto – '*Ni neart go chur le chéile*', 'No strength without unity' – was a fitting creed.

It was a symbolic time in general for the association there. In February 2020, Larry McCarthy made history by being elected fortieth president of the GAA, the first-ever overseas candidate to hold that office. The Bishopstown man, who would replace John Horan in 2021, won an All-Ireland club football title with Thomond College in 1978 and worked as a teacher in Dublin before emigrating to the Big Apple in 1985 to do a master's degree. He worked as a lecturer in sports management at Seton Hall University in New Jersey and his election was a massive boost for New York GAA, a shining reflection of their efforts over the decades – work that was never more important than now, as the members of the Irish community fell into need.

'Take the delivery of groceries, doing runs for the elderly and the community – that's who we are.' Henchy shrugs. 'That was no big deal. There's no better organisation in the world than ours to look after its own, I'm convinced of that. But the additional assistance our members offered during covid will never be forgotten. They helped feed families and keep them together. What better legacy could you ask for?'

She was director of operations in the fight, both on and off the playing fields. 'On the field we managed just a condensed championship at the end of 2020 and progressed to both a league and championship in 2021 and 2022. But the whole thing of running games programmes in that environment was a frigging nightmare.

'We often have excessive heat out here, but protocols still had to be strictly observed. Our players didn't always like change, but they complied because they understood the reasoning behind it. We didn't drink out of someone else's water bottle. We didn't clamour into dressing rooms on top of each other. Small things added up and we kept the virus at bay within our own community. We had just two recorded cases during the games' programme of 2020 and none in 2021.

'Despite the misinformation and the fake news, there was a huge take-up of the vaccination programme. Out of ten clubs we surveyed, eight reported that one hundred per cent of their membership were vaccinated. The other two reported a seventy-five per cent take-up. Croke Park allowed us to follow our own mandates according to the state and federal guidelines, and that was significant too.'

Away from the fixtures and the games, Sláinte 2020 raised more than $500,000 in the first three months of the crisis, with thousands of beneficiaries, lots of them under the age of eighteen. That money helped pay for rent, food and medical bills, or was used to help cope with the cost of unemployment.

One message left for the organisation read: 'Thank you from the bottom of my heart and my two kids, you have brought me hope. I felt so alone and so far away from my family . . . this has helped me immensely. You have not only helped but you have made me feel that we are not alone. From a very emotional Kildare mammy, overwhelmed with gratitude.'

They tried to keep the submission process simple. It involved identifying which of the five Irish organisations the applicants were affiliated with. Most were of GAA stock and so came under Henchy's watch. It was complex. Sensitive data pertaining to their legal status or otherwise in the US had to be gleaned.

'Seeing young families struggle was the most upsetting,' Henchy says. 'A lot of people were saying, "Hey if they are undocumented, it's their own fault." But it wasn't. The option to become documented in the US is just not here. Our immigration system is broken. I've been with the Irish reform movement for thirty years and there has been no change. For many, there is no pathway to gain citizenship or status.

'Most undocumented Irish here are paying taxes. They have their own business and employ people. They have American-born kids and give back so much to the community. They are willing to pay back-fees to the US government. But the option to become documented is not an accessible one.

'I know we are no different to any other nationality, but, on the ground, we are so accepted here. Too well accepted almost, because people seem blind to the plight of the Irish immigrant status. They mainly see us as white, English-speaking, hard-working – and see us easily blend in with society.

'We're not seen as vulnerable. Our men, women and children fully participate in society, they are constantly putting back into the economy, and they just want to make a life here. But it appears there are no deals to be done,' Henchy adds.

She knows natives who returned to Ireland during the pandemic and reckons they have little chance of getting back to the States, even if they wanted to.

'From what they report back it's not easy to re-establish residency in Ireland either because there are layers of bureaucracy. You can't just walk into a bank and open an account; you need a home address and a utility bill proving you live there. And the availability of housing at home is low, with the rent sky high. Insurance is so costly: we are hearing of all these issues from friends who have moved back. But they had no choice. Their lives in New York ended when the pandemic hit, with jobs lost in hospitality, construction and home aid.'

Henchy has the perspective of someone who left Ireland during the recession years of the 1980s when the government, she says, were almost giving you extra dole money to get you out of the country.

'What happened this time was that the rug was suddenly pulled from under the feet of so many. There was no sense, no rhyme or reason to it. We heard about the virus one day and the next New York shut down and an entire way of life with it.

'Irish bartenders, waitresses, hotel managers, builders – they suffered so much. Girls working as nannies, home-help aids, companion aids, they all lost their jobs.'

The state's covid benefit scheme only helped those paying taxes, but Henchy points out it was far more multifaceted than that.

'No doubt about it, some people learned that they should have been putting money away for tax purposes and should have been paying something over the years – but a huge number were doing all of that and still had no benefits. We had people here on legal and valid visas who were not eligible to draw virus or unemployment payments.

'They could get a stimulant check, but even as taxpayers they were not eligible for unemployment benefit. If they drew welfare, the narrative was that they could potentially never get visas again. That was a Trump policy. That was the system.'

But knowing that she and the other organisations could help made a real difference. The administrators even left their personal numbers available for people to call any time of day or night.

'From mass unemployment to single moms with no support trying to raise a child, we saw it all. Another girl was the victim of savagery, domestic violence and abuse. There were cases where we had to reach out to counsellors at the Aisling Centre or Pieta House, if we thought further care was needed.'

Calls came round the clock. A wide checklist of fears centred around Medicare, bills, the process of legalisation, being undocumented, whether they would meet the threshold for benefits – everyone had a different concern.

The aftershock was significant. The hospitality sector, once an open door for every Irish man, woman and child who arrived at JFK or Newark, is no longer an automatic route to pursue.

'What a learning that was,' Henchy says. 'I have seen so many of our people leave that sector to go back into offices and construction. They are taking a massive drop in money and salary, but what they have instead now is consistency, a job that starts at 7 a.m. and finishes at 3 p.m., or else the stereotypical 9-to-5. There is no overtime, no plámásing over a counter and getting $20 in tips in a bar or restaurant. But it's steady work. That's all people want now.'

Several people who received aid from Sláinte found their feet again and quickly sought out New York GAA to give something back, whether it was helping on gates for matches, doing fundraisers or donating money. Henchy is proud of that. She senses the bond among the Irish who have remained in the city is stronger than ever.

'Once we got past the ease and accessibility of having a Zoom meeting and prioritised human interaction again, people were just overjoyed to see each other, to be back playing games and be among each other.

'Life is slowly moving on. We are fiercely protective of each other now. We always were, but the sense of identity, of being Irish and of being part of something, is more significant than it ever was. The pandemic hit hard, but I think it has reinforced who we are as a society.'

It's more than twenty years since Henchy took the first steps into administration, helping the Kerry club in New York. Along the way, in 2019, she shattered a glass ceiling to become the first female leader of their county board.

At the start of lockdown she often confided in her husband, Brendan, and two daughters, Tara and Shauna, her fears at the magnitude of the task ahead. She wondered if a two-decade-long slog to help the community had culminated at the worst possible time.

Turns out New York GAA had the right person in the right place just when she was most needed.

London Balling

London senior football manager Michael Maher admires the vitality of New York and what it stands for. He spent three years trying to instil new life and similar values into his own set-up.

'Most people wouldn't have an idea what goes into playing for London,' Maher reckons. 'You give over your life to play for the team. On a typical day you'd go from Dublin to Kilkenny in the time it takes our lads to get just twenty miles across city traffic just to go to training. But they give it all they can. And I'm really proud of them.'

Trying to hold the threads of his squad together whilst implementing a philosophy during three interrupted seasons was tough. But not having a game of note for twenty-three months and enduring a seven-hundred-day break without a competitive outing was torturous.

'It was gutting, frustrating. I was climbing the walls, to be truthful about it,' he admits.

Imagine a creative director putting together a hungry new cast, honing them over four months on stage only to have the show pulled as the curtain was about to lift. That's what it was like for Maher, who had a home-grown, holistic project underway when Gaelic Games shut down.

In Ireland, hints of hope flickered across parts of the 2020 and 2021 seasons, allowing for the resumption of training and games once the public-health situation was stable. There were no such glimmers for London, however. They were bereft of any action and consigned for two years to a halfway house, neither here nor there.

Their final pre-pandemic outing came against Wicklow in Division 4 at McGovern Park on 29 February 2020. They didn't play again until 29 January 2022.

'One minute I was on the phone to my liaison officer, changing names on flights as we prepared to travel over to Dungarvan to play Waterford in our next game in the 2020 league,' Maher recalls. 'The next we went into a deep freeze. I turned on the RTÉ News and saw Leo Varadkar address the nation on

St Patrick's Day. I knew then we wouldn't be seeing action any time soon.'

He tries to see the logical side of it all. In January 2021, London had the highest daily death rate in the world, according to figures collated by an Oxford University research platform. By the early stages of 2022, it was no better – the UK had 18.9 million cases and 160,000 deaths. Due to those numbers, quarantine restrictions and their geographical location, London simply had to stay on the sidelines as GAA life restarted back in Ireland. Maher's squad was the only one across the four divisions who didn't see any further action in 2020, nor league or championship in 2021. There wasn't much anyone could do about it.

'You have to be realistic,' Maher admits. 'The NHS and the government here faced a big struggle for a long time; it was a time of crisis. Sport was not a priority. Even when games and events did begin to re-open, flights to Ireland were still not allowed, for instance. That confounded our hopes of getting a game in 2021.

'We would have loved to have been part of it, but in fairness Croke Park made us aware of every consideration and challenge all the way through. Realistically, there was no chance of us featuring in either of those two seasons. Frustrating, but you learn to live with it.'

They had grand plans. Players outside of the normal pool were earmarked, London even found themselves competing with the likes of Harlequins Rugby to identify new talent and new structures were harnessed. They were thinking outside the box.

Just as well. It was the end of 2020 when clubs in London finally received the green light to resume contact training, months after Irish units were back. But two lost seasons meant a drain of players. Ten of the 2020 squad had returned to Ireland.

Trying to maintain conditioning levels for a team devoid of action for so long was another headache. Yet Maher knew the day would finally come when they would have to dust down the cobwebs and thrust themselves into a compact and condensed fixture calendar.

A PE teacher with a background in sports science and physical activity, he had his team ready for that day and enhanced by new levels of conditioning. They stuck with his policy of developing native players. They had thirteen Londoners in their squad when life resumed; two more from the under-17s panel were marked out for development.

'It is so important that we build from within,' Maher feels. 'That's the future. The last two managers, Paul Goggins and Ciaran Deeley, started that policy and the pandemic gave me time to draw up more structures for players aged fourteen and upwards to keep developing. The goal is to have an under-20 team and a homegrown junior team, ensuring a pathway and consistency in the journey towards being a senior player.'

Hailing from south London with a Kilkenny and Kerry heritage, he wants to use his term to ensure that those like him, with Irishness in their blood, get the chance to play Gaelic football at school or community level. If things are right, they won't have to depend on visitors or floating footballers coming over from Ireland for short stints.

He knows this template can work. Working at St Paul's Academy in south-east London, where students predominantly hail from African, Portuguese and Brazilian backgrounds, Maher assembled a side to make up the bulk of the South

London under-14 team some years back. They landed six All-Ireland Féile titles on his watch.

In 2019, a team mainly containing players from African backgrounds beat Galway giants Corofin and Kerry champions Austin Stacks on their way to the All-Ireland Féile Division 1 final. Eventually, they went down to Dublin giants Kilmacud Crokes.

But while Maher could no longer oversee the upcoming fixtures, he looked on as the county's senior hurlers and footballers made an impact in the community, fundraising for the London Irish Centre, located in Camden, which supports elderly and vulnerable Irish people, especially those living alone.

During restrictions they provided food parcels twice a week, hot meals to people's homes three times weekly, a health and well-being advice line, and made phone calls to the elderly to check in on them.

These activities took place around early May 2020, when the footballers should have been hosting Roscommon in the annual Connacht Championship fixture.

'The biggest game in the London calendar,' Maher acknowledges. 'A huge day for everyone, no matter who we play. A guaranteed five-thousand crowd. And for the players who travel hours on end for training, that day is their reward. These guys get public transport across the city just to train. Their slog starts in November and goes right through until the end of the league. There is a lot of unseen work to prepare for that championship day.'

Without that landmark, they could only prepare for the future. And when games came thick and fast again in 2022, it was very intense very quickly. Two nights a week training and a match at weekends, meaning planes, trains and automobiles for a trip to Ireland.

'We're not like the other counties,' the manager points out. 'When we travel for a game, it's for a whole weekend. An early flight on a Saturday morning and not back home until Sunday night. All in it together. You'd really have to want to be there. We really only have each other.'

Out of a thirty-two-man squad, only thirteen remained from 2020. They had rebuilt on the hoof.

Against Carlow in the last weekend of January 2022, the boss gave nine players their league debut. They fell 10 points behind but dug out of that deep hole to win. Next, they beat Waterford, then Leitrim. After three rounds they were top of Division 4.

It was the first time they had ever won back-to-back games. They pushed hard for promotion, only tailing off near the end of the campaign. In the championship they only lost out to a late goal from Leitrim and set their sights on the Tailteann Cup.

They were back in the thick of it again.

'There's a long road ahead of us, we know that. But look, at least there's a road,' Maher acknowledges. 'We didn't have one for two years.'

6

THE WAY BACK

A WELCOME RETURN TO PLAY

In mid-July 2020 confirmation came that games would resume in Ireland.

Pressure had been building to re-open club grounds and let players into fields for a puck or kick around, even a socially distanced chat. Missing that sense of belonging was tough.

A debate over people's wellness and well-being developed too, but HQ strictly adhered to public-health guidelines both north and south of the border. Their covid-19 advisory group worked in graduated fashion, taking guidance from the road maps of the respective governments.

A significant update was expected from the southern government by May, but with the very slow downward movement of the 'R' rate (rate of infection), there was no immediate sign of restarting games at that point.

The initial 5km boundary restriction put on hold any prospect of opening clubs up for small training pods, though walkways were made available at designated times for locals. There were numerous variables and uncertainties. It was messy.

Players began training in small clutches of under four people in local parks and public places, but with people still dying and falling seriously ill, the Croke Park administration didn't veer from their stance.

The virus was having the greatest impact on people aged sixty-five or over, with almost ninety-two per cent of confirmed deaths occurring in this age group from 11 March to 15 May 2020. It was one thing lobbying for local clubs to be re-opened, but could you facilitate that and still protect the vulnerable and elderly in your circle? What would happen if one of those players brought a strain of the virus back into the family home and loved ones suffered? Where would the responsibility lie?

These were questions that the administration frequently asked of themselves. The consequences of any cases being linked directly to GAA activity were stark, so they held firm. They retained a strict observation of all public-health guidelines through March, April, May and beyond, even though it was feared that players or coaches could go underground and start holding unofficial training sessions.

Cross-blowing and unpredictable winds of change led the association to hand powers to its management committee, adding a new policy allowing for 'Special Emergency Circumstances'. Essentially this gave the GAA the freedom to respond quickly to the dynamic public-health situation.

The Gaelic Players Association also briefed its members to prepare for the possibility of no championship in any form in 2020.

Clouds were gathering. The air was heavy with tension.

And then, like a bolt from the blue, a crack of lightning.

Perhaps sensing public morale dipping and recognising the hard work sporting organisations were undertaking to maintain protocols, the government announced that if the 'R' rate continued to fall, club games could soon recommence. This was a major breakthrough. Expectation levels rose.

Croke Park seized every morsel of momentum and ran with it. At Easter, their games development department held virtual skills sessions for kids and attracted 11,000 users. It was a reminder of the insatiable appetite for interaction – even in an online setting.

Perhaps it was a wake-up call for the government too, in terms of the importance of physical activity for kids, because soon after the Cabinet released a revised road map, allowing slightly increased gatherings, indoors and outdoors.

This created a pathway for the hugely popular GAA Cúl Camps to return. Co-ordinator Charlie Harrison produced a plan demonstrating how the camps could feasibly take place amid the pandemic. Everything was on the table, from holding virtual events to the possibility of traditional or regional gatherings. The goalposts hadn't moved in a while, but now they were swaying in the winds of change.

At the start of May, Leo Varadkar suggested there could be an inter-county championship in 2020 – but possibly without spectators. He deemed 20 July as the date for resumption of activity. It would be baby steps. Club gates would only re-open to a maximum of four players in pods.

Large chunks of the public pushed for a quicker re-opening. It was all happening too gingerly for them. Unprecedented fine weather, lockdowns and working-from-home routines had resulted in a huge fitness resurgence in the country and droves of people were out walking, cycling and running. Grassroots felt the concessions were not significant enough. They argued that club teams should be trusted to resume dutifully and that inter-county set-ups could see five coaches split across the county borders to safely resume training in pods.

They complained that 20 July was a long way off. The GAA, meantime, tried to keep all members in the loop, even though information was at a premium.

'Ordinarily, our communications flow through the province or county before reaching our club network,' Alan Milton says. 'But covid challenged that approach, leading to us sending more information directly in eighteen months than we had in the previous decade.

'There were good reasons for this. When new advice came from government or our own committee, it needed to flow through the organisation in uniform fashion. Even allowing for the challenges of dealing with two jurisdictions, and at times different rules and protocols, it was always our aim that new and updated information would arrive in the inboxes of club secretaries at the same time. This would not always be possible if routed through county committees where our officers are volunteers and working in their professional lives during the day. The potential for rumour and conjecture, with updates arriving at different times in different counties, was too great and this led to us adopting a position where clubs would be communicated with at the same time.'

With the virus, we were learning faster than we could be taught.

Regardless of whatever way the information filtered down, it looked like there was never going to be anything other than a phased re-opening of sport. The core issue remained – how could the GAA resume in a safe manner with the country still in the grip of the pandemic?

* * *

'Pulling together the "return to play" guidelines was our hardest job,' Feargal McGill admits. 'Not just for playing, but how would we return to normal activity? How could we hold meetings? Socials. Medal presentations. Fundraising. That was a big job.'

They created a policy paper to map out a way forward. It covered everything from the establishment of training pods and handwashing stations to the completion of health question-naires, recording of temperature, non-use of indoor dressing-rooms and insistence of separate travel.

When the government, HSE and GAA covid-19 advisory group formally approved the return of the Cúl Camps from 20 July, it gave a specific target to aim for. Harrison hit the bull's-eye.

The camps are a phenomenon, with almost four million children attending them since 2006 and, despite the turbulence of 2020, eight hundred camps were mobilised to host 71,000 children; kids who had been out of school and out of sync.

Just one case of the virus was detected from that entire series, and that case had no direct link to any camp. It was an aston-ishing success. It provided great hope of what was possible.

'The most important thing was to give camps, fun, games and interactions to as many as we could,' Harrison says. 'In the year that was in it, kids needed social interaction and physical activity more than ever. I could see from my own nieces and nephews that some sort of normality was very important. There had been no school and no sport. We fought tooth and nail to make sure the camps would happen.'

None of the above happened by accident. Harrison contacted sports officials in New Zealand and Denmark, who were both a month ahead of Ireland in re-opening their games activities. Along with the GAA's e-learning manager, former Dublin hurler David Sweeney, they put together a template, educating parents, coaches and coordinators of guidelines and protocols that would need to be observed in advance of the camps resuming.

A child protection and safeguarding course – which is normally conducted face to face – was held online for the first time ever with the help of the association's national children officer, Gearóid Ó Maoilmhichí. They brought 3,500 coaches up to speed with every possible scenario and guideline. The wheels were quickly in motion and the government was suitably impressed.

On 5 June official confirmation came that a club series would be held. Children and juveniles would resume normal club training at the end of that month, with all games initially behind closed doors. There was still no use of dressing-rooms or changing-room facilities – players arrived separately and returned home immediately. To participate in any activity, parents and players first had to fill out a covid-19 health questionnaire.

Only players and a limited number of coaches could enter grounds or premises. Games were streamed on board websites for supporters to watch. Two to three venues in each county were proposed to host domestic championships and a general tweaking of existing competition structures was recommended to facilitate new, compacted tournaments. It was left to counties to decide their own formats.

Meanwhile, it became apparent that the inter-county series would also be greatly compressed and possibly played at the end of the year.

The advisory group's 'return to play' booklet meant that amid the fog of confusion a clear picture was finally emerging. All grounds and pitches re-opened for non-contact training in June, and full contact across all levels was permitted by the end of that month.

The window to start local championships was brought forward to 17 July, with county boards given an eleven-week window to run off their affairs. There would be no provincial or All-Ireland series at that level.

Once club championships were completed, inter-county matches would commence in mid-October. Even though the country gradually moved towards Level 5 restrictions, with the country finally submitting to a second full lockdown on 21 October, the government confirmed that inter-county Gaelic Games activity would be given elite sport status.

This meant that inter-county teams could train, prepare and play games despite the country effectively being locked down. It was a huge boost, designed to help lift the national mood by giving people a sporting focus in their lives. It also meant that county players could train without fear of breaching any protocols.

This was providing every box was ticked and every precaution taken by each unit. From that point of view, there were still rigorous procedures to follow before players and teams were allowed to assemble.

But the buy-in was immense, from the kids' camps right up to the completion of the 2020 club and inter-county series. From the summer of 2020 until October 2021, McGill discloses that twenty-five million health questionnaires were completed and submitted, as players, coaches, parents and officials did whatever was necessary to resume activity. The questionnaire was designed by the advisory group, digitised and rolled out to clubs via the games administration department and Tomas Meehan in the IT department.

'The absolute key challenge was how we could make sure that people who turned up for training sessions or matches were not infectious,' McGill states. 'Fundamental to that was the online health questionnaire system. We put huge trust in our membership to see if they would repeatedly fill the forms out and if they would be honest. It was a fantastic exercise in self-policing. We took a leap of faith in 2,200 clubs that were affected by this, stressing that if they had any symptoms they should stay away. Recording temperatures, completing questionnaires – it all just took off and became a staple of the 2020 season. No one blinked an eye.

'What I would be most proud of, though, is the role the GAA played in keeping the responsibilities of people high in their minds. Every time someone had to fill out our forms, it was a reminder to them that the disease was still there. A subtle reminder that, while games were returning, these were still not normal times. We made a serious contribution to the fight against the virus because your peers called you out on it if you didn't conform.

'It was all taken so seriously. We think sport is exceptionally important and, for us, we feel Gaelic Games are the most impor-tant, but for probably the first time we saw where sport really fits in the grand scheme of things. It was only important in the context that public health was good. Realising that, people dug really deep to get games back up and running.'

Fields were soon filled with players who ran the legs off them-selves. Medics were masked, water bottles were no longer shared by all and sundry. Referees produced cards with a renewed zest. Restless coaches strode up and down the sidelines, fretting over their next move and half-questioning their last one.

With glorious weather, the likes of which had not been witnessed in Ireland for decades, and people having more spare time, parishes and towns were reinvigorated. The county championships ran off splendidly, and Irish people all over the world were able to stream the games. Inter-county players were fit and available to their clubs; there was action every week and everyone knew where they stood.

Indeed, the 2020 club championships were so successful, so engaging and concise, that the clear outline of a new structure emerged. The GAA began to wonder if they could ever go back to the old format.

It looked like they had found a new northern star.

7

THE ETERNAL YEAR

LOUGHMORE-CASTLEINEY'S DUAL DEVOTION AND THE MIRACLE SEASON

For just a little while, Liam McGrath must have thought he could see that guiding light glistening from the other side of the world. He was on a party boat in Sydney Harbour, 18,000km away from Semple Stadium, as his club, Loughmore-Castleiney, stood on the verge of winning the 2020 Tipperary hurling final. Until disaster struck and they conceded a goal with the second-last puck of the game . . . and saw their dreams of a championship go up in smoke.

A week later he downloaded a stream of the county football final, which his club also lost in a last-gasp dramatic finale. As his cousins, best friends, clubmates, uncles and neighbours sank to their knees in despair, he detached himself from the carnival atmosphere on the boat, never further away and yet never feeling their pain more either.

The story was not going to end there, however. It was just the midway point of a meandering, spirited journey for both player and club.

Loughmore-Castleiney are fuelled by ferocious ambition and a pure love of hurling and football. Drawing from a pool of just a thousand people, they are not brimming with resources, but what they produce year on year is loaves-and-fishes stuff. They are blessed with talent, generational gifts in some instances, and play with style and intelligence. They also have an inner-built sheer bloody-mindedness to never give in.

Eddie Connolly epitomised that determination. He grew up excelling in both codes to such an extent that he played for the Tipperary senior hurlers and footballers at various stages. He passed away in 2015 after a courageous battle with cancer. He was just twenty-nine.

If Loughmore-Castleiney are the essence of spirit, skill and hardiness, Eddie was the essence of them. After being diagnosed with a brain tumour and forced to undergo heavy surgery and crushing cycles of chemotherapy, Connolly made one simple promise on the road ahead – to fight every step of the way. And, by God, did he fight.

Six weeks after the tumour was taken from his brain, he hit the treadmill and ran 5km in 23 minutes. Eddie being Eddie, he was raging with himself for not coming in at under 20 minutes. Almost twelve months after the operation, he declared himself well enough to bench for Loughmore against Mullinahone and received a thunderous ovation from everyone in the ground when he came on. He tried all he could to stay well, including undergoing a new form of treatment in Spain, before the illness finally took hold. Brave as a lion, his legacy lives on, his valour and courage a beacon for everyone at the club to look up to.

If at any stage the boys of 2020 and 2021 were looking for inspiration, they didn't have far to look. Eddie would have loved the easy rhythm of how it all fell into place, games in both codes, week after week, how the pandemic presented a new championship structure. It would have reminded him of the double he was part of that they managed in 2013.

As a club, they like to keep things simple, but in 2021 they astounded sports scientists, nutritionists and physios by handling nineteen championship games in nineteen weeks, with covid dictating that a much shorter series take place. The year before it was seventeen games in an equally confined period.

They just want to play. Against whatever is put in front of them. Deeply rooted in a footballing tradition, their hurling pedigree is as rich as any of the celebrated Tipp clubs. And they're single-minded about protecting both codes.

It was a long way back from the heartbreak of 2020, but the mist didn't linger for long on Loughmore's lowlands all the same. While McGrath watched them lose that county football title by a point, and the hurling by two points, he was back with them in 2021 when they won both Tipperary finals by a point.

He takes up the story.

'I knew deep down I could have been there helping my team-mates, but life had to go on too. Earlier that year I had decided to go travelling.'

A first cousin of Tipperary greats Noel and John, Liam had been motoring a long time, captaining the county minor footballers to an extraordinary 2011 All-Ireland title and subsequently starring for the senior footballers. He is also one of the best club hurlers around. Once in Australia, the plan was to tour the country, but just as McGrath arrived in Sydney from Cairns restrictions started.

'Lockdown in Sydney was nothing compared to Ireland,' he shrugs. 'Five minutes from the beach, you could go for a swim and walk along the coast, the restaurants and coffee shops were open, and you could meet up with people for a coffee or a bite to eat.

'There was never a house arrest, and I just don't know how people back home got through it. Things got very bad for four or five weeks in Sydney, but then it passed quickly. I was just off Coogee Bay and the 5km radius was one of the most scenic in the world! You could live with that. It was unreal. Sure, that's the luck of living so close to the beach. The place was surrounded by Irish, too.

'I always knew there was a chance that you could miss something special with the club. In hurling, we were there or thereabouts, and we're always capable of winning the football. Losing both was pretty devastating, to be honest, but at least I was miles away from it. I didn't have to face getting up the next morning, meeting people at the shop who only wanted to talk about the game.'

One man who couldn't escape that was club veteran David Kennedy, an everlasting servant who entered his twenty-eighth year of service in 2021. Kennedy was only fifteen when he played senior for the club for the first time, a challenge match against Roscrea. Short of a few players, the selectors spotted Kennedy, still in his school uniform, and threw him in goal. The education he received in the classroom was nothing like what he was taught that evening.

'It wouldn't happen now,' he says, laughing. 'But that was my introduction to senior hurling. Uniform and brown shoes.'

In 2020, he played in goal on the team that beat Moycarkey-Borris in the first round of the Tipperary SHC and stayed in situ until they lost to Kildangan in the dying seconds of the county final. In between his debut and then, Kennedy enjoyed a golden outfield career, winning two county senior hurling titles and four football championships, as well as helping steer Tipperary to Liam MacCarthy Cup glory in 2001.

Having spent the bones of a decade living 120km away in Naas, where he was based as a garda, there were three years, 2015 to 2018, when he didn't make the Loughmore senior team.

'But I was always on the panel, if needed. In 2019 I got back in, as they were looking for a goalkeeper. People made a deal of the fact that I was still playing at my age, but I didn't see the fuss.'

He did, however, grasp the enormity of losing the 2020 county final to that last-second goal. 'That disappointment is still there. I knew in my heart and soul that was my last chance. We led with time up and I was there, thinking, "Jesus, this could actually happen."'

But it didn't.

Bryan McLoughney struck the killer goal for Kildangan and upon Kennedy's despairing restart the final whistle sounded. Even from Sydney, Liam McGrath must have seen the despondent Kennedy slump helplessly as wife Karen and their children came on the field to console him. Not a word of comfort could be uttered, however.

When the team went back to the Templemore Arms for food, they recounted those agonising final moments.

'The last play was broken down and explained in full, and I was traumatised all over again,' he remembers. 'It was just sickening. I had two or three drinks and got a lift home. The next few days were just a blur.'

Nineteen of Kennedy's teammates were also on the senior football panel and their pain only worsened seven days later when they lost the football final to Clonmel Commercials on a 1–16 to 1–15 scoreline. The club had gone all the way to the peak of both codes but never got to pin down a flag at either pinnacle.

Would that group ever scale such heights again?

In typical Loughmore fashion, they rode out the aftershock, waited for calm and quickly sat about navigating a fresh ascent. Whatever championship format the virus would allow in 2022, they would be ready for the hike.

'We just have a way of gently getting on with things here,' says Tom McGrath, father of Liam, and another club devotee. 'People from outside were praising how both codes helped us, but when we lost both 2020 finals the talk turned to how one code was hurting another.

'We just play to who we are. The tradition is there in football; we had two members of Tipperary's "Bloody Sunday" team – Bill and Jim Ryan. And since the late 1960s we have been working very hard in our development of hurling. We're dead serious about both.'

Most of the team returned to the drawing board for the 2021 campaign. Wounds of the previous season may not have fully healed, but there was nothing like a new challenge to draw the steel from their soul.

Liam McGrath came home for his sister's wedding and ended up staying put, as Australia closed its borders because of the virus.

The same management team remained for both codes: Taffy McGrath, Eamonn Sweeney, Maureen Connolly (Eddie's mother) and manager Frankie McGrath. Neither consistency nor burnout would be a problem.

Mick Dempsey, once the right-hand lieutenant in Brian Cody's Kilkenny hurling dynasty, joined them. No one talks much about Dempsey's role, but 'steel' is a word that keeps coming up in conversation. Likewise, whenever Dempsey is quizzed about the club, 'values' is the first term he uses.

Neither term is thrown out lightly. The steel was shaped, perhaps, from the trauma of 2020, but it was their tradition and impeccable approach to Gaelic Games that drove them to take off on another iconic run.

'We were hammered in our very first Cahill Cup game by 27 points. With only a handful of seniors,' Kennedy recollects. 'But no one panicked. Everything in 2021 was for the players, and Frankie and the management were happy to let them at it. When the government allowed pods of fifteen, we went along with that. If pitches were closed, we had three groups rotating on a field up the village. Everyone knuckled down. You had two groups working away at any one time and the players just went for it. One night Noel would take a pod and John Meagher would take one. Another night John McGrath might take the lead. Different training sessions were organised, and maybe the management sensed something was happening for those few weeks because they just let us at it. It was incredibly enjoyable.'

They started the season very slowly, with no big dramatic sessions, speeches or promises.

'When we lost Joey Niland – one of our best players, with a knee injury in 2021, and then travel and work commitments in 2022 – I wondered if we could really do it. But then we got word that Liam McGrath was coming home. If Liam was able to stick around, you felt things might take off again.

'We suffered an unmerciful trimming against Moycarkey-Borris, got less of a trimming against Toomevara, and then drew with Kilruane, our first decent performance. Off we went.'

Liam was home about two hours when he was hauled right back into the thick of it. They brought him to watch the hurlers in a county championship game, and once the jetlag cleared he was flying up and down the training field himself. His addition was crucial, not just because of his intelligence and playmaking skills but because the club essentially draws from the same playing pool, with twenty-seven players across both squads and just three unique to the footballers and hurlers. They need everyone, especially someone with skill levels such as his.

A seemingly never-ending trek across Tipp ensued. Most of the panel featured in three Mid-Tipperary hurling games, three group games in the senior hurling and football championships proper, a preliminary hurling quarter-final and quarter-final proper, semi-finals and finals in both codes.

It didn't knock a breath out of them. 'Sure, we're doing that all our lives.' Kennedy shrugs. 'In 2013 we did the double and hardly a word was said about it. The pandemic meant games came thick and fast, and that just happened to suit us.'

'We leave other clubs to do what they want and what they feel is right,' Liam McGrath adds. 'We did the double at under-12 and under-16 too, and from the time we were born this is what we do. Play what is in front of you. Hurling or football.'

Tom summarises it well. 'If they weren't playing matches, they'd only be above in the field training anyway, or organising challenge games. So they may as well just play away.'

They came from behind to win the 2021 Tipp football final with a late John McGrath goal, this time defying Commercials. And having drawn the hurling final against the famed Thurles Sarsfields, they won the replayed decider by a point. They forced fortune's wheel to turn in their favour.

The double ranks as one of the most remarkable achievements by a group of club players at any period in the GAA's history. Exactly nineteen weekends on the spin and, if anything, they got better with each outing.

'A lot of it comes down to management,' Liam stresses. 'You could only do what we do with the same management team for both codes.'

Kennedy isn't sure there is much more to it.

'Our people are humble and maybe there is something in that. There is a lot of fuss about what we do as a dual club, but we're surrounded by other dual clubs. Good ones at that, like JK Brackens. There is no secret sauce, just people wanting to play sport, people who love hurling and football and their club.

'We're also blessed with some of the best hurlers and footballers of a generation, the likes of Noel and John.'

The McGrath family connection is indeed powerful.

Brian, younger brother of the two lads, is another class act. Their first cousins from different branches of the family include Ciarán and Aidan, Liam and Michael, all top drawer club players.

Manager Frankie is their uncle.

If you delve into the extended family, both Tomás McGrath and Conor McGrath are related too. Meanwhile, Willie Eviston, Joseph Hennessy and Evan Sweeney are extended family members. All key members of the set-up.

'What the McGraths have done is incredible,' Kennedy states. 'In a small, rural community, if you go back to the lads' grandparents, Mick and Tess McGrath, their impact on this club has been massive.

'There was one weekend in 2021 when Mick and Tess had twenty-seven grandchildren who won county medals. The McGraths, Evistons, Campions and Shortts all come from the one family tree, and the grandkids won titles with Loughmore Castleiney in hurling and football, Drom-Inch in intermediate football and Drom-Inch in camogie.

'That's a really important ingredient – we have a number of strong families in the parish with a real passion for our club.'

The general plan runs along these lines. A weekend spent playing hurling gives way to two sessions of football the following week. A football match then, on Saturday or Sunday. Back to two hurling sessions and a match in the week after.

Once they beat Commercials in the 2021 football final, Liam reckons all the pressure lifted. 'We really wanted to win the hurling, but beating Commercials was a big weight off because it meant we finally had something to show for the year – and maybe the year before too.'

It took composure to take Sars in the replayed hurling decider, but aptitude is a feature of all Loughmore teams. They always find a man better placed. They hunt in droves, keep shape at the back and work their way into attack, playing heads-up hurling.

'That team played together from under-12 to under-14, and we are more or less the same age group and have the same mindset,' he maintains. 'Apart from Ciaran Connolly, Brian McGrath and Conor McGrath, everyone is within three years of each other. We have been playing together since we were children.'

Now to the essence of it all.

'We are a tight club on the field, very tight. There is some craic around the place too, everyone is at one with one another. There are no divides. If there is a row between someone, it is sorted very quickly. When we go for a few pints, the lads are nearly always together too. We are best friends; we all went to school together and we have been in one another's pockets since we were five years of age. The way covid fell, it meant a lot of games in a short space of time, but when a group of lads come together all on the same wavelength sometimes things just click,' McGrath finishes.

And in Loughmore-Castleiney, that's as close to hype as you will get.

8

SPLIT DECISION

COVID LEADS TO HISTORIC WINDOWS FOR CLUB AND COUNTY

'Two things made the 2020 and 2021 seasons particularly special,' David Kennedy, Loughmore's ever-faithful servant, maintains. 'One was managing to play games in the environment we were in. There was huge grief and tragedy for families who lost loved ones and for society in general; there was weariness. Everyone just wanted a distraction and a purpose.

'Secondly, as an unintended consequence of covid, we finally got a proper structured club championship. A split season. When the GAA went club first in 2020, it changed everything. They simply had to implement it again in 2021, such was its success. It was a blessing for clubs everywhere.'

Kennedy is right. By accident, through the chaos that the virus caused, the administration landed on the optimum fixtures format – defined seasons for both club and inter-county. There would be no crossover and room for both to thrive.

Loughmore's glorious odyssey may never even have started, never mind concluded, but for the decision to make the split in 2020.

Most clubs recognised this was the way forward. Once that series ended, the clamour to keep the two championships separate only intensified. It was a gift horse that couldn't be ignored.

'Loughmore nearly always had players on two or three different county panels at the one time,' Kennedy explains. 'Hurling and football, senior and underage. It was so hard to have structured training sessions. Then you come back half injured and not used to playing with the club boys.'

He remembers his own Tipperary days when he reverted to club duty to play with fellas that he hadn't seen in six months. In terms of game-plans and understanding, it felt almost alien being back among his own.

'It was ridiculous. All the county lads would tell you the same thing. Players only ever wanted certainty and predictability, and that applied to senior, intermediate and junior. All codes. They wanted to put down dates for games in the calendar, know the weekends they were on and be able to take a break with friends, partners or families when they were off. But lads in my era could never do that.'

The new system, however, allowed for greater harmony. Club teams connected better. Everyone was around. Games flowed. There were no distractions. The county scene would follow, and everyone would be just as enthused about that.

'The virus changed everything for good,' Kennedy states. 'The club-first plan meant no inter-county commitments to take our best players away. We had proper training and cohesion. We built an understanding. Got a buzz going. Jesus, it was unreal. I waited over twenty years to see the day and it finally came.'

Kennedy wasn't the only one shouting from the rooftops. Supporters loved the new format too. Like fat bees buzzing from flower to flower, they filled up on as many games as they could as play resumed.

For years the fixtures crisis had pained countless administrations. Finding a solution for club players who floundered for three months without a match, as the county scene took over, was like clutching at straws in a gale.

The unsettling imbalance led to such serious frustration and bewilderment that it ultimately prompted the establishment of the Club Players Association (CPA), founded by Monaghan man Declan Brennan at the start of 2017.

The CPA's mission was to 'fix the fixtures' and seek the establishment of a 'balanced fixture programme' for club players. Its administration included several high-profile figures, like hotelier and former Wexford manager Liam Griffin, ex-Dublin footballer Kevin Nolan and former Armagh footballer Aaron Kernan.

They were invited by Croke Park onto an official fixtures review committee, but their members didn't stay long in that group. They failed in their bid to be officially recognised at Congress 2017. A year later, just one of their motions got through only to be well defeated. At Congress 2019 they were called out for not providing a 'more detailed sample' of how they would 'fill the blank canvas on fixtures which they talk about'. The CPA argued they had presented multiple proposals on how the fixture crux could be solved.

Leaving aside the tension between Croke Park and the CPA, the crucial issue remained – typically, counties would resume training for the inter-county season in October and from January, and could be tied up right until the end of September. Only then would the club championships get a real window – often in dreadful weather.

The pandemic, however, prompted Feargal McGill and John Horan to ensure that club action would commence first in 2020 when games resumed. That meant all players got to play – and not just the elite. The inter-county series would be compacted into ten weeks at the end of the year.

That format worked so well it was duly retained in 2021 and made a permanent fixture in 2022, with the All-Ireland senior finals to be completed no later than week 29 of the calendar year. It was a huge call. Usually, the inter-county series would only be warming up at that point.

Yet there wasn't a dissenting voice to be heard at Congress 2021, as the association gave its purring approval to officially separate the season between definitive inter-county and club blocks.

From 2022 onwards the structure would flip, meaning inter-county would go first. Training for the inter-county season could only commence in December. The county season would start earlier and run for only twenty-seven weeks of competitive action.

From July, the club scene would take centre stage across the country, allowing for an uninterrupted spell for completion.

It didn't take long for this new format to come under scrutiny. By the middle of the 2022 championship there were already accusations that games were being run off with indecent haste, that the championship was too condensed, that the gap from July to January without any inter-county action was too wide. Supporters balked at under-17s having to undergo a penalty shoot in the Munster minor final rather than have space for a replay the following week.

But the players seemed to embrace it. They had an opportunity to go on a summer holiday, a rarity in a top GAA player's lifetime, and enjoy things outside of sport.

McGill feels the structure will need time to fully settle but states that it was one of the biggest developments in his time in Croke Park.

'The thought of split seasons was always there, but we felt people would never wear it. Covid forced us to, though, and when people saw what played out, it was like, "God, this can work."

'It will take five years for the format to fully settle, I think,' he reckons. 'And it will be our biggest takeaway from this pandemic.

'The split season does two things: it helps address the "club versus county" imbalance and it takes the pressure off the inter-county player. Some context needs to be provided for that. A recent ESRI [Economic and Social Research Institute] survey stated that those elite players give forty-three hours a week to prepare for their county. That time commitment aspect simply had to change.

'Now we go from thirty-five weeks a year to twenty-seven. Straightway, inter-county players will have an extra eight or nine weeks where they aren't part of an inter-county set-up.'

In March 2021, following that momentous Congress, the CPA formally disbanded, declaring their work done and happy that a rich vein of hope for the club had been found.

What had caused chaos and irritation for several administrations over countless decades was finally streamlined. Only for the disruption caused by the disease, the GAA may never have turned in this direction.

Funny how it goes, sometimes.

9

THE GREEN LIGHT

THE CHRISTMAS CHAMPIONSHIPS

With the club scene in rude health, all attention turned to the 2020 inter-county circuit. It would be different from any championship ever held – only forty team members had access to stadiums on match days and there would be no spectators. Due to their elite status, Croke Park could at least proceed with top-flight games – even amid Level 5 restrictions, the highest level under the government's plan. But all had changed – utterly.

Having no crowds was going to thrust the organisation into even deeper financial ruin. The inter-county scene is the GAA's golden goose. The revenue it brings in allows the association to invest in areas of games development, infrastructure, marketing and general structure. Basically, it lets the association be as self-sufficient as possible. Typically, eighty-three per cent of everything the GAA takes in at central level is redistributed to provincial councils, counties, clubs and schools through coaching and games development and infrastructure. In 2019, just shy of €14 million went back to county boards in various guises.

But all that depends on a buoyant county scene, where league, provincial and All-Ireland games attract huge crowds and interest. Indeed, such is the appetite for the inter-county game that there have been occasions when crowds of close to 20,000 have turned up to watch pre-season clashes.

Without that beating heart, the pulse of the GAA was weakening with every passing month. The chances of a championship being held looked slim.

'We needed help,' John Horan admits. 'I had developed a very good relationship with government officials, such as Simon Harris [Minister for Health], Jack Chambers [Minister of State for Sport], Leo Varadkar [Tánaiste] and Taoiseach Micheál Martin, and after he took office I contacted Micheál asking for a small chunk of his time.'

Horan attended the meeting with Tom Ryan, the GAA director-general, and Martin Fraser, secretary general of the Department of the Taoiseach. Horan stated that he wanted a championship to happen, that he suspected the Taoiseach did too, but that the association just wasn't in a position to stage one.

They painted a picture of where they were at, mooted how the government could help and received some reassurances at the end of the meeting. But there was nothing concrete.

In May 2020, staff at Croke Park were informed of pay deferrals. Further cuts were expected in June. A conference call around that time informed county board officials that the GAA could lose over €60 million that year if there was no inter-county fixtures calendar.

Every effort was made to safeguard jobs and existing structures. In the north, some county boards put their coaching staff on the government furlough scheme. The effects of that were significant, as thousands of children were unable to participate in the GAA summer scheme while younger children missed out on the Cúl Camps. Without gate receipts, broadcast revenue and other incomes, and lacking a dividend from the Croke Park stadium company, a serious financial crisis developed. The outlook was dire.

Unlike the FAI and IRFU, it had no international governing wing to fall back on either. Knowing this, Horan stayed in constant contact with government ministers and kept communication channels open, as the most unpredictable year progressed.

'I was impressed with them,' the Taoiseach says. 'Obviously they needed help, and came looking for it, but they were realistic about where they were at too. I knew that if we gave a commitment, they would look after everything else. They were stringent in their approach to running games and that impressed us.'

As winter set in, those words of admiration kept coming, but three months out from Christmas there was still nothing in the bank. It was crunch time. At September's Central Council meeting, Horan came under pressure from county board officials, who were being hounded by their own people looking to know what was happening. Horan applied the same logic that a former science and maths teacher naturally would in a classroom – he laid out the problem and set about building the steps to work through it.

Key to securing the financial aid were people and relationships. It was slow and often silent work. There was constant correspondence and networking behind the scenes. Varadkar and Harris called to see the work of the testing centres at the Cusack Stand tunnel at Croke Park and saw at first hand the practical impact the organisation had on the country's fight.

By then Croke Park was one of twenty GAA venues around the island made available to the HSE as part of the national effort to assist mass testing. Speaking to Varadkar and Harris,

Horan said the GAA was determined to stay helping for the long haul – but reminded them they would need government assistance down the line too.

The time for talking was over. The September Central Council meeting would determine whether the battle for the Sam Maguire and Liam MacCarthy cups would take place. It was time for the rubber to hit the road. For promises to be kept.

'I left the meeting to take the call from Minister Chambers and it transpired that Jack still had not received anything in writing,' Horan recounts. 'But on that morning he was able to give us the word of Michael McGrath [Minister for Public Expenditure] and Micheál Martin that funding would be found and would be there to support us.

'That was enough for me. Once he gave that assurance I went straight back to the meeting, passed the information on and the decision was made to go ahead with the 2020 championship.'

They had lift-off.

It would all be played behind closed doors, but counties could now press ahead and prepare.

The tension lifted. At that critical juncture, even a slight delay would have been an organisational and logistical nightmare. In fact, just one further day of interruption or uncertainty could have pushed the 2020 series into 2021 – not unprecedented, but totally undesirable. But because communication lines were open all along, fixture plans were well advanced when funding was finally assured.

Weeks later the GAA would receive a total of €31 million in government aid, including €15 million specifically for running the championships behind closed doors. The other €15 million was confirmed as part of Sport Ireland's protection fund for sporting organisations and saw Croke Park receive a further €9 million, a €5 million package for clubs, €1 million for LGFA and €795,000 for camogie.

'It was a huge development,' Horan said. 'We always knew we could run the games safely and swiftly, and now we had the means to do so. And I think it gave the people of Ireland a massive distraction when they needed it most.'

The next task was to get the infrastructure in place to televise as much action as possible and bring the games to the people who were not allowed to attend. That job fell to Noel Quinn, the association's broadcast and marketing senior manager.

'At a time of such uncertainty and fear, people turned to the GAA for a sense of "normality" and togetherness,' Quinn says. 'In the first instance I think we helped the HSE get essential messages to the public through our nationwide network of clubs.'

In the absence of attendances due to outdoor restrictions, the GAA put a huge emphasis on broadcasting games for members here and overseas. Broadcasting the 2020 series would prove a source of release, distraction and recreation.

'It might have even shaped part of the conversation that people were having in every village, town and city in Ireland in the days following the final whistle,' Quinn says. 'Now they had something, anything, to chat about other than the pandemic, illness and the economic or social impact it was having.

'There are close to two hundred games made available on linear television every year, but the magnitude of providing live coverage of all games during lockdown was unprecedented,' he explains.

'GAAGO was set up in 2014 to provide coverage to our diaspora overseas, but it had to suddenly pivot into the domestic marketplace to ensure coverage from all inter-county games was produced. It was an endeavour undertaken somewhat in the national interest.'

Over one weekend in October 2020 when the Allianz League recommenced, for example, there were sixteen games streamed live on GAAGO.ie within a 30-hour period. This included eight games on a Saturday and eight on a Sunday.

At home people feasted on the fat of endless live coverage. It was a godsend.

'That service was in addition to the triple-header of live linear TV coverage across both days of every weekend,' Quinn explains. 'As well as that, there were numerous GAA county board streams from the lower tier hurling leagues.

'It required a massive effort from the GAAGO team to deliver a huge operational, technical, marketing and support plan throughout 2020 and 2021. They worked through the pandemic and delivered hundreds of games to those who were not allowed to watch in the flesh. They worked tirelessly with the production teams of RTÉ, Sky, BBC and TG4 at all the venues. RTÉ head of sport, Declan McBennett, also played an instrumental part in getting crews to games everywhere.'

Quinn reveals that complimentary GAAGO passes were also made available to county boards for local hospitals and care institutions.

'This meant that those less fortunate could watch their county take to the field.' For 70 minutes at least, there was a source of distraction and enjoyment for those people. It meant the world to them.

10

REBOUNDING FROM ROCK BOTTOM

HOW DOMHNALL NUGENT CAME BACK FROM THE BRINK

It wasn't just the supporters who needed games. Players craved them as much as anyone.

'I certainly wanted as much pitch time as possible,' Domhnall Nugent stresses. 'When you're a recovering addict, you need people around you. Instead, I had a very tough eighteen to twenty-four months to endure with everyone staying apart.'

The covid experience was proving tough for everyone, but Antrim hurler Nugent was reconstructing his life in the wake of drug and alcohol addiction when Ireland locked down.

'Life at my lowest point of addiction was a very lonely, draining and very scary place. I didn't want to be around anyone. I hated the world, and I thought the world hated me. I was riddled with depression and anxiety, but I was comfortable with being uncomfortable. By that I mean I did not want to be alive.'

Breaking out of the hell of recovery amid strict lockdowns and restrictions was never going to be easy.

'All structure went out the window. When you are in rehab and getting treatment, they advise you to surround yourself with likeminded people. When you come out, the counsellors ask you to stay around those people and try to look for a better life. But the public-health advice was to restrict contact. So, the big thing was not getting too high, nor too low.

'With regard to hurling then, I wanted to work my way back into the Antrim team but needed games to do that. We didn't get to play a lot in 2020, so I didn't see much game time. It was about the same in 2021. I had no routine on or off the field for six months at a time across the two years and that wasn't simple.'

Another temptation was to answer when his past called.

'With addiction, the demons in your head often call for you to go back to old ways. It really helped that in lockdown AA meetings were held online and there were Zoom calls. While you weren't meeting anyone in person, at least you were still engaged.'

People looked in on him as best they could. Antrim hurling manager Darren Gleeson especially.

'He was always on the blower,' Nugent says.

'Days before we went to Dublin to play the Christy Ring final in 2020, he rang because he knew the temptations I would face – win, lose or draw. On the evening of the final, he gave me the keys of his car and said to pop out anytime I wanted. I don't know what the boys did that evening because of restrictions, but I took Darren's car and got a pizza and a coffee. He went all out to ensure I would be okay.

'Others were just a phone call away. Look, I knew there was a much bigger picture out there, too. People lost jobs, loved ones and a lot more. They lost things in life because of the virus. I just had to get on with it. I had to stay strong. Rather than suffer and sit in an apartment alone, I had to continue doing what was good for me. Interaction. It just came in a different form. Phone calls, Zoom calls, texts – a bit of connection that way. It wasn't ideal, but it helped.'

* * *

It was in June 2019 that Nugent took his last drink. In a desperate attempt to claw his way back to life, he contacted the addiction treatment centre at Cuan Mhuire, Newry. They had a space for him nine days later.

While he was there, Nugent wrote in a journal at the end every day.

'Be excited about who you want to become.'

It was a simple message but a strong one.

After years of addiction to alcohol and cocaine, Nugent was at a crossroads. 'There were two options,' he remembers, drawing from a trove of smothered memories. 'Stay on the road you were on, which would kill you, or go get help.'

He had drifted for years, but dips in and out of society had become dangerous and upset those around him. Summers were spent in Boston or the UK. He was hiding.

Prior to leaving for England, he also left his club, St John's, for chief rivals Lámh Dhearg, a move you rarely see in the Gaelic Games world. He lined out for his new team in the 2017 Antrim SFC final, predictably enough against St John's. Padraig, his brother, was in goals for John's and Lámh Dhearg prevailed to win.

In that decider, his brother went to kick a ball out from the goalkeeping tee, but Nugent kicked it away. Padraig reacted and was sent off. The two had grown up dreaming of winning a championship together. It was never meant to be like this.

'That time of my life is just a blur. I obviously regret leaving my club and doing what I did that day. There's still not a day that goes by when I don't think about it.'

He's back with St John's since.

'I want to make amends for what happened. A county title with them is my goal.'

The turnaround began in Cuan Mhuire. Mentally, he was beaten and battered but somehow still unbowed. He walked into the centre shaking with nerves and was placed in an assessment area. Over the next two weeks he detoxed, questioned all he had done and moved into St Joseph's, the principal treatment house, for ten weeks.

Official business began each morning with a 6.15 a.m. meditation before breakfast and therapeutic work. Group therapy sessions led him to re-engage with his faith. He chatted over meals. Slept a lot.

'It was all straightforward, but that was what I had been missing. I had a difficult childhood, my parents' marriage broke up, and I had been getting counselling since I was sixteen, but I was never really honest with myself until I went there.'

During troublesome years, hurling and football had always been an escape route. Until he started drinking.

'Self-pity was a huge thing. I was lucky; hurling and football became my escape. But then I started drinking and that became my escape. From there cocaine was another escape. I don't know about anywhere else in the country, but it is easier to get cocaine in Belfast than a packet of cigarettes. You don't have to leave the pub because boys bring it to you. They don't even always look for money there and then – you run up a tab until they knock on the door when you haven't paid up. That brings its own issues. That's the road I was on. I didn't need the GAA any more because of drink and drugs. At least that's what I thought.'

In the early summer of 2019, at the age of twenty-two, Nugent came back from hurling and working in Warwickshire with £20,000 in savings. That could have helped him pivot in life, but he blazed through the money. One night after training, a St John's teammate offered him a lift home. Nugent politely declined.

The truth was he had no home any more, as he had lost his apartment on the Falls Road. He went for a pint in the Rock Bar in Belfast with little left of the sum he'd brought home. When closing time was called, there was no place to rest his head. He slept on the porch of his grandmother's house.

'The next morning I could see Granny's face and what I had done to her, how worried she was about the state I was in. That was a low moment. About the lowest of the lot.'

Rock bottom became the solid foundation on which he rebuilt his life.

In Cuan Mhuire, he reflected on everything.

'I wrote a lot in the journal. Wrote letters to people I had affected, those I couldn't look in the eye any more.'

Padraig, his brother, received a letter which kickstarted the healing process. The brothers met in his second month at the centre, talked through some issues and the fall-out from that county final. More healing.

He spent three months inside. He'd walked in dishevelled. He left with hope that life could still mean something.

Hurling was an immediate focus. It wouldn't be an easy road back either. The struggles of addiction had taken their toll on him in different forms. He was three stone overweight for a start.

That fightback began at Cuan Mhuire too. He rose at 4.45 a.m. and ran the perimeter of the centre each morning, all the time targeting playing championship again for St John's.

It boded well that club legend Andy McCallin was waiting for him outside as he left the centre on his final day. Nugent still struggles to put into words the boost that gave him.

'Just to know that someone felt, "This fella is worth sticking with." It meant a lot.'

He needed more people like Andy and solid structures to support him if he was going to stay on the straight and narrow. He was wary of what lay ahead.

'You were going from a sanctuary back to the big, bad outside world, and I knew I needed more help. Willy O'Connor, who is involved with the Dublin ladies football team, had been helping me at Cuan Mhuire and contacted the Gaelic Players Association to help me readjust to life on the outside.'

Nugent had been on the Antrim panel for the 2017 season but wasn't technically a county panellist when he rang the players' group.

'It didn't matter to them,' he insists. 'The GPA arranged a counsellor to come and visit me in Belfast, who I met once a week. I wouldn't have been able to afford the services, but they paid for everything. They were a huge help in finding the road back. I went to all my AA meetings too and that support structure helped me recover.'

The GPA run a player welfare service called Beo360. Nugent, who now hosts an aptly named podcast called 'Let's Face It', feels other players who struggle with issues would benefit from the service.

'Beo360 is there to help county players with their well-being, lives, careers and transition from playing into retirement and that's a huge support structure for players to be able to call upon. I hope players who are struggling show courage and avail of it. Would you be embarrassed about coming out of a bookies' after losing all your money? Would you be embarrassed about rolling out of a pub at 2 a.m. off your head? But why would you be embarrassed about going to seek help somewhere? This programme will help normalise having issues in your life. People do struggle, but something can be done about it.'

* * *

There's a photograph of Darren Gleeson on the ground at Croke Park, bear-hugging Nugent at the end of the 2020 Joe McDonagh Cup final win.

Nugent holds it close to his heart and would love to create more images like that to look back on when he retires.

'I want to take my life to a different place now. I still have uncertain times, but consistency is the key. I keep it simple; I have an easy life. I don't stretch myself going off looking for complicated things.'

By and large people have given him a second chance. 'Since I went and got help, I think a lot more people actually respect me and that's nice too. They mightn't have looked at me two years ago.'

Settling down in his grandparents' home has been another positive, living with his uncle Eamon and his grandmother,

Marie, through and beyond covid.

'I had been living on my own since I was seventeen, but I'm back living with Granny. I have a job at Robert Murphy Motors in Antrim and Robert has been very understanding. If I have to go to meetings, he gives me time and space. I want to build consistent structures in my life, and in sport my goal is to become a regular first-team player with Antrim. I'm working on that the whole time.'

'People are there to help, but ultimately I had to dig deep myself or I was going to die,' he finishes. 'The lockdown and pandemic were pretty hard, but I faced up to them. It is nice going to bed at night knowing that you are trying your best every day.'

11

CURTAIN CLOSES OFF-BROADWAY

SUDDEN SWANSONG FOR SLIGO'S STALWART

A week before the 2020 inter-county championships commenced, a Sligo footballer displayed covid symptoms and rapid testing of the entire group followed. This would have dramatic knock-on effects for the long-serving Neil Ewing and his teammates.

When the results returned on Monday, seven positives were identified, with other cases proving inconclusive and four more players deemed close contacts. In a flash, Sligo were down to twenty-one players. Out of that number, one or two had just recovered from injury, while others hadn't played county football in some time.

Further positive tests emerged and more close contacts were identified too. At the county board's management committee on Tuesday night, as the players convened remotely to see if there was any way their season could be salvaged, the executive took the decision to withdraw.

The players were understandably disappointed. They felt a re-fixture was reasonable. Their championship was over without a ball being kicked.

It was a decision taken after prolonged consultation between the board, Connacht Council and Croke Park, and in ways it painted a portrait of the challenges the administration faced with the virus. The whole affair was dominated by talk of symptoms, mass testing, close contacts and positive results.

When the dust settled, however, it still seemed tough on Sligo that they didn't receive a week's grace to regroup. The Connacht final was scheduled seven days before the three other provincial deciders, so, technically, it might have been possible. Official regulations stated, however, that there should be thirteen days between the semi-final and final to allow for a re-fixture. There wasn't in this instance. And with so many close contacts out of action for fourteen days, a postponement wouldn't have helped.

A year later, Tyrone withdrew from the 2021 All-Ireland semi-final due to a similar outbreak, but Kerry offered them extra time to recover and the GAA facilitated it. Tyrone gratefully accepted that gesture, beat Kerry in the semi-final, and then Mayo in the final.

Could Sligo have been afforded similar mercy in 2020? One of Croke Park's leading administrators, Feargal McGill, says they were completely different decisions.

'If a team couldn't fulfil a fixture in the allotted timeframe, they had to withdraw from the championship. Our competition regulations for covid postponements of inter-county games state that for all championship round-robin or knock-out games, where a county is unable to fulfil a championship fixture due to issues related to covid, the game will be awarded to the opposing team [a walkover] without any further penalty being imposed. But All-Ireland semi-finals and finals are listed as exceptions to the normal.'

There are other exceptions to that rule, besides All-Ireland semi-finals and finals. Where there is a clear thirteen days between the original fixture and the next scheduled round of the competition. And any game in which direct relegation to a lower tier is a consequence of a walkover.

'Regarding the Tyrone scenario, the postponement was only possible with the agreement of the other teams that remained in the competition,' McGill states. 'I come from Leitrim, where there are similar playing numbers to Sligo, so I fully understand the landscape. Sligo had to withdraw from that Connacht semi-final because the final had been scheduled for the next week. They were excellent to deal with, and they realised they had no choice but to pull out.'

Ewing, a stalwart of the Sligo team, retired soon after. He officially walked away in 2021, but once that Galway game went by the wayside he had sensed his time was up.

'Could the GAA have done more to help us?' he asks. 'Probably not. In fairness, they were pretty clear in their communications all the way through.

'Could Sligo have been a bit stronger for themselves? For the sake of the players, probably a bit. Maybe it feeds into something I see out there on a more general basis. I sense a lack of ambition among some lower-tier counties, maybe a willingness to accept your place.

'Some Division 2, 3 and 4 counties have accepted that stance over the past ten years. The attitude seems to be "there are six standout teams in the country and the rest of us will do what we are told".

'I think it reflects a more general way of thinking. Ticking the boxes, getting the fixtures played on time, getting the grants that come in, and looking after matters at club and county level. I appreciate the task facing county boards is huge. But the gap between top and lower counties is big too, and there seems to be an acceptance from some: "This is where we are at."'

In April 2022, the Sligo board did demonstrate serious strength and spirit when they refused to concede home advantage for the Connacht under-20 football final with Mayo. This was despite the provincial council wanting to move the fixture to the Centre of Excellence in Bekan to facilitate TV coverage.

Sligo's home ground, Markievicz Park, doesn't have floodlights and wasn't suitable for TV. But the county board clearly spelled out its position, refused to budge and showed a lot of the resolve Ewing was looking for.

'There are huge challenges for all boards,' he acknowledges. 'The target is to make the county as vibrant as possible whilst they are addressing those. At senior level, a county like Sligo, on the law of averages, would be handed out beatings by the likes of Mayo, but it's really concerning if it happens at underage too. It would mean we don't have our house in order from under-6 at club level right up the grades. And that shouldn't happen either.'

Meanwhile, Ewing won't countenance any contrasts with Tyrone, who gained that re-fixture in 2021 during their own crisis.

'Fair play to Tyrone. They made their case and took a stand. I heard people criticising them, but I wouldn't for a minute go there. They played the perfect game to get the extra two weeks they needed to recover from their own issues.

'Some people were exasperated when they went on and beat Kerry and Mayo, and felt they had been playing games, but it's not for any of us to say what the health situation was up there. I just admire how they made a stand, put the ball into the court of the GAA and forced their hand to get the best result for Tyrone. They deserve no criticism for that. Fair play to them.'

And so, what seemed like the longest year finally ground to an end. With the shortest championship campaign that Ewing had ever known.

* * *

Neil Ewing was thirteen years in the mix with Sligo when he called it a day. Six months previously, he ripped his hamstring and it never fully came right. Inter-county toil was relentless and his body couldn't handle it any more. He didn't want to make a mistake on the pitch because of injury and face retirement with that baggage. Every facet of his preparation as a Sligo footballer centred around optimum performance. His conditioning levels never waned, even when the county team bowed out.

'I played for two teams and pushed hard for success with both. I had dreams and ambitions with the club and county,' the Drumcliffe/Rosses Point clubman insists. 'Why would you go back to your club and not put the very same effort in? You were there to set standards. I trained the same for the club as I did for the county. It was intense – twelve months a year for thirteen years – but that's how I wanted it.'

He reckons he was a nutritionist's worst nightmare. He constantly scoped for any inch that might benefit him or his recovery. Everywhere he went he was a GAA player.

'I took a lot of slagging for always having a few boxes of grub with me. Carb cycles and matching those to the intensity of your workload, having protein and healthy fats on non-pitch days. It was a well-oiled routine.'

Even during the scorching covid summer of 2020, when the country's ice-cream vans did a roaring trade and fast-food delivery services went into overdrive, there was still no slackening.

'If anything, I went overboard with my preparation in that period, wondering how nutrition could help my injury. I was taking lots of vitamin C and collagen supplements to help with tendon repair. I was reducing carbs and upping the fats, so I probably didn't ease off during lockdown at all.'

Subconsciously, though, the pandemic did quell the burning fire within. In normal beast mode, Ewing left home at 7 a.m. and returned at 8.30 p.m. Those were just gym days. On field session days, it was even more demanding. He left at 7 a.m., returning any time after 10.30 p.m. He then prepared food for the next day.

The 'journeyman' and 'weaker county' labels are easy to slap on – a few gruff platitudes easy to throw out – but the rigours were unrelenting for Ewing all the way through his career. Just because some players struggle to break out of Division 3 and 4, it doesn't mean they are doing any less than the big boys.

The grind without any gold takes its toll, though. Just weeks into lockdown, and for the first time, Ewing began to wonder what it was all about.

During the early restraints, he and his wife Siobhan headed out for strolls any chance they could and, as straightforward as that was, he got a glimpse of a different world.

'Jesus, it was so refreshing to get out of the bubble for a little while. Just to cook dinner, go for a walk, chill out for the evening and maybe enjoy TV or something. This was a new life for me. Yes, I had short seasons with Sligo, which you imagine might have left me with more spare time, but I was somewhat addicted to maintaining the level of training and keeping it going for my club. We went through the ringer with the club, losing three intermediate finals in a row, so there was seldom a break, really.

'When we eventually won and turned senior, we had some relegation battles to manage, and it meant playing well into October. It was always a twelve-month season.'

When covid hit, Ewing fell off the hamster wheel he never realised he was on.

They say the only regrets are the chances you didn't take, but he was never found wanting on that front. No, the hardest part of stepping aside was doing so with Sligo still rooted in the bottom tier. He'd made his debut in Division 4 against Kilkenny and that's where they remained as he bade farewell.

'Somebody has to be down there, I know that, and Sligo are there as a reflection of what's happened over the past few years, but I really feel we should be able to compete in Division 2, if things were right. It's no slight on any Division 4 team, and I have no delusions of grandeur, but I just hate to see us down there.

'That was my only dilemma, walking away. Was there anything more I could have done to help them get out of Division 4?

'I fretted over that. Maybe I still had something to offer, but then again, if I was on a pitch and a play developed that I wasn't able for because of fitness, would I cost Sligo? And if I did cost them, I would struggle to handle that.'

The fear is that younger generations of Sligo players won't commit if they stay rooted to the bottom. At least the new structure, with the Tailteann Cup catering for Division 3 and 4 teams, allows for increased time on more level playing fields. And their

2021 minor and 2022 under-20 Connacht titles have energised everyone. Those wins were badly needed after a fruitless period.

'We had talented guys from underage teams. Brilliant individuals had joined panels, but you could almost detect from them a resignation that "this is where Sligo are at, this is where we'll always be at". I just had the feeling that some lads didn't envisage winning a Connacht title with Sligo. It scared me.'

The new breed coming through offer much promise. Ewing would like to draw on his experiences to help those young players.

'Look, I have taken more positives from football than I ever could imagine. I have had experiences to share with friends and family. I loved the sense that playing with Sligo could make other people happy, people like my granddad and others around you that take a sense of enjoyment from it.

'I made great friends along the way, and we still have that tight network; you will never lose that, even if you are no longer a Sligo inter-county footballer. That relationship is still there.

'Leaving the scene during the pandemic, through injury and the team withdrawing from the championship – none of that was ideal, but good, bad and indifferent I learned a lot and I will bring all that back to the club now, share with younger players and help them to have a platform to be the best that they can be. As footballers, and off the pitch too.'

As he said himself in his retirement statement, in a nod to the movie *Cool Runnings*, 'peace be the journey.'

There was disappointment in how it ended, how the pandemic robbed him of a swansong, but Ewing found comfort at the finish line. He had left nothing in the tank. He had emptied it for the love of the game. For the love of Sligo.

12

REMEMBRANCE DAY

UNFINISHED BUSINESS FOR THOSE COMMEMORATING BLOODY SUNDAY

The contentment that Neil Ewing experienced having given his county everything was a precious feeling. That feeling of serenity, of having done everything the right way, was something the GAA were seeking when they set out to honour those murdered in their principal stadium in 1920. There was unfinished business in that regard.

The committee formed to mark the hundredth anniversary of Bloody Sunday was heavily influenced by the words of Elie Wiesel, an Auschwitz survivor who became an expressive eyewitness for six million Jews murdered during the Second World War. A renowned lecturer, professor and author, Wiesel scorched the memory of the Holocaust on the world's consciousness; his powerful quote – 'If we forget, the dead will be killed a second time' – resonated with the committee.

One of those who was struck by Elie's words was Michael Foley, author of *The Bloodied Field*, a brilliant and definitive recollection of the fateful events of 21 November 1920, when a challenge match between Tipperary and Dublin at Croke Park altered the course of history. As has been well documented, that game between the two most imposing teams of that time was held to raise money for the Republican Prisoners Dependents' Fund.

Beforehand, tensions had run high across Dublin due to fears of a reprisal by Crown forces following the assassinations of some of their officers earlier that morning. Still, some 15,000 gathered in Croke Park for a scheduled 2.45 p.m. game, one that was delayed by 30 minutes due to crowd congestion.

Five minutes in and an aeroplane flew over Croke Park, circled the ground twice. A mixed force of Royal Irish Constabulary (RIC), Black and Tans, auxiliary police and military then stormed onto the field and opened fire on the crowd. There was a rush to all four exits and crushes ensued, as the army prevented people from leaving. They opened machine-gun fire to push them back. On the Cusack Stand side, hundreds of people braved the 20-foot drop and jumped into the Belvedere Sports Grounds.

Shooting lasted for less than 2 minutes, but in that time fourteen people, including Tipperary footballer Michael Hogan, lost their lives. Between sixty and a hundred people were injured.

Much is known about Mick Hogan, the twenty-four-year-old Grangemockler farmer and GAA martyr. In 1925, the association named a stand in Croke Park after him. But little is known about the others who perished that day: James Burke, Jane Boyle, Daniel Carroll, Michael Feery, Thomas (Tom) Hogan, James Matthews, Patrick O'Dowd, Jerome O'Leary, William (Perry) Robinson, Tom Ryan, John William (Billy) Scott, James Teehan and Joseph Traynor.

In 2015, five years out from the hundredth anniversary of the event which later became known as Bloody Sunday, the GAA's communications manager, Cian Murphy, formulated plans for commemoration. A former journalist and author, he had recently begun his new role in Croke Park. This project would consume much of his time.

'The initial thought was to have 80,000 people at the service,' he says. 'But everything changed because of covid. We ended up having eight.'

Murphy was always definite about what direction the association needed to take in honouring the victims, the tone the memorial had to take. 'We needed to reconnect with the families of the Bloody Sunday victims. The GAA hadn't always done a good job of looking after the memory of the people who died that day. There were some incorrect facts on record; the number of actual deaths from that day was wrong in some places, while other records were non-existent. We had to try to fix it.'

The project was inspired and supplemented by the incredible research and workings of Foley.

'If England hadn't played rugby at Croke Park in 2007, a lot of stuff mightn't have happened,' Murphy adds. 'When they came to play, Michael went looking for material to help with an article that he was writing, but he couldn't find the information he needed. In typical fashion, he researched it himself. That led to his wonderful book, and it led to more families coming to the GAA's attention.

'For the 95th anniversary of Bloody Sunday, one of my jobs was to work on the match programme for the Ireland versus Australia international rules series. In the programme Michael had a thousand-word article on the events of 1920 and it just blew me away.'

One of the standout lines in Foley's piece revealed how several of the dead from Bloody Sunday still rested in unmarked graves. That shook Murphy.

He went to then director-general Páraic Duffy, relayed what he had read from Foley's piece, and asked to research and perhaps rectify the situation in the five years leading up to the hundredth anniversary. Duffy instructed him to do what needed to be done.

On the morning of the 95th anniversary, the GAA joined with the surviving relatives of Jane Boyle to erect a headstone on her previously unmarked grave in Glasnevin cemetery. Hailing from Lennox Street, just off the SCR, twenty-nine-year-old Jane went to the match with her fiancé Daniel Byron, one week out from their marriage at St Kevin's church on Harrington Street. Shot in the back as she and Daniel fled around the halfway point of what is now the Cusack Stand side, Daniel felt her hand go limp in his before the stampeding crowd swept her away. On the day she was due to be wed, she was instead laid to rest in her wedding dress. The Boyle family and the Croke Park museum cooperated to erect her headstone.

Murphy received permission to formally initiate a Bloody Sunday Graves project. This entailed verifying final resting places of the other victims and contacting surviving relatives.

'Our job was made easier because Michael had done so much work and was an invaluable asset in terms of helping us make contacts and verify facts. We were on the one path in trying to learn about these people and bring them back to the awareness of the GAA community.'

The next number of years were spent laying headstones on graves and marking the passing of those who had perished at the hands of the British Crown Forces.

* * *

In January 2020, with the world still spinning at full pelt, Murphy contacted representatives of all twelve bereaved surviving families – the bloodlines of two clans have died out – and invited a representative from each to Croke Park to meet then president John Horan and museum director Niamh McCoy for lunch.

'Niamh outlined an extensive programme of commemoration that was planned, including a major exhibition. One of our museum colleagues is education manager Julieanne McKeigue, who is directly related to Michael Hogan. This was another inspiration and a reminder to us of the importance of what we were trying to do.' That exhibition launched, but was cancelled just as quickly due to intense protocols.

Meanwhile, it was also proposed to 'finish the match' of one hundred years earlier between Dublin and Tipperary. The 1920 game was without a score when it was stopped after 10 minutes. Tipp had surged forward and were about to take a free when the shooting started. The plan was to present the two counties wearing the replica gear of 1920, finish the game and hold a tribute afterwards. Invites would be sent to Dublin and Tipperary to send fifteen players each, with a further thirty coming from the other counties in Ireland to reflect the national involvement in the ceremony. A unique medal would be presented, and the plan was to stage this event before that Ireland versus Australia international rules test. They hoped Croke Park would be packed out. When the country came to a halt in 2020, however, those plans were dashed.

'With all the uncertainty, we operated three different strategies,' Murphy recalls. 'One where we would be free to do everything; one where there would be some restrictions to contend with; and one where we weren't allowed to do anything whatsoever. Deep down, because of covid, we sensed it wouldn't unfold how we first wanted.

'The international rules game was an early casualty. And ultimately we had to ask the Department of Tourism, Culture, Art, Gaeltacht, Sport and Media what the bare minimum was in terms of how we could commemorate the anniversary. We were going to be happy with whatever was allowed – we just wanted to honour the fourteen people who had passed.'

They continued with outline preparations and at a gathering of the families one morning at HQ Murphy met a woman outside the stadium pulling hard on a cigarette.

'She looked nervous, so I asked if she was okay.'

'I've never been in here before,' the lady replied.

'She was not a young woman,' he elaborates, taking up the story. 'Turns out she'd grown up not far from Croke Park but had never been. Her family told her not to go, as bad things had happened there. She had grown up with that narrative and inherited that shadow. It had followed her family all the way down the line.

'Now, not all families had that story, but they all carried some kind of baggage from it. As they would. They each had a family member that was murdered.'

He was struck by her words. And more determined than ever to do right by her and the others affected.

'As bad as it was to have someone murdered for simply going to a match, what must have been worse is to have felt forgotten about. I felt we stood accused of that. We had forgotten the families. We couldn't change what had happened; we could only make a statement on who we were now and what we planned to do.

'Those who were killed were our people. They went to one of our games and never came home. At that lunch we promised the families we would do our best to make sure they were remembered.

'Those families have something terrible that they carry. They have a huge part of history they don't want to have. For most of us, Croke Park is known only as a cathedral of games. A place of joy. But for those families it goes much deeper. There was no easy death there that day in 1920. Each one was horrendous. There was still huge trauma for all those who followed.'

The GAA agreed that any commemoration would remember the fourteen who died as people and paint a full picture of their lives. One year before the anniversary, the last of the seven unmarked graves in Glasnevin had headstones erected on their final resting places.

'We like to look out for each other in the community,' Murphy adds. 'For example, you see a club at its best in times of tragedy, when people mobilise to look after their own. But 1920 was a time of war, and Ireland was being terrorised by the Black and Tans and the Auxies. I've no doubt that people at that time wanted to do far more for the Bloody Sunday dead than they did. But there was a culture of fear. The War of Independence blew immediately into the Civil War.

'I don't believe these people were intentionally forgotten. I do believe that the whole nation was traumatised by what was happening in this general period of upheaval. It added to the sense of responsibility that existed a hundred years on.'

At each headstone unveiling, there were GAA representatives to pay tribute.

'I know to this day that John Horan, when he goes on a walk, cuts in through a side gate in Glasnevin and looks in on the grave of Jerome O'Leary. Jerome has no surviving blood relatives left that we can find. He was a ten-year-old boy, shot in the head as he sat on the wall of what is now the Canal End, behind the goal. There are GAA people who look in on him.

'John William Scott was known as Billy to his friends, and sadly his line of relatives cannot be traced either. He was a fourteen-year-old boy who grew up on Fitzroy Avenue, just off Jones's Road, a stone's throw from the pitch. He went to the match with a friend but was shot in the chest. He was carried to a neighbour's house, where he cried for water, prayers and for his parents. By the time his frantic father had located which house he was in, he had been taken to hospital. When his neighbour, Mrs Colman, put his glasses and tie pin into his hands, he knew his boy was dead.'

They had just gone to watch Dublin play football.

When HQ unveiled John William Scott's marker in Glasnevin in 2018 on a cold November's morning, Dublin CEO John Costello and then manager Jim Gavin were there to pay their respects.

'We started to learn their stories,' Murphy remarks. 'You could see yourself in them. Fathers, kids in school, a fiancée. The more we learned, the more we agreed these people could not be remembered as numbers any more; they had to be remembered as people.'

A short list of those to attend the restricted commemoration was finally confirmed. They included President Michael D. Higgins, Taoiseach Micheál Martin, Minister for Tourism, Culture, Arts, Gaeltacht, Sport and Media Catherine Martin, three musicians, two flag bearers, Rachel Dobbs, and Michael Joyce from Artane School of Music. Alan Brogan represented Dublin, while Declan Browne was there for Tipperary.

Restrictions meant none of the Bloody Sunday families could attend. But it didn't stop the GAA from making them the sole focus.

'My former colleague Lisa Hayden played a big role in helping create digital content for the commemoration and produced a series of short videos or vignettes which were stitched into one main video,' Murphy adds. 'They helped us remember the victims as real people at a game that day and reached the modern, digital and social media generations. We had a 360 approach to the event and supported a podcast, TV documentary and radio documentaries. There were articles in newspapers in America, China and New Zealand, and it truly went around the globe.'

Level 5 restrictions meant that only a small televised ceremony was permissible. It would precede the meeting of Dublin and Meath in the 2020 Leinster football final. A master of ceremonies was required, too.

'There was never even a list. Only one name. Brendan Gleeson. We knew he was one of us; he goes to Croke Park, Parnell Park, he's from Dublin and has Tipperary roots. He was a perfect fit. A Gleeson of Thurles and Tipperary, but a true-blue Dub, who was born in the capital and spent his summers in Tipp.

'He is a national treasure and a GAA person, a Hollywood A-lister with no airs or graces. I'd seen him once being interviewed on *The Late Late Show* and he had become emotional talking about St Francis Hospice, and you knew how strong he was on social justice. Everyone loves him because he is the real deal in every way. So humble.'

Robert Smith is the Croke Park entertainment director and producer on match days, and his contacts helped get Gleeson on board.

'Brendan was over in Canada playing Donald Trump in a film,' Murphy explains. 'But the irony is covid brought him home and ensured he was in Ireland for the tribute. The virus had derailed our plans, but it also ensured that an enormously busy actor – in fact, one of the most in-demand actors in the world – was back home.'

Smith produced a subtle but powerful service built around fourteen torches on Hill 16 and at Gate 43, just in front of where Michael Hogan was fatally shot. A wreath-laying service took place to the air of a specially commissioned piece of music called *More Than a Game* by the renowned Colm Mac Con Iomaire, who was accompanied by Lisa Hannigan and Catherine Fitzgerald. A video tribute played over the music before the poignant oration delivered by an inspired Gleeson.

Stitching the elements of the ceremony together was stadium announcer Jerry Grogan. Croke Park fell into complete darkness, save for the illumination of the fourteen torches of flame and a corresponding beam of light which pulsed out from Dublin 3 and into the November night sky.

'Robert and Jerry always bring their A game,' Murphy stresses. 'And with Brendan, the thing was just to stay out of the way of genius.

'Michael wrote the script. By that stage Michael must have written fifty pieces on Bloody Sunday, but a real sign of his class is that no two were ever the same. He handed the script to Brendan – it was like a brilliant chef getting the best of ingredients.'

111

As the lights of remembrance shot up into the night sky, Gleeson spoke at the foot of Hill 16, reading out the names of all the victims, pausing before speaking of each one, how they lived and how they perished on that dark day. A flickering flame gleamed through nightfall as he told their stories.

Gleeson spoke to an empty stadium, but almost an entire nation at the same time. Coverage beamed into households the length and breadth of the country.

In the Croke Park gantry, Foley was co-commentating on the event with RTÉ's Darragh Maloney. He held his head in his hands as the lives and times of those killed were recounted. Emotions ran high in the stadium and in every living room where the ceremony was relayed.

'It was highly charged,' Murphy admits. 'On a personal level, along the five years of planning, Michael's dad and my mam had passed away. So that was a personal thing. Then the more you met members of the bereaved families, the more respectful you were of them.

'There was a weight of responsibility attached. Just two weeks out I ended up in hospital and only got the final permission for the event sealed and delivered while I was emailing from the hospital bed. We got the official approval for the event just twenty-four hours beforehand. It was stressful, but we all kept going because we knew we couldn't let these people down.'

The last line in Foley's script, relayed powerfully by Gleeson, knocked everyone for six: 'They are our family. Our friends. Our people. *Cuimhnímís orthus uilig*. We remember them all.'

That they did.

13

WHEN HOPE AND HISTORY RHYME

EMOTIONS RUN HIGH AS EIGHTY-FIVE-YEAR WAIT ENDS

There are ties in the GAA that help bind the generations; historical symmetry unites young and old. Tipperary football folk have a deeper connection to Bloody Sunday than most, and nearly a hundred years to the day that Mick Hogan and the thirteen others were shot dead, there was a beautiful symbolism to the 2020 team ending an insufferable eighty-five-year wait for a Munster senior title.

'Feels like a lifetime ago now,' says Brian Fox, casting an eye back. That November Sunday when they won their first provincial title since 1935 in an empty stadium will stay with him forever. 'It was down to both faith and fate. We took our chance when it came, but I think there was nearly a sense of destiny about the whole thing, too.'

When the government allowed play to resume, Tipp restarted the 2020 season on something of a high. 'We just appreciated sport more,' explains manager David Power. 'Sport means a lot to the Irish and I remember the buzz of being back on the first night, 20 September. Six months of calls, antigen tests, social distancing, texts, Zooms, Microsoft Teams – and then finally we were back together. Nothing like it.'

Tipp didn't realise it, but, though covid had played havoc with people's lives, the stars had somehow aligned for them. Several of their top players planned to go abroad for 2020 but when restrictions rendered international travel out of bounds, they instead found themselves staying put. As the virus spread, others who were overseas cut their stay short and returned to Ireland, home being a shelter for all storms.

Even at that early point, it seemed like a higher power was making sure that all of Tipp's finest were back on terra firma and ready for whatever would come.

That's certainly what Power, the spirit keeper of Tipperary football, felt. He had previously led the county to Munster minor and All-Ireland glory. And done a lot more besides in almost every age group. As the months passed, he got the sense something extraordinary might happen for his senior team.

'Covid threw it all upside down. Lads that we had planned without started to come back into our thinking. The fellas who were supposed to be travelling were around home. We were looking closely at the Sydney Swans AFL side and whether they would release Colin O'Riordan to play for us. That didn't happen for a while – even when he returned to Ireland when Australia shut its borders.'

If Power is the heart and soul of the game in Tipp football, O'Riordan was its beating pulse. O'Riordan's presence is immense. He is a rare breed who can command a dressing room with words but then go out on and back up everything with action. When Tipp beat Dublin in an epic 2011 All-Ireland minor final, he was only fifteen but already leading the way. Those qualities transcended codes. Ten years later, the Swans named him their 'Clubman of the Year'.

He had signed for the Swans in 2016 when the county reached an All-Ireland senior semi-final. Would he have helped them reach an All-Ireland final? Who knows, but even without their talisman they still only lost by five points, having seen another leader, Robbie Kiely, black-carded early on.

When the pandemic brought O'Riordan home in 2020, there was an unexpected chance to play for his county again. All-Star Michael Quinlivan and midfield powerhouse Liam Casey were also available after their wanderlust was put on pause.

O'Riordan initially linked up with the squad just to stay fit. He acted as water-boy at the Leitrim, Offaly, Clare and Limerick league and championship games at the end of 2020 but simply couldn't take watching from the sidelines for much longer.

After the heroics of Mark Keane, a fellow AFL player at Collingwood who sent Cork to victory in their shock Munster semi-final win over Kerry, O'Riordan asked his club for permission to play for Tipp in the final. The response was negative.

Undeterred, he wrote a heartfelt email to Sydney joint captains Josh Kennedy and Dane Rampe, explaining the significance and historical thread of the game, coming almost a century after Bloody Sunday. He explained his love for the county and for football there. After they read his heartfelt letter both players grasped the significance of the upcoming final. They agreed to speak to coach John Longmire on his behalf.

Once the joint captains fully understood the situation, O'Riordan knew there was a chance. The club duly agreed to let him play for Tipperary in the forthcoming decider against Cork – and subsequently for as long as their championship campaign lasted.

This spun Tipp's fate on an entirely different course. All key players were now within a short radius of Thurles once again.

The band was back together.

It's hard not to think fate was intervening.

Tradition played a huge part, too.

In his email to the club, O'Riordan was able to tell the story of Bloody Sunday and the historical and emotional connection to his county.

'When he got the nod the second or third time of asking it was because of the significance of playing for his county,' Fox says. 'The leadership group had discussed the possibility of him coming back in with other players, and I remember saying there were no guarantees he would get a jersey. That he would have to fight for it. But even in the short time he was home Colin had already reminded us of what a leader he was. We were thrilled. You'd listen to him talk; he simplified everything, explained stuff, and made so much sense. Sure, he was going to be an automatic name on the team. We all knew it.'

Power says the respect the team holds for O'Riordan could be traced back to when Tipp won the All-Ireland minor final.

'At just fifteen, Colin led the charge. In the Munster semi-final against Kerry, we were eight points down at half-time when he gave a speech in the dressing room. Back we came. In the final against Cork, he told us he had never lost to Cork or Kerry and didn't plan on starting now. I had to remind myself he was only a kid. When he was finished talking, I genuinely couldn't add anything. We just went out and won. It's just that drive in him and that's why he's in Australia.

'But now he was back with us again. And though it meant that lads would lose a place on the starting fifteen and the twenty-six-man squad, at the end of the day you don't get a load of opportunities to win Munster finals. You must throw everything at it.'

They did, too.

'Looking back, it's still mad how everyone re-assembled,' Fox continues. 'The virus came, we stopped training. Casey and Quinlivan, top-drawer players, didn't get to travel, and Colin came home. For ages everyone had just focused on their own targets – be that staying fit, getting ready to go back to Oz, or making alternative travel arrangements. But with restrictions extending we all ended up on a pitch together.'

Tipp took on Clare in the Munster quarter-final and won.

Against Limerick in the semi-final, they were awful, but managed to inch through.

'That's Tipp football,' Fox laughs. 'We try to play a nice brand and when it goes well, we look fantastic. When we are off it, we go the other way. We looked poor that day, and I think Colin and a few more wondered what we were at.'

They only reached the Munster final courtesy of a sensational late winner from the left sideline, courtesy of captain Conor Sweeney. It was as sweet a score as ever seen on a Gaelic football field.

Afterwards, county secretary Tim Floyd asked if the squad was happy to wear the green and white jerseys of Grangemockler, Mick Hogan's club in the Munster final.

'I had a quick word with players, and they were happy to do so,' Power reveals. 'But it was important to get that made public and sorted before Cork and Kerry even played in the other semi-final. I asked the board to issue a press release. All sorted.'

There were still two weeks to the decider. Emotions could settle. The team could focus.

It was later that evening, hours after Tipp beat Limerick, that Cork caused a sensation of their own by beating Kerry.

'That result changed everything,' Fox reckons. 'We had no fear of Cork. We had beaten them at senior level before and at underage plenty of times. We knew the chance was there for us.'

Power agrees. 'When we are at it, Tipp know that we can beat Cork. Against Kerry, it's tougher mentally. But when Cork beat them, everyone in our camp believed we could win the final.'

* * *

22 November 2020. Tipperary 0–17, Cork 0–14. History.

With the game coinciding with the Bloody Sunday centenary, it was always going to be a day when grown men cried.

The occasion was even more emotive with Tipp opting for those green and white hooped jerseys, as worn by the 1920 team.

So it wouldn't have mattered if Tipp went down to Cork to play hopscotch on that particular weekend; there were going to be tears anyway. The build-up was intense. In the fortnight beforehand, historical events were pencilled in everywhere. The magnitude of the game threatened to bear down on the footballers. Fox was aware of the sentiment. A teacher in St Anne's secondary school in Tipperary Town, he'd been with the senior panel since 2008 and knew this was not just an ordinary game.

Once more, covid's disruptive nature helped them.

With the virus mutating, all the commemorative events were cancelled. Now there were no distractions whatsoever. After a decade of toil, this bunch quite simply had to get the harvest home.

'Everything else was put to one side,' Fox insists. 'This was our own chance to end the famine.'

The 2011 All-Ireland minor-winning team had helped feed the All-Ireland senior semi-final team of 2016, but, besides a few league titles here and there, Tipp hadn't claimed much since on the national stage. In fact, Fox had lost five Munster finals (one at minor level, three at under-21 level and a senior loss to Kerry). In contrast, several of the Dublin minor side they beat in 2011 graduated to enjoy stellar careers, thriving in several senior triumphs.

'You wondered if we would ever break through,' Fox admits. 'We knew our players were good enough, we had a lovely brand of football, but the turnover was huge. Lots of great players reached minor level and then chose hurling. In other counties, if you are close to making the football team you stay there, work hard and progress. In Tipp, if you are on the fringes of the football team, you will instead most likely focus on your club hurling team, which is every bit as much of a priority. You can nearly pick out ten of the minor hurling panel each year who could have played for the senior football team. Year after year we lose those guys. It's a pity.

'Hurling is number one here. But we felt that if we could beat Cork and win that Munster title, we could give young lads coming through the system something to think about.'

The day before the final, one hundred years to the day that Mick Hogan died, there wasn't a Tipperary man alive with a

Munster senior football medal. Just 24 hours later there were forty-one of them. A 3-point win. And a result that will forever remain with those players.

The poignancy of the whole weekend had hit home at different junctures, but it hadn't distracted them. Michael Quinlivan recalls watching the Bloody Sunday anniversary commemoration on RTÉ with his parents with not a word spoken between them for 20 minutes afterwards, such was the impact.

The following day Quinlivan, who should have been in the US, Australia or Dubai, went out and kicked five points.

Emotive minefields could have been triggered anywhere. But Power handled that side of things expertly.

'The lads wore the commemorative jerseys in training to get used to them and deal with the emotion that way. When match day finally arrived, we were well used to them and able to focus on the job at hand.'

The only pity is that the game was played behind closed doors at a time when the second wave of the virus was in full flow. But it was what it was. At the final whistle anything that had been suppressed finally poured out.

'Wow,' Power says, thinking back. 'All I know is the feeling is still there whenever I reflect on that day. It was just so emotional – not just because of the history but because of the battles Tipp football has faced, the eighty-five-year wait. And because of stalwarts here who worked tirelessly for forty and fifty years. I don't know if they ever believed they would see the day. All that emotion and history could have derailed us, but we just played great stuff and could have won by more.'

Fox longed for his parents and family, his wife Siobhan and his two young children at the end, but the place was empty. Instead, he wrapped himself in the warm embrace of his teammates. And how they celebrated. Whooping and hollering, lifting each other to the skies. Power hugged his father Michael, the county board treasurer and a football diehard. A son doesn't often see his father shed tears, but this was special.

O'Riordan walked around in a daze. How did this happen? He was meant to be at the far side of the world.

'I was hugely disappointed for those people who couldn't be there with us,' Fox adds. 'We missed our supporters. There are not many of them and we know them all. I would love to have met older players, too. A lot of them texted afterwards and let's just say there were more tears.

'I was an absolute wreck myself. I went from laughing to nearly breaking down. I couldn't control my emotions.

'It was a very special day and a weird day. But do you know what? That's Tipp football for you. Even in our finest moment something had to be held back or missing. Covid prevented a huge celebration.'

Later he met his family in Ballyporeen and got to hug little Tadhg and Lily. There was no cup because the GAA wouldn't allow it to be taken out of stadiums for fear of fuelling celebrations during the ongoing public-health crisis. There were no photos because it was freezing cold and pitch black.

'One man I am so glad I saw was one of our greatest supporters, Petey Savage,' says Fox. 'Petey missing a game like that was heartbreaking for everyone.'

Clonmel, the nerve-centre of Tipp football, was silent that evening as the town and country remained shut down. Power travelled back in the car with selector Charlie McGeever – the two were in their own bubble – as phones hopped with callers literally bawling down the lines. Power himself did a TV interview with Virgin Media the next day and broke down.

'We came off the motorway and saw the crowds lining the streets in Ballyporeen and that's when it hit us. We decided not to even get out of the car, because if we got out, we might never have got back in. I'd imagine there would have been ten to fifteen thousand people in Thurles to welcome us, if all was normal.

'To miss out on that was tough for the players, but the biggest disappointment of all is that when we did have the cup, we could not bring it around to the schools. I think that would have been a big, big thing for Tipperary football to promote the game. I think we turned a few people in the county towards football,' he explains. 'Hurling is number one and that's fine – most lads will opt to play hurling before football – but it's a big county, with space for both codes.'

They never got to mark that win or close it off properly. Two years later, Power still hadn't sat down to have a pint to celebrate with the players. There was no medal presentation until midway through 2022. And maybe because they never got to draw a line under it, Tipp struggled to keep going after winning that title.

But Power was happy that their golden generation, including warriors who soldiered along the hard shoulders of Division 4 to the smoother motorways of Division 2, were at least rewarded.

'Lads like Colin and Bill Maher have now won Munster medals at minor, under-21 and senior level. Incredible achievement. Any Tipp hurler will have a load of Munster medals, but for a Tipp footballer to have that array, they can be so proud of their careers.'

It was no easy journey. Fox was there for almost every mile.

'Philly Austin and I were coming home from training one night and reckoned that in our first four years with Tipperary football there was a turnover of three hundred players.' He smiles. 'That's three hundred players that came in, trialled, trained, played league, played championship – or did all the above. Countless lads came and went. I think we saw most of them.' He grins. 'But there was perseverance, too. That was the story of Tipp football. It probably still is, to be honest.'

Power nods. 'But even in the dark years – and, by God, we had lots of those – Tipp always had a cut. Historically, we are up and down, I know that, but we are an attacking county, and if I'm proud of nothing else it was our style of football that Munster final day.'

In true Tipp mercurial fashion, they went out against Mayo in the All-Ireland semi-final, coughed up eight goal chances, were caught asleep at the back and fell badly behind by half-time. They rallied well and scored 2–8 in the second half before losing out. The extraordinary odyssey ended under a blanket of fog in a deserted stadium on 6 December.

O'Riordan and others soon went their separate ways.

Another lockdown was implemented after Christmas and the exalted spirits of the group slipped when the players were forced to train individually again.

'We said we'd stay going and try to kick on,' Fox recalls. 'But by the time the 2021 season eventually restarted, lads were burned out and we had probably over-trained due to pure eagerness. Then you had a condensed league and championship. It didn't go well for us.'

In the space of just seven months Tipp went from boxing with the big boys in an All-Ireland semi-final as proud kings of Munster to being relegated to Division 4, as Kerry snatched their provincial title back from them.

Fox knew the game was up. He announced his retirement almost a year after the 2020 final, at thirty-three years of age. Without him, and with only eleven of the 2020 championship squad available for a variety of reasons, Tipp began the 2022 league campaign in slow fashion before rearranging to stack five successive wins together and earning promotion. In the championship, they played Limerick, with just five of the provincial title-winning side in the team, lost, and were beaten by Carlow in the Tailteann Cup.

'We're in transition once more,' Power says of Tipp football's endless roller-coaster ride. 'We gave nine players debuts in 2022. I'd question whether the necessary development work is going in at underage, and the structures need looking at. When we were helping to get it going, we searched the county, from Puckane to Drombane, looking for talent. Is that work still going on?'

On the night they gained promotion to Division 3, the core group of the squad finally got to celebrate the 2020 Munster final with a few pints. It was a late one. In every sense.

The long road back starts again.

14

CAVAN FEVER

MOMENTOUS DAY AS CAVAN OVERCAME ALL ODDS

The chances of two earthquakes rocking the Gaelic football world on the same day were slim, but as he drove to Armagh for his county's Ulster final against Donegal, Cavan full-back Padraig Faulkner was ready for more upheaval.

Faulkner listened to the closing stages of Tipperary's famous win in his car and wondered why Cavan couldn't have some of that.

'It's the year for the upset,' he thought to himself. 'If they can do it, anyone can do it.'

His manager, Mickey Graham, was listening to the same commentary and immediately thought of a stat that had been doing the rounds. Dublin, Tipp and Mayo had all reached the 1920 All-Ireland semi-finals and a hundred years later three of those were now through to the last four again. The fourth team a century ago was Cavan. If they beat Donegal a few hours later, the same quartet would again line up for the 2020 semis. Like David Power before him, Graham wondered if a higher power was at play.

If Tipperary's win was against the head, it was no wild shock either, but when Cavan beat Donegal by 4 points, it most definitely sent tremors through the GAA world. Like Tipp, Cavan benefitted from several knock-on effects caused by the pandemic. They had unexpected access to six players they imagined were unavailable, big hitters including Conor Moynagh, Dara McVeety and Killian Clarke. Even still, 2020 was slow to bear any fruit. They were relegated to Division 3 of the Allianz league and covid issues ripped the core of their community and team.

From there, they found a vein of form and followed it. After the league, they regained composure to beat Monaghan, Antrim, Down and Donegal in the championship.

They looked dead and buried more than once in some of those games, trailing Monaghan by 7 points and falling 10 points off Down at one point in the Ulster semi-final. They also withstood two black cards in their sensational final win over Donegal.

Football has a curious character. Just one month after being relegated they were crowned Ulster champions, taking an unforgiving preliminary round route to land their crown.

Raymond Galligan reflects on that season with a smile, though he can't make much sense of it. 'Sometimes you just prepare the best you can and go with it.'

At twenty-two, Galligan was in his pomp as a classy forward. In one of his first national league games, against Roscommon, he demonstrated the complete range of skills, hitting 10 points from all sorts of angles. There were high hopes for him.

But life moves to a different reality and sometimes so swiftly it can scuttle you on a different track in no time at all. A few years on, he had drifted from the county panel.

His clubmate, Terry Hyland, took over as Cavan manager in 2012 and re-opened the door to his top-flight career. But it was only partly ajar. Hyland wanted him as a goalkeeper. There would be absolutely no guarantee of game time.

'And I don't know what it is about Cavan, but we always seem to have huge competition for the number 1 jersey,' Galligan figures. 'I didn't know what to think. I wasn't sure because I felt I could still do a job as a forward.'

The new Cavan set-up instantly recognised that the most important thing they needed from a goalkeeper was a definite kick-out strategy. With Hyland estimating that his team would have an average of twenty-five to thirty restarts per game, he needed quality and reserves in the position.

Hyland knew Galligan was a brilliant free-taker and had seen a catalogue of YouTube clips where he converted frees with both feet from impossible angles. But when Galligan came on board, he found two goalkeepers, Conor Gilsenan and James Farrelly, ahead of him in the pecking order.

Former Dundalk soccer net-minder Gary Rogers was designated to work with the trio with the focus on restarts, kicking, shot stopping, the aerial game and peripheral vision.

Some plans are formulated with the end goal in mind, but more are of a 'come in and see what might happen' nature. Galligan's was definitely in the latter category. But he was highly motivated to wear the county shirt again.

* * *

A rural county, once described as full of hills with water collecting at the bottom of most of them, Cavan was one of the hardest hit with emigration. Traditionally, young men moved to England and football suffered. They were top of the tree for a while, winning five All-Ireland titles between 1933 and 1952. The cream of Ulster football, they had thirty-nine Ulster titles in the trophy cabinet by 1969.

But just one followed and that was almost thirty years later. The 1970s passed with no title claimed, and what a culture shock that was. The 1980s were just as bleak, with only one final appearance. A mini revival unfolded in 1997, when Ulster-title success came under the watch of Martin McHugh. But it was brief.

Following football is a birth right in Cavan, but whereas once upon a time a county obsessed with the game sent missionaries such as John Joe O'Reilly and Mick Higgins to coach weaker sides, coaches were now summoned from outside to apply aid within.

The period from 2006 to 2012 brought some dark days, including a menacing memory when, following five wins on the spin, they needed to beat Waterford to gain league promotion to Division 1. The year before, in 2005, Cavan had put seven goals past them, with Mickey Graham banging in four. Before the 2006 rematch, the Waterford lads read in the match programme that a home defeat would be 'the biggest disaster since the sinking of the *Titanic*'.

Well, they did hit an iceberg that day. Waterford beat them.

When Hyland took over, they were rooted in Division 3 and ripe for a plucking in the summers. But the new boss had blooded players at under-21 level and recognised there was quality coming through.

Hyland brought the senior team to a level of competitiveness, changed the players outlook, and wasn't afraid to challenge them.

'I genuinely think we owe Terry for the work he did,' Galligan says. 'I do, anyway.'

Galligan probably owes Mickey Graham, too. When Graham took on the managerial role in the winter of 2018, he took Galligan aside before the start of the McKenna Cup and made him captain. It was some vote of confidence for a man who'd made his Cavan debut twelve years earlier but had been marooned in their junior team for a period.

They reached the 2019 Ulster final and lost by 5 points to Donegal. By the time they repeated the feat of qualifying for the 2020 decider, they had more experience. Seventeen of their twenty-six-man squad had tasted underage success of some sort. Galligan says they felt they could achieve something.

'It's funny,' Galligan says. 'I will look back from 2020 to 2022, and while those years were dominated by covid and adapting to the various cycles, an awful lot more happened too. Outside of football I think we all had perspective. Your health is your wealth – that's the biggest takeaway I've had.

'Our county was hit really hard with cases and illness in 2020 and our team was too. For a few weeks, just as the league reached its climax, we were working with just thirteen players,' he reveals. 'We didn't make it public, but the camp was devastated by the virus. We played away, but it cost us a tilt at Division 1.

'Afterwards we felt sorry for ourselves a little. Other counties had earned public sympathy for having to cope with covid issues, but we kept our challenges in-house; no one knew what we were dealing with. We took flak in various places for our performances. Once it came to the championship, people didn't expect much, but we had everyone back fit by then and our mantra was: "Let's show them what we can do."'

* * *

They were as good as their word.

Having trained individually during the early lockdowns, all physical targets were easily met by the time the championship rolled around. This meant management could trust the players but could also devote more time to significant tactical work in training, rather than fretting about fitness levels.

Raging underdogs against Monaghan, Down and against Donegal, they won all three games, playing amid the backdrop of an intense hush. In each game they attacked the opposition as though they were personally affronted. Their tactics varied. They could run the ball, or go directly into the arms of Galligan's brother, Thomas. They used diagonal, long and short ball deliveries, and when they didn't have possession, they hounded opponents for turnovers at every opportunity. That doggedness and breadth of play caught opponents on the hop.

'We were so fit from having trained by ourselves,' Galligan says. 'The lockdowns allowed us to build a base to play such a high-tempo game. We were able to hunt in packs.

'We were also playing for the people of Cavan and what they were going through as a society. A good few of my family had covid at various points and, while everyone got through it thankfully, some really struggled.'

At one stage in the winter of 2020, the electoral area of Ballyjamesduff in Cavan had the highest fourteen-day incidence rate of coronavirus cases in the state. It stood at over five times the national rate.

'It just puts things in perspective,' Galligan adds. 'Gaelic football was the outlet for people in that time. People who suffered could look forward to our games either online or on TV. I think the GAA helped change the conversation. One day it was all positive cases, close contacts and who has it now? But when the Cavan team got going, it was who would play where, what will the match-ups be?'

Realistically, at half-time, Monaghan should have had the game over. They missed three goal chances.

'I will never forget the dressing room. The management gave us five minutes to get our thoughts together and give us space,' Galligan recounts. 'That was significant because a few of us took over the room. We were 7 points down, but now had a breeze at our backs. We just had to keep chipping away. There was no panic. Going into the last quarter, it was down to 3 points. Monaghan kind of went back into their shell and that allowed us more scope.'

The victory was sealed when Galligan landed a long-range free deep into injury-time for a 1-point win over their next-door neighbours.

'When it went over, I was so emotional because I had kicked thousands of frees over the years and always wondered, "Jaysus, wouldn't it be great to kick a winning point for Cavan some time!"'

It was as good as he had imagined.

And just like Tipperary, destiny kind of led the way from there.

Cavan beat Armagh well, scraped by Down and set up another Ulster final tussle with a star-studded Donegal outfit.

'Along the way we gained this resilience that we never previously showed,' he adds. 'Like against Down in the semi-final.'

Galligan says playing without fans in the stadium was strange, but, against Down, he considers the momentum they achieved, the clarity of their play – from kick-outs, tactics and possession – and reckons everything clicked because the players could clearly hear each other talk on the field.

'We could really drive each other on and heed the different calls, get the squeeze on. Had it been a normal Ulster championship day, we wouldn't have heard a word. We may not have been as tight and together – you missed the atmosphere – but there was this other side to it, too.'

Especially when they won the final. A 4-point win in the end, 1–13, 0–12. Totally against the grain, with Conor Madden's goal securing a historic triumph. The fairy tale was only enriched for manager Graham, a key player the last time the county lifted the Anglo-Celt Cup.

Remarkably, Cavan's win meant the 2020 All-Ireland semi-final line-up of four teams would be the same as 1920, the year of Bloody Sunday.

'There are some things you just can't put your finger on.' Galligan shrugs happily. 'The emotion of that win was massive. For the people of Cavan and even beyond. It's there with you for the rest of your life.'

Once they grasped the enormity of what they had done, it was back in the trenches. For the greatest battle of them all. They went down to play Dublin next.

'I spent the whole day obsessed with the cogs on my boots. Trying to change them, then breaking them, driving back to Cavan so my dad could fix them, then back down to Dublin to practise in St Jude's before a cog came off again. We were facing the best team of all time and my entire day was spent trying to get my boots right.'

They set up well and looked adept at times, but never laid a glove on the Dubs.

'I was very disappointed because we had been training to an unreal standard. We probably didn't get enough direct ball into Thomas, but what really shocked us was the tackling ferocity from their half-forward line. We couldn't break through it. The way the Dublin forwards tackle, we just didn't realise how workmanlike they were. They turned us over and it was a massive learning curve.'

Yet the year ended on a high. Only a few years previously Galligan was fretting over his inter-county future. In 2020, he was selected as an All-Star, taking the number-one slot on that team. Thomas got one too, as did defender Faulkner.

'You just didn't ever envisage stuff like that happening,' he says. 'I was the third choice not long back and just wanted to nail down a place on the team. It was just fantastic for our parents, club and family. I was delighted for all of them.'

Like Tipperary, Cavan found 2021 a totally different proposition. Both teams were relegated in 2021, promoted in 2022, whilst they also ended up in the 2022 Tailteann Cup final, which they lost to Westmeath.

'We never got to put 2020 to bed either. Rather than sit back and draw a line under it, we strived to train harder and get better. But it just didn't work. The lockdowns continued into early 2021 and we were flat by the time we resumed play. We got nowhere near our levels.'

Despite all the frantic highs and disappointing lows, there was always a bigger picture for Galligan to reflect upon. He manages a day service centre for people with intellectual disabilities in Rathfarnham and those in his care were his top priority during the pandemic.

'Our mission kind of changed,' he states. 'The aim is to

help our people settle into the community and employment. It's very interactive. During covid it simply boiled down to making sure they were all safe. Everything was geared towards temperature checks, mask wearing and social distancing. We tried to hold sessions on Zoom, but we couldn't engage like we wanted to.'

Wherever he goes, Galligan is conscious of who he represents and works with daily. When in team meetings, his mask was worn; he observed every restriction all the way through.

'For young people with disabilities, wearing a mask can be quite tough. So it was the least I could do. I found it an unbeliev-able time, linking in with their families to make sure they were all okay. But it was very rewarding. And we had a bit of craic too. Before our All-Ireland semi-final with Dublin, I brought in a load of Cavan gear and got our people and the whole school decked out in the blue and white. I really enjoyed that.

'Keeping the centre open was the key. It was tough on staff because they were not getting the same input. Whereas they were previously trying to educate, safety was the only priority at that time.

'You do appreciate the football stuff more outside of that, I guess. What happened with Cavan was a kind of fairy-tale story, one that I will probably only stop to consider when I retire.'

15

TAKING STOCK AFTER A SEASON OF SILENCE

BEHIND THE SCENES AS A NEW COURSE IS NAVIGATED

Finally 2020, a year without precedent, ended.

The GAA issued nineteen different advice notes to clubs and county boards over that period, such was the disruption and uncertainty that they experienced. Whenever the government made a move, Croke Park dissected it and tweaked their own approach.

'Each time there was a change in government policy, I would listen to the Six One News on RTÉ, watch Micheál Martin walk down the steps of Government Buildings, record his speech on my iPhone, and then replay it to fully decipher and interpret what he said,' Feargal McGill says.

'The second the Taoiseach spoke, everyone involved in the GAA was trying to get us on the phone or email, enquiring what the latest changes would mean for their training session, juvenile match or whatever.

'That was really tricky, and it meant plenty of Friday nights were spent getting advice notes out there once I had spoken with the president and the director-general and asked the advisory group to sign off on our interpretations.'

There were several occasions when the GAA gave their best interpretation of what the Taoiseach had signalled while they waited for civil service confirmation of changes to come.

'That was the hardest part,' McGill elaborates. 'The time lag between the government broadly saying what was happening and then interpreting it whilst awaiting the specifics. It wasn't easy for anyone – government, civil service, health workers or anyone who depended on clarity.

'The first two or three times when there was a big government announcement, there was chaos, absolute mayhem. Then, as it went on, people understood the GAA would interpret it once we had taken all the information on board. They trusted us.'

It wasn't easy to keep up with it all. By December, living through the pandemic had driven dramatic shifts in our workplace and lifestyle habits, childcare arrangements and even our sense of time, which seemed to be distorted. Virtually no one was left untouched after twelve months of upset.

By the end of 2020 worldwide figures showed that two million people had died from the virus. In Ireland, the Central Statistics Office (CSO) showed that more than four thousand covid-19-related deaths occurred that year, with more than a thousand of those deaths occurring in the four weeks before Christmas. There were 535,786 people either on the Live Register or in receipt of the Pandemic Unemployment Payment (PUP). A CSO survey showed that forty-two per cent of respondents rated their overall life satisfaction as 'low'.

The number of hours worked per week decreased by 8.5 per cent across the year and almost a quarter of companies planned to

CLOSED FOR NOW Celbridge GAA Club and others would soon be preparing for the relaxation of covid-19 Restrictions.

A PENNY FOR YOUR THOUGHTS Feargal Logan looks pensive as his Tyrone side takes on Monaghan in the 2021 Allianz National Football League Division 1 North Round.

THREE-IN-A-ROW Injured Limerick talisman Cian Lynch stands alongside captain, Declan Hannon, and lifts the Liam MacCarthy Cup aloft after they clinched the three-in-a-row with a sensational win against Kilkenny in front of a packed Croke Park in the 2022 All-Ireland final. It was Limerick's first championship win of the covid era to be played in front of a capacity crowd.

MORNING AFTER THE NIGHT BEFORE Brian Fox is back teaching at St Anne's secondary school in Tipperary Town the day after his Tipperary team made history by winning the 2020 Munster senior football final. Fox is met by teachers and students outside, saluting at a distance.

HOME FROM HOME New York's GAA president, Joan Henchy, took on a serious leadership role by guiding the exiled Gaelic Games family through the pandemic in the 'Big Apple'.

THE SLIGO STALWART Neil Ewing saw his inter-county career end with a whimper due to his team's withdrawal from the 2020 championship. He is pictured here with Drumcliffe/Rosses Point clubmate Kevin Dufficy after they won Division 2 of the Sligo league to return to the top-flight.

FAMILY FIRST, THROUGH THICK AND THIN Antrim's Domhnall Nugent came back from the brink with the help of his loving family. Here he is with his uncle, Eamonn and grandmother, Marie.

LIKE FATHER, LIKE SON Legendary Cork medic, Dr Con Murphy, devoted his life to helping others and continued that work during covid. During this time he passed the responsibility of looking after Cork's GAA teams to his son, Dr Colm.

© Sportsfile/Stephen McCarthy

FAITHFUL FOREVER The pandemic saw Offaly GAA's fortunes change dramatically – mostly for the better. It started with the community eagerly supporting the board's fundraising ventures, continued with some sensational moments on the field of play and was crowned by the backing of champion golfer Shane Lowry.

© Sportsfile/Ramsey Cardy

NAVIGATING TOUGH TERRAIN Feargal McGill, GAA director of club, player and games administration, played a key role in guiding the association through the pandemic.

DEFINING MOMENT Covid-19 presented former GAA president John Horan with the biggest challenge of his administrative career.

WHERE WE ALL BELONG East Belfast GAA made huge inroads by establishing itself in a traditionally loyalist area and quickly attracting 1,000 members. These pictures show one of their underage teams playing in their first ever blitz, hosted by neighbours St Paul's. Meanwhile, Kimberly Robertson and Richard Maguire receive the 2021 Community Outreach award presented to them by Ulster GAA.

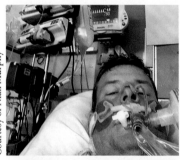

MURPHY'S LAW Never give up. Belfast barrister Niall Murphy is seen applauding front line workers at the very start of the pandemic. He described them as his 'guardian angels' in his lowest moments after the virus struck and left him battling for his life in the ICU ward.

FROM THERE TO HERE In the darkest covid times Marianne Walsh inspired a nation by overcoming a cancer diagnosis to win a Kilkenny Camogie Championship with her club, Mooncoin, just months later.

CLOSED UNTIL FURTHER NOTICE

Croke Park, a haven for Gaelic Games lay empty for long periods as the country battled covid-19. The historic stadium and the games played there would never be taken for granted again.

© Sportsfile/Ray McManus

A GAME OF 4 QUARTERS

Covid saw water breaks being introduced to the GAA for the first time. Some loved them, some didn't. Here, in mid-December 2021, Eire Óg Ennis players take in some fluids as they paused against St Finbarr's in an AIB Munster club football clash.

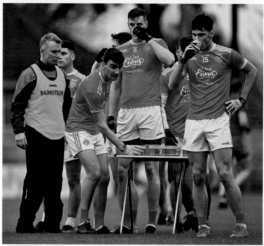

© Sportsfile/Eóin Noonan

THE MEATH MIRACLE

The Meath ladies footballers, led by Eamonn Murray (pictured with his family after their 2021 All-Ireland win), have enjoyed the best moments of their history despite tough times during the pandemic.

Courtesy of Eamonn Murray

© Sportsfile/Ray McManus

THE GAA REMEMBERS The 2020 Bloody Sunday commemoration. It was meant to be an event for 80,000 people. Covid ensured that only eight were present but its impact was nonetheless powerful.

© Sportsfile/Stephen McCarthy

TRUE BLUE Dublin actor and Hollywood legend Brendan Gleeson was the obvious choice to narrate the Bloody Sunday commemoration. A true GAA man, from Dublin, with strong roots in Tipperary.

LEADING THE WAY Taoiseach Mícheál Martin led the country for much of the pandemic. He always maintained the GAA had a huge role to play in Ireland's fight against the virus. He says his son, Cork senior football goalkeeper Mícheál Áodh, was never short of advice for him either!

ONLY A CALL AWAY David Brady got on the phone at the start of the pandemic and very rarely came off it as he helped the elderly and the isolated cope with covid times.

ADAPT AND ADJUST The GAA went from record revenues and attendance to almost seeing the entire organisation vulnerable in the matter of weeks. Commercial & Croke Park stadium director Peter McKenna among those who found ways to adapt as the virus wreaked havoc.

THE POWER AND THE GLORY Little needs to be said as Tipp's footballers break historical barriers by winning the 2020 Munster title behind closed doors as their manager struggles to get his head around the emotion of the occasion.

NOT THE SAME WITHOUT FANS Colin Fennelly of Kilkenny lifts the Bob O'Keeffe Cup following his side's Leinster final win over Galway in 2020. The ground was empty due to ongoing restrictions imposed by the Government to contain the spread of the coronavirus.

LOUGHMORE LEGACY You can be a dual club and still thrive and promote codes. Loughmore showed this when they lost both the 2020 Tipperary hurling and football finals but came back in 2021 to win them both. Here, they celebrate their 2021 replayed county hurling final win over Thurles Sarsfields at Semple Stadium.

make remote working permanent. Meanwhile, there was a near collapse of air and sea travel, with 31.4 million fewer arrivals and departures in 2020 compared to 2019.

With so much going on and such turbulence, it was remarkable that the administration got to complete the season, witnessing the most poignant moments and incredible drama.

Apart from the Tipp and Cavan heroics, there was Cillian O'Connor's masterful 4–9 haul in the All-Ireland semi-final. Under a veil of darkness at Croke Park, Dublin won six football titles in a row. Limerick's occupation of hurling's main pillars was reinforced when they beat Waterford in the hurling final.

Off the field, money was tighter than ever and, to manage overheads prudently, HQ set up a centralised template for squads and backrooms, keeping mileage and other expenses to a minimum.

Peter McKenna feels the GAA only prevailed through the crisis due to the collective efforts of membership, financial aid from the government and goodwill from sponsors.

'The government stabilised the economy with the PUP and gave significant help to sporting bodies too,' he says. 'Truthfully, that stopped us going into a colossal recession. What I found amazing, though, was the reaction I received from our own sponsors when I told them of the uncertainty around our 2020 season. It was probably the biggest morale boost I ever got. They all had the same outlook: "The GAA is a community. How can we help?"'

One sponsor said their company would pay a hundred per cent of that year's contract and would review the situation at the end of 2021. Another also pledged full payment – and even offered further support. McKenna was blown away.

'They said, "We sponsor you guys because you are a community." It showed the relationship was deeper than transactional. These people had their own targets to meet and boards to respond to. I was ringing, expecting them to say, "We will give you sixty-two per cent [of the contract fee] because you guys can only deliver on sixty per cent of the contract." That didn't happen. We averaged eighty per cent in the end. And from the broadcast point of view, RTÉ and TG4 streamed all games so people could see them. They did it without a problem. Everyone worked together; it was real public service broadcasting.

'It came down to the human side, though. I will never forget Sean McGrath, the CEO of Allianz, and others like him, who offered their full support. It just reminded me of who we represent.'

Throughout 2020 Croke Park's pitch manager, Stuart Wilson, and his team kept the sod primed for action in case play did resume. A shadow crew oversaw stadium operations, always with an eye trained on a return.

Twenty-five miles of pipework had been laid under the turf to regulate the temperature and moisture of the soil, and staff maintained the preferred heat as the year progressed.

And whilst games did come back to Croke Park at the tail end of the year, they were inevitably without crowds.

'An outrageously hollow experience,' McKenna recalls. 'I sat in the stand and, apart from one or two in the media, or John Horan, I was alone. Games were like challenge matches in terms of hearing every word that was said. It was surreal.'

Croke Park stadium announcer Jerry Grogan still thinks back on the bizarre nature of the 2020 series and says he will never forget the effect of biting cold winter championship days either.

'It was still an absolute privilege to be there. When you saw the amount of people trying to get into these games, you just realised how lucky you were.

'In fairness, Peter tried to keep things as normal as possible, even by holding Mass at 9 a.m. in the museum on All-Ireland final day, although there were only four of us allowed – Peter, John Horan, Mick Leddy, the chief steward, and myself. He tried to stick to traditions whilst acting safely and responsibly too.

'For me, two things stand out. There were just the four of us at the Mass and only fourteen stewards were on duty when we would normally have two hundred. But we got on with it. In a way there was more time to talk to people. I remember Kevin McManamon coming down the Hogan Stand after Dublin had won their sixth All-Ireland in a row and he came over. I saw Kevin play as a kid at Croke Park but wouldn't have known him well. He came over and just mentioned that it had been a pleasure to hear me call his name out on the tannoy over the years. I thought that was lovely.

'There was also a nice chat with another Dublin player, Niall Scully, after the final. I was able to remind him how I had seen him play both hurling and football with his school in the stadium when he was a child. In normal circumstances would those chats have ever happened? I don't think so. The lads would have been dragged here, there and everywhere after the final whistle. So those were positives amid a very weird experience.'

McKenna maintains the softly-softly approach to resuming play was the right call. He reckoned the GAA's alliance with the IRFU and the FAI demonstrated to the government that the sports organisations held a collective expertise to deal with the challenges ahead.

'The government gave us a guideline and we responded with solutions,' McKenna elaborates. 'If games continued behind closed doors, we were not going to live much longer. We came back to play with crowds of two hundred and five hundred, creeping up to 2,500 and eventually reaching fifty per cent capacity for the 2021 All-Ireland finals.

'We didn't want to be a source of infection, so we actually pulled back in the enthusiasm to welcome spectators back when people were shouting "move forward, move forward".

'There was a lot of pressure to let bigger crowds back. An example of that was the 2021 Munster football final between Cork and Kerry at Killarney, which would have been a massive event for the town. We didn't budge in the limit we set. Instead, we looked at how people would exit, and the signs were that there would be a big mixing zone outside the stadium.

'We went through everything to the last degree, and we had no recorded onward transmission of the virus from any game we had. That was the competence we knew we could deliver to the Department of Sport.

'Staying safe was the focus until it was safely back to one hundred per cent at the Aviva Stadium for the 2021 autumn rugby internationals. That successful and phased re-introduction showed the government we had professional expertise in managing crowds and crowd movement, amid all guidelines. It was a huge positive.'

The road was never too smooth for too long, though. It chipped, cracked and even pivoted at various points.

With the 2020 club season coming to an end, all bar eleven domestic championships were completed when Croke Park had to call a sudden halt to the action.

That directive came on 7 October and was implemented with immediate effect. All club games were suspended following several breaches of public-health guidelines linked to matches and celebrations.

The GAA's management committee took the decision in the interests of public safety following those incidents, which it said were both disappointing and problematic. It came soon after Nphet's recommendations to impose Level 5 restrictions.

One scene of celebration in Cork saw droves of people gather, as players, squad, management and fans marched towards each other from opposite directions, met in the middle and started celebrating on the street with no social distancing observed.

In any other year, this gathering would have been a perfect example of how the GAA can bring a parish together, but in Ireland at the end of 2020 society was anxious, uncertain and frustrated.

Positive case numbers were increasing once more. Public patience was thin. Stern clampdowns were implemented, including extremely low numbers permitted at funerals, and the court of public opinion carried more thump than ever.

When social media footage of club celebrations spilling over emerged, there was more uproar. It wasn't easy shutting county championships down, but it was done quickly.

McGill says they had to pull the plug. 'Through the end of September and the start of October, we had recognised the celebrations were very hard for us to control,' he says. 'We controlled everything inside the pitch, made sure that people were not sitting on top of each other, that everyone wore masks, that players didn't use dressing rooms. Everything and everyone was sanitised.

'But the second the cup was taken out of the stadium we lost all control and it became more of a societal issue. What was happening in celebrations was beyond the GAA's control at that stage. For two to three weeks, we monitored it very closely, and when incidents emerged, we communicated with people in various clubs and counties, informing them that they were bringing a bad light down on the association.

'It was not good for us to be giving regular and rigorous communication on health and safety advice, and having footage of club championship celebrations emerging at the same time. With the best will in the world, our people tried to stop what was happening, and club and county board officers were among some of the most disappointed. They had given their utmost to try and control the situation.'

On the first Monday morning in October, John Horan called McGill and said they had to react.

'We got together – John, Tom Ryan and I – to discuss our options. We were going to have to put a stop to all county finals until things calmed down. We issued a statement confirming that.

'It was open-ended at that stage, and we didn't know when we would return, and I know it hurt counties. One case that will always stick in my mind was Donegal. We made the decision on a Monday and they had their final that Wednesday. But it was like, "Sorry, lads, this has gone too far and it's not doing any good for our communities or for the GAA as an entity."'

McGill also empathises with how it was hard on clubs who were doing everything right and hard on players who had done all that was asked of them – filled out questionnaires, washed hands, travelled alone, stayed out of dressing rooms.

'But what could we do?' he asks. 'The hardest thing was that we couldn't guarantee when the finals could be played. And, as it turned out, things gradually went downhill, with rising case numbers until the end of the year, so we definitely made the right call.'

Those outstanding championships were later completed in early 2021.

* * *

That was just one of numerous obstacles the association faced. There were plenty more.

When the 2020 national leagues eventually resumed, Leitrim had to give Down a walkover in their first league game back due to an outbreak in the squad. It immediately led to countless debates on the integrity of the 2020 season and the possibility of more games having to go by the wayside.

Around that time the Gaelic Players Association also surveyed its membership to see if they wanted to proceed further: fifty-two per cent wanted the season to go ahead, twenty-four per cent wanted to play with improved safeguards, with the remaining twenty-four per cent reluctant to play in that environment.

'It meant a lot to get the 2020 inter-county season completed, and you simply can't overlook the role the players had in us getting there,' McGill says. 'The players took a really great approach. They realised we were facing a dark winter, with very little distractions and the whole country locked down.

'They knew they could play their part in lifting the national mood simply by going out and giving it their all. Our players were put in the frontline, and they were the ones who had to go and respond.'

Was there ever a fear they would say no and refuse to make themselves available?

'No, not a bit. We wondered if it was fair to ask them when the rest of the country was locked down, but my communication with players was that they felt they were very lucky to be able to represent their counties.

'Those players and their management teams had to buy into difficult protocols that we put in front of them, and we set the standard very high in terms of what we asked them to do. Overwhelmingly, they delivered.'

Ending the 2020 season with all inter-county senior competitions concluded – and all bar those eleven club championships outstanding – was even more impressive when you consider the regular restriction changes enforced by the government.

Here's an example. In early April, Simon Harris, then health minister, stated that it would be highly unlikely there would be any mass gatherings for the year ahead. This was news to the GAA, as it had not been communicated officially.

Often restrictions were tightened or loosened without any advance notice, meaning that the GAA – and other sporting organisations – were frequently left scrambling to adapt.

Sometimes senior politicians made announcements that caught even their party colleagues – never mind the GAA – by surprise.

There was serious tension at junctures, like in August when Croke Park officials asked the government to provide 'empirical evidence' to explain the decision to ban all spectators from sporting events until at least 13 September.

Up until then, two hundred people had been allowed to attend outdoor events. Plans were in the pipeline to raise that number to five hundred, but they were put on hold due to rising infection levels.

The news to scrap the two-hundred-person crowd limit was totally unexpected by the GAA, who, in quick-tempered fashion, called upon Deputy Chief Medical Officer Dr Ronan Glynn and Nphet to present evidence which provided the basis for their decision.

The GAA's letter to Glynn was heavily criticised by those who felt that anger had swallowed their reason. On the other hand, the government's view that having so few supporters at a game could be a threat to public health also came in for flak.

Managing a virus that always seemed one step ahead of us was a fluid situation. The government made hard calls and later assessed and reassessed them to see what had worked. Nothing remained the same for very long. The goalposts changed constantly.

'Without doubt that was the most stressful part of the whole process,' McGill admits. 'We fully accepted that the government couldn't consult with everyone. They were doing what was right for the country and they did a very good job.

'They picked Fridays almost exclusively for their announcements, and with good reason, as they had to accumulate all the relevant data from earlier in the week before finalising decisions,' he notes.

'It just meant that we had to be ready to tweak and adapt to their latest set of restrictions, or easing of restrictions, and with the vast majority of fixtures taking place at weekends it didn't leave much time to turn around new policies.'

While the 2020 fixtures behind closed doors were a soulless experience, with no crowds allowed and only forty people per county permitted, McGill was taken aback at the acceptance of every directive.

'All over the country there are lots of stewards, volunteers, officials and others who wanted to go to games but were told they couldn't. And they abided by that. Incredible going. These people have given their lives to the association, their clubs and their counties, and they continue to work as hard now in a voluntary capacity as they ever did.'

Even though he was to the forefront of the GAA's response to covid, McGill also refused to attend any inter-county games in 2020, including the All-Ireland finals.

'Of course I wanted to go, but I was leading such a strict line that if you didn't have a role on match day you shouldn't be there,' he states. 'I remember going to Pairc Sean MacDiarmada at 8 a.m. for a pitch inspection before Leitrim played Mayo in the Connacht championship. Michael Doherty from the stadium committee was there and said he would see me later.'

McGill replied that he wouldn't.

'It was "essential people" only,' he says. 'I only tell that to illustrate the effort of the thousands of those who stayed away, hundreds of thousands of volunteers who looked after the tea rooms, the press box, the grounds, checked tickets at gates – the people we rely on to keep our inter-county championships running. To a person, they never once complained. They are the reason we got through 2020.'

The All-Irelands were completed days before Christmas. And just in the nick of time, too. Not even a fortnight later, on

31 December, the country was placed on Level 5 restrictions and fully locked down for a third time. The following day, Ireland recorded the fastest and highest spike in cases in the world.

In fewer than eight weeks the 2021 GAA season was due to start, but already that was in doubt. There was scarcely time to draw breath.

16

FROM CANCER BATTLE TO CAMOGIE CHAMPION

MARIANNE WALSH AND THE FIGHT OF A LIFETIME

In late winter 2020 Marianne Walsh was sitting at her desk in the Oncology Unit at Waterford University Hospital labelling patient blood tests when she felt a little lump on her collarbone.

'I did think it was unusual, a cyst or something, but I didn't think too much more about it either,' she admits.

A few days later she tried to give blood but couldn't because her haemoglobin levels were too low.

'I went for my flu injection then, and asked my friend and colleague Corrine about the lump. Just got her to have a look at it. Corrine asked a few questions, but whatever symptoms I was quizzed about I had a reason for them all. Like, sure I was tired, but nurses are always tired . . .' She smiles. 'I genuinely did have an answer for any other symptom I was displaying.'

Still, they arranged an X-ray and within five days of it she received a call from her GP. 'I was told there was a large mass on my chest,' Marianne recalls. 'I knew exactly what was coming from there. I had very few symptoms at that stage, but what they found was at Stage 3.' That was the diagnosis. Grade 3 Hodgkin lymphoma.

Everything happened fast from there. Confirmation came on 9 December, exactly a month after she had gone to check her symptoms.

'I knew something was up, but I didn't know what type of cancer I had and when it was Hodgkin's I was actually relieved,' the twenty-six-year-old says. 'With my line of work, I see people who have really bad cancer and thank God the one I had was very treatable.

'But I would say the week between having a biopsy and scans to getting diagnosed was the worst week I put down in my whole life. It was the same for everyone here in our house. We didn't know what type I was going to be diagnosed with.

'Once we knew I was able to plan. I had it all sorted. Fertility treatment, hair sorted, my PICC [peripherally inserted central catheter]. Some people say ignorance is bliss, but I don't agree with that. I would always rather know what I am getting into. I think that if I wasn't working in the area that I'm in, I wouldn't have coped. Especially with all the restrictions in work and outside. I saw patients on their own and that was tough to watch.'

The hospital is just 20 minutes down the N24 from her home in Mooncoin and not long after her treatment started Walsh received a phone call from Joe Wall, her camogie manager. Due to the nature of her diagnosis, Wall enquired if Marianne would like to be regraded from the Mooncoin first to second team.

Walsh replied that she would like to stay put and push herself. She had an unshakeable faith in her ability to recover and play again.

'Everyone at work thought I was a lunatic,' she says, and laughs. 'They felt there was no way I should be pushing anything bar recovery for the year ahead.'

But hurling and camogie are rooted in the Walsh family. Marianne's father, Michael, won Kilkenny hurler of the year in 1994 and is renowned locally in the game. Plus, his daughter had played in three junior county finals for Mooncoin and lost them all. It didn't sit well with her.

Receiving chemotherapy and treatment during this period, with patients isolated and families kept apart, wasn't easy for any who had to bear it. Typically, she had a positive outlook.

'Genuinely, I was one of the lucky ones. Because I work at the hospital, I had colleagues and friends around me. I was so grateful for that. There were times when you would feel low and drained. When you throw all the restrictions in, and with the country shut down for large parts of the year it could definitely get on top of you. But there was always someone around to come and see me.'

Others didn't have that.

'Yes, I saw the strain on people's faces. Staff and patients alike. Having to deal with all the extras, making sure the PPE gear was secure, checking on patients who had no one.'

That's not to say her own recovery was straightforward. Walsh received her treatment as a day case patient each Tuesday. She clocked in that morning and finished up in the afternoon. This cycle was repeated every two weeks. Every minute in between was needed to summon the will to go again.

'Each time I was flattened after it. The side effects were so strong. When I started getting chemo, I was getting sick, then I had dizziness, and from there it was every symptom in the book. The lads had a hard time managing me,' she adds, referencing colleagues who were treating her. 'Nothing they gave me worked. You had to learn to live with it all. If you didn't, you were finished.'

* * *

On 11 January 2021, the night before Walsh started chemo, a few girls from the camogie team went down to her house to check in. They had collected a few euro to buy her materials she would need during treatment. Walsh says that gesture sustained her in the early days of her recovery.

The comeback started the next day, with her first session. The treatment continued until 15 June. Mentally, she dragged herself through those six months, even though she was sick all the time. In between, around mid-March, she was told she was cancer free. There was no immediate elation.

'I was just so sick,' Walsh explains. 'It was obviously great news, but the realisation was there that I still had four months of treatment ahead. I know you should be enjoying such good news, but there was no enjoyment at the time. I had months of misery left.'

But it's mad what can be achieved when you have a purpose. By the time training for the camogie season resumed in April, she was ready for a bit of participation, no matter how small it was.

The Mooncoin team received a pre-season training plan. It involved two runs a week, with the players required to send in their times for management to monitor them.

'My times were shocking,' she says, 'but I was just focused on getting it done. There were 3km runs on the road and 2km ones on the field. There was a circuit class as well. I had been going to a personal trainer through the whole treatment, so I was determined not to be left too far behind.'

A personal trainer, even with the sickness?

'Yeah, just to tip along, always taking it handy, but it was a real focus to me, something to help take my mind off treatment. It was a reminder, too, that there would be better days ahead.'

When chemo finished and the sickness eventually stopped, Walsh still didn't feel inclined to shoot from the rooftops.

'No, I felt very lost, to be honest with you,' she reveals. 'I had been living from appointment to appointment from November 2020 to July 2021, when I had my last scans. When you are finished, they tell you to go off and do what you want with your life.

'But that's not easy. Your brain is wired to look no further than the next treatment. I didn't know what to do. For months it had been nothing but appointments, getting bloods done, treatment, clinics. That was the sequence. You didn't look too far beyond it.'

That's when camogie kicked in. From wondering when her next scan would be, Walsh's attention steadily veered towards the next training appointment and showing incremental progress from session to session. The dial was changed.

Throughout her treatment the management team had treated her with huge respect and little fuss, and it was much the same in between the four white lines. Just how Walsh wanted it. They were very supportive. When she managed one lap of the field, they would mark that milestone. In training they didn't stand off her, but they didn't go out taking the head off her with a high tackle either.

At least not at first.

'Those girls definitely pulled me through some dark places. Right the way through. Hopefully, I helped keep them going too. There were times when training was hard for them – remember, we were intent on winning a title and the bar was raised high – but I would say the sight of me dragging about with the PICC line hanging out of one arm and the hurley in another drove them on. I would imagine they felt like, "Jaysus, if that one is doing all this training, we better cop on and do it too."

'The managers also played a massive role: Joe, John Grant, Derek Comerford and May Murphy. Just for believing in me. Just for believing that I could play for them again.'

Playing in a county final at that. She underwent her first full session in July and got through it. In August, she played her first match with the second team. Every week from there was one of progression.

'I played eleven full matches between the first and second teams and could see improvements in every game,' she recalls. 'The girls started tackling me properly then; there was no laying off or minding me. That's what I wanted – just to be treated like another player.'

To say things went well is an understatement. The corner-back helped her side finally land that elusive Kilkenny camogie junior title, beating Piltown in the final. And less than twelve months after her diagnosis, she was nominated for Kilkenny's junior camogie player of the year.

Incredible.

As the final whistle sounded against Piltown, Walsh's father hopped the fence and made a beeline for his daughter. She saw him racing towards her and copped her mam Margaret and her two brothers, Bill and Pat, celebrating behind him, too.

'You can imagine how we all felt at the final whistle.' She smiles. 'Like, it was tough for us all at home. When I was so sick, I knew I had to stay going for the family. If they saw me miserable, they would be too, and I couldn't have that. They were the ones who were looking after me all the time. They were so proud at the end of the game, but I was proud of them too. And of my friends, teammates and management.'

The evenings after the county final were spent in glorious splendour, celebrating that famous win.

The Mooncoin junior hurlers landed a county title of their own in the same weekend. Despite the times, those were among the best of days in the village. Marianne threw herself into the thick of the devilment, her voice croaking as the week went on.

Back to her old self?

She takes time to ponder.

'It was only before the final that I felt close to that. It took a lot of time. I lost all my hair. I put on four stone. I lost my identity and appearance. I couldn't even look at myself in the mirror. That's the truth. That's how it was for a long time.'

The volunteer-led Solas Centre offered another blanket of reassurance to wrap herself in. They provide quality cancer support services in the south-east – counselling, relaxation, reflexology, and they help families too,' she says. 'It helped me so much.

'Various people are focused on physical recovery, but there is the mental side of things too. The lads in work knew; they always warned me of that. When I was trying to get through every day, they wouldn't really mention the body. Instead, they would ask, "How's the head?" The Solas Centre is well tuned into that side of it also.'

Defiance and resilience are the cornerstones that Walsh's story is built upon. She faced every battle with the dignity of a champion.

'I just wanted to keep living like a normal twenty-six-year-old. Even going back to work at the end of 2021, with so much unease still there with covid, I wanted to get back out working.

'People were nervous, but the way I look at it, covid will be with us in some form for quite a while and I wanted to come back a year after I had been diagnosed. That felt like a good time to start a new chapter.'

17

BREACH OF TRUST

NOT EVERY COUNTY ABIDED BY THE GAA'S RULES

Life was coming at the GAA thick and fast. The warm glow of completing the 2020 championships dimmed, new challenges emerged, and it wasn't long before a cold front approached.

The first setback of 2021 came in February, when the government clarified that inter-county Gaelic Games activity was no longer covered under current Level 5 exemptions for elite sport. In other words, while the country was fully locked down the GAA would not be allowed to continue. Meanwhile, competitions such as the League of Ireland soccer could continue under the exemption.

Losing the 'elite sport' mantle was a sudden and surprising blow. Taoiseach Mícheal Martin explained that the exemption for senior inter-county football and hurling activity granted in 2020 was 'always timed to end at the end of the year'. He added that all decisions with sport were designed to 'keep activity levels low in society'.

Minister Jack Chambers added that the GAA had not shown 'massive appetite' to return in the 'medium term' and confirmed that Nphet had not been in communication regarding the GAA specifically.

This led John Horan to publicly state that any reluctance on their part to push again for the exemption was based on health and responsibility to the community. We were already covid weary at that point, but now there were renewed fears of missing out on a championship – this time the 2021 series.

Instead, the GAA took a more medium-term view of the situation. Their advisory group clarified that the deteriorating public-health crisis was the only priority for the time being, but everything would be reviewed. Until then a return to inter-county training or games was prohibited.

The date for the 2021 pre-season activity to commence was initially identified as 15 January. Now it would be Easter at the earliest. It meant that contingency plans for the master fixtures programme had to be revisited once more, though officials couldn't do much until they had a clear picture of what restrictions the country was likely to operate under in the year ahead.

In the meantime, counties were warned that anyone who breached that date would be penalised heavily for misconduct, discrediting the association.

Cue the second crisis of 2021. No sooner was that directive out than it was challenged. A number of counties decided to hold training gatherings.

On the first weekend of January, video footage emerged of the Cork footballers training on a beach in Youghal, which was not in breach of public-health guidelines – but was in breach of the GAA's covid restrictions. Despite a stout defence from the Cork camp, stating that the session was covid-compliant, as it happened in a public place, HQ suspended Ronan McCarthy, then senior team manager, for twelve weeks.

McCarthy very strongly contested his twelve-week suspension, brought his case to the Central Hearings Committee (CHC), Central Appeals Committee (CAC) and later to the Disputes Resolution Authority (DRA). But the ban was upheld.

In the same week, there was more embarrassment when the GAA ruled that a gathering by the Down footballers was also in contravention of their guidelines. This came after the Police Service of Northern Ireland (PSNI) were summoned to a session at a secondary school after a phone call from a member of the public.

A total of eighteen Down players had met in Newry in two separate groups to receive individual training programmes.

The police force found that there were no grounds for action, as it did not contravene health guidelines in the north, but Croke Park bosses nonetheless suspended for twelve weeks also, though the ban was later reduced to eight.

Both Down and Cork were hit with Rule 6.45 of the official guide, which prohibits collective training outside of permitted windows. These training breaches coincided with a spell of record daily case numbers in the country. For the week ending 8 January, that number was 26,343.

Around the same time, Mayo decided to ban three members of their senior football backroom after it emerged that they had broken covid-19 guidelines to gain entry to the December 2020 All-Ireland final. Officially, twelve backroom members were permitted into grounds for the 2020 championship games, but the GAA were forced to ask Mayo officials to explain the presence of three further non-accredited personnel at the final, who were pictured on CCTV inside the stadium.

After an internal review, Mayo stated, 'All unaccredited members of the backroom team admitted their mistake, apologised sincerely for their actions and have been suspended for three months.'

The Mayo board and senior management stated they had no knowledge of the presence of the people at the game. 'These individuals attended the game without the knowledge of the county board's officers and the team manager,' the statement continued.

But every violation drew the eyes of a nation ever closer to Croke Park. The scrutiny was intense, and another advisory note was dispatched to all units, urging them to hold the line until 19 April, the official starting time. There was just three weeks to sit out.

The note was uncompromising. 'It is more important than ever that no collective training sessions are held between now and the government's indicated return dates. Breaches in this context will not only be dealt with under our own rules but would likely put the broader plan to return to activity in serious jeopardy.'

Leading officials were livid to read the *Irish Independent* the very next day. The newspaper published pictures of some of the Dublin football squad training in the early morning at the Innisfails clubhouse, off the secluded Carr's Lane close to the Malahide Road. The news broke on April Fool's Day, but it was no joke.

Innisfails had served as the Dubs' low-key winter training base in the past. Now it was front and centre of every media outlet in the land. The spotlight was firmly thrust on Dublin and with it an incredible glare foisted on their squad and management.

They had just made it six championships in a row a few weeks earlier. Seven of their stars automatically joined the immortals of the game, as they now held eight All-Ireland senior medals.

In winning the 2020 title, their manager, Dessie Farrell, who replaced Jim Gavin, also joined an elite group – alongside Jack O'Connor and Mickey Harte. They had all guided their county to All-Ireland titles at minor, under-21 and senior level.

But all hell broke loose when the GAA's red-letter team, with the highest profile, the most successful outfit in modern-day Gaelic football, were caught breaking protocol.

The Dublin board quickly recognised there had been 'a serious error of judgement' and said management and players 'apologised unreservedly for their action'. Before the GAA issued any sanction, the Dublin board suspended Farrell for twelve weeks.

That swift response helped draw some of the sting out of the backlash. The point had been made that the pictures published showed players were exercising outdoors in a socially distanced fashion – but it didn't weaken the robust reaction to the breach.

Maybe this was because it was the Dubs, the champions who were up on a permanent pedestal; maybe it was because others wanted them to fall. Or perhaps it was down to the fact that the country was simply not in a great state at that time. When the *Independent* ran those pictures of Dublin training, some businesses had still not re-opened, secondary school students hadn't returned from the Christmas break and hundreds of thousands remained on the government's PUP scheme.

The subsequent ban meant that Farrell would not take charge of the team again until late June 2021.

Later in the year, some Dublin players went on the record to apologise. Dublin GAA CEO John Costello echoed those words in his annual report, whilst also reflecting that, in his view, some of the media commentary was extreme.

'The tone, at times, was one of "these lads should be arraigned for treason" and that they were guilty of burgling the bank of youth from the young citizens of the country,' he wrote. 'For almost two weeks, some media organisations turned over every stone to see if they could squeeze yet more mileage out of the story.

'Was the same attitude applied to other teams who were also in breach? Or to a team from a different sporting code who broke restrictions to go outside the jurisdiction for social events? And that's before even mentioning any political "socials". Most certainly not.'

The incident did little to help Dublin going forward. They retained the Leinster title but lost to Mayo in the All-Ireland semi-final, their first championship defeat in a record-breaking forty-five appearances. It was their first loss in that competition since 2014. They floundered further from there. Goalkeeper Stephen Cluxton never returned to the panel, flying half-back Jack McCaffrey had left the season before and he never came back either. They had to do without Paul Mannion, too. Those were three of the best footballers in the land. After losing their first four league games of 2022, they were relegated to Division 2 for the first time in fourteen years, and only the fourth time ever, before they eventually regrouped and found some form and retained the Leinster championship.

The following week it was Monaghan's turn. Their board also admitted a breach of regulations when some of their senior football squad took part in a group training session.

A dossier detailing the breach had been sent to several different parties, including the Department of Justice. A video, as well as photographic evidence, appeared to show Monaghan footballers engaged in a training session.

The board also acted swiftly and suspended then manager Seamus McEnaney for twelve weeks, though the spotlight on them was nowhere near as intense as the bright gleam pitched on Dublin.

Within Croke Park, patience was wearing thin at these contraventions. Officials were furious.

Other counties were allegedly training too, but evidence of their sessions didn't reach the public domain. But most teams had abided by the rules, gone out of their way to meet protocols and take the necessary steps to ensure a safe return to play. They were livid to see what played out.

'The nervous undercurrent in society led to a situation where everyone was watching everyone, and a number of training incidents – not least of all high-profile inter-county teams – catapulted us into a space we wanted to avoid,' says Alan Milton. 'But those incidents were few and far between, and need to be placed in context against the efforts and contribution of the wider association – something reflected in the generous government support the GAA received.'

Still, the outside world was wondering why the GAA couldn't keep its house in order. Minister for Sport Jack Chambers issued a sharp reminder that any breach of public-health rules was unacceptable.

'The latest reports will cause great anger to all those who have been adhering to the rules and have made great sacrifices,' the minister said. 'Any breach of the public-health rules like this is unacceptable. It undermines public-health messaging, when our GAA stars and sports teams should be supporting them and leading by example as role models. My officials from the Department of Sport have been in touch with the GAA to re-emphasise that all breaches undermine the broader public-health messaging.'

At that juncture of the covid nightmare, people were sacrificing things to keep in line with restrictions and most – including GAA membership – were sticking rigidly to restrictions.

It didn't go down well.

'I think what the other counties did was wrong,' Peter Keane, then Kerry manager, said. 'I think it was unfair. I think it was unfair on society in general. The view was that we were all in this together and, look, some of these counties breached the covid guidelines and I don't believe they should have.

'Did it bring pressure? I think, in the early part, yes, it did. We took a view down here that we weren't going to do it. We were going to try and look out for all these people. There was a good number of months [where] my own mother, I didn't see her. We've to be conscious of all of these people that we were minding, vulnerable people.

'So it puts pressure if you do see, or hear, that other counties are doing something,' Keane added.

Longford chairman Albert Cooney felt the punishments handed down were too lenient.

'The counties who broke the training ban have been treated very lightly, as far as we're concerned,' Cooney stated in an interview with the *Irish Examiner*. 'We're very disappointed. The problem is the GAA didn't lay down the law beforehand. They should have put in a rule that said any county caught breaking the regulations would be removed from the competitions. I guarantee not one of them would have taken a chance then.'

New president Larry McCarthy, who had just replaced John Horan, admitted the organisation's reputation had been hit hard by the contraventions.

'I think it has done us reputational damage, which we're going to have to work to get back. There's no appetite for any breaches in society at the moment. So undoubtedly it has. But we'll continue to work to get that confidence back from the public again. And hopefully there won't be any more breaches.'

There were no more. It begged the question, though, would the breaches have been prevented had the Level 5 sport exemption still been in place? And should there have been a greater push to retain that elite status to help contain such violations?

Just a short time earlier the GAA had been hailed for their monumental efforts. Now there was anger from inside and out.

Mention the training breaches to McGill and his disappointment is obvious.

'There were not many of them, but they were probably among the most disappointing things that happened in my twenty-one years as a full-time administrator of the GAA,' he says. 'I don't want to single out the counties who were involved because there were others, but to not be able to honour a request in a pandemic for the good of the people involved – themselves, their families and communities – and for the good of the whole GAA, is disappointing. There is not a whole lot more I want to say about it simply because it was so disappointing.

'In each of those counties there is someone who thought this would be a good idea. I am not necessarily saying it is a team manager, but whoever it is, they need to reflect on it. It was an exceptional error in judgement, and I hope that if they are ever in that situation again, they will reflect and not be that foolish.'

John Horan is still at a loss to see why they happened.

'Firstly, the impact of the GAA on Irish society is huge. Everyone in it and how we behave is subject to public scrutiny. That annoyed me to see those counties training when they shouldn't. Having been involved in teams myself over the years, I just couldn't see the benefit that would be gained with those breaches. They were not appropriate at all.'

18

THE PANDEMIC PRESIDENCY

JOHN HORAN AND THE GREATEST CHALLENGE OF HIS CAREER

Incoming GAA presidents usually have a good steer on what lies ahead of them. There is nearly always an issue of the day, a burning reform, or a rules or restructuring policy that will define one's term in office. After that it's about getting out to the membership, dealing with domestic affairs. John Horan had specific targets for his three years but seldom was a term of office so unpredictable as his.

'Starting out, I had a goal to change our football champion-ship structures and bring the Camogie [Association] and Ladies Gaelic Football Association (LGFA) closer to the GAA. Those were two priorities. But a lot happened in my final year, and I guess my presidency is now best known for the pandemic.'

In that regard, Horan is certain his background as principal of St Vincent's secondary school at Glasnevin helped.

'In school, people came to you with problems, and they wanted solutions,' he says. 'Sometimes you must be able to see the problems before they arise. Either way you need to be able to identify answers or offer a way out. As a principal, your energy can potentially drain as the day progresses because you're juggling several things and trying to sort matters as they arise, and dealing with the pandemic as GAA president, I was able to draw on that experience.

'I couldn't really have asked for better training for what was to come. It was a time for gathering information, interpreting government advice, coming up with answers to problems on a GAA level and quickly implementing our strategy. Then doing the same when everything changed again. But there was a common denominator to both school and the association – I was surrounded by good, solid people.'

Horan's progress through the ranks was low-key but steady. His early work centred around schools' games, alongside several roles with his club, Na Fianna, and later Dublin underage and development squads. He was selector with the Dublin minor football team that reached that 2001 All-Ireland final – beaten by a Sean Cavanagh-inspired Tyrone in a replay.

When he became chair of the Leinster Council in 2014, he marked himself out as a serious figure in the committee room – firm and definite. In 2017, he quipped that he 'wasn't renowned for my speeches'. Yet his reign at the top saw him deliver clear and consistent messaging.

Appearing on RTÉ's *The Sunday Game* at the end of May 2020, Horan ruled out a return to play whilst things stayed as they were. It was a dramatic moment, considering the public yearned desperately for games.

'If social distancing is a priority to deal with this pandemic, I don't know how we can play a contact sport,' Horan stated. 'That is what Gaelic Games are. It is a contact sport. Our concern has to be the players on the pitch, their families and their work colleagues.

'When this is all over and we are back to normal life, I would hate to think we have made any decision that has cost anyone a member of their family.'

On first digestion, his words knocked the stuffing out of those who had the flasks full, ham sandwiches packed and were only waiting at the diesel pumps to fill their car up and hit the road to Croker. Horan, however, insists he left the door open – maintaining that Gaelic Games would return later that summer, just on a gradual basis.

'I was aware of most of the country looking on that night,' he says. 'A lot of preparation was put in with the communications department, working out all angles that could face us. The key message delivered on the show was in the context of the two-metre social distancing being sacrosanct at that stage.

'At the same time, if people go back to that clip, I did say we'd be back in July 2020, but in a careful manner. We would not rush it. It was very easy for people to have opinions, but bringing it back in a safe manner was all we were concerned about. If it wasn't safe for our members, it wouldn't happen.'

No handbook could help. Things were moving too fast.

Soon after that TV appearance, all changed and changed utterly. Horan's *The Sunday Game* slot had severely dented hopes of top-flight games being played, but data then emerged that people were nineteen times less likely to pick up the virus in an outdoor environment.

That was a complete game changer.

The GAA quickly reacted to that finding. The covid advisory group, which studied the fluid and dynamic environment, began outlining a pathway for a safe return to games based on this information. The target was to create circumstances in which people could carefully assemble again.

Outdoors was where it was all going to be.

The president trusted others to help lead the way.

'I always take the view that in leadership it is key to have good people around and you must empower them. Setting up the advisory group was one of the best decisions we made, and it resulted in our medical and safety experts meeting each Monday at 5 p.m. and giving up their time to help.

'Feargal McGill has a huge network, and his team of doctors and professionals were key people and very practical. Feargal, Shay Bannon, who chaired the group, Tom Ryan and I were the GAA's inner circle. We used professional expertise to guide us. We had Paul Flynn from the Gaelic Players Association too. It was also probably the closest the three playing groups – us, the LGFA and the Camogie Association – have worked together.

'On the day we all shut our facilities down, all three groups issued a communication note and our social media expert, Niamh Boyle, quickly created a page with the three logos across the top – it hadn't happened before that day in March 2020 because we had never collectively communicated strategically like that before.

'For the next twelve months, we worked in that practical manner, operating away in our own organisations, being independent, and then coming together on key elements. This process of integration must evolve even further now.'

Through all the comings and goings, one key request Horan made of his covid committee was that they would act solely as a consultative group.

'I didn't want people speaking on behalf of the GAA about information that emerged. Data first had to be clarified by our management committee, collated, and then a final statement would come. I wanted to avoid any conflicts. Even at that early stage you could already see the strain between Nphet and the government, and we didn't want that. Instead, the group would advise us, and the GAA would put the relevant interpretation on it. These people were professionals in their own field and very happy for us to work in that manner. There was a great balance on the committee, but the presence of Professor Mary Horgan and her expertise gave us the confidence to progress.'

Inevitably, however, there were moments of contention.

In August 2020, when bigger crowds were allowed inside pubs than in 50,000-capacity stadia, there was that request made of Assistant Chief Medical Officer Dr Ronan Glynn to provide the GAA with 'empirical evidence' of why more spectators weren't allowed to attend games.

Croke Park had a recognised pattern of embracing all public-health guidelines and even going the extra mile to implement them. They were doing everything right and much more besides. They were quietly hoping for small crowd increases and this development caught them by surprise.

Their abrupt request for more data from public-health officials didn't go down well.

Professor Philip Nolan, the chair of Nphet's epidemiological modelling advisory group, labelled the GAA's words as 'a bit headmaster-ish'. Ironically, Professor Nolan was a past pupil of the school of which Horan became headmaster.

The former president insists they simply had to represent their membership.

'I know we clashed with Nphet, and, at the time, I wouldn't have apologised for that,' he states. 'We were very frustrated with the latest decision and couldn't see the logic that you could have people sitting in a pub watching a match in greater numbers than in a stadium with a 20,000 capacity.

'All our members were making unreal efforts to comply with our own safety regulations. Our health questionnaires and protocols were rigorous and if we didn't speak up, I felt we would lose our own membership and their buy-in. We were asking masses of people to be compliant at that stage and did everything asked of us – and more. We had to challenge what appeared not to be a good decision or it would be seen as weak leadership.

'I chatted with An Taoiseach soon after and, while he understood where the GAA was coming from, his priority was clearly to get schools back open that September. He simply had to hold his ground on other matters to get the schools back. When I got that explanation – and it didn't have to come from the Taoiseach, by the way – I could live with the decision not to allow supporters inside grounds, especially as a dad and school principal. I could see it was important that everything would be done to ensure schools would return. But that reasoning had never been communicated to us and communication eases a lot of conflict.

'It was never personal. But as president I felt that I had to represent the membership and that's what I did.'

At a high level, it had been previously agreed that when games did finally resume the club series would roll first. That was another big call but was vindicated emphatically as grass-roots burst back to life. People who hadn't played in years came back to tog out for the shortened club season. Indian summers were enjoyed.

Not all inter-county managers were happy at being in dry dock for longer than expected. Croke Park was adamant that two thousand inter-county players would get their chance. First, though, the need of the many had to outweigh the need of the few.

When the inter-county series did eventually resume, there was a large volume of fixtures to navigate in little time. Knockout games only added to the drama. And while Horan felt 'lonely and unusual' to be in Croke Park – alone, for all intents and purposes – it was much better than having no games at all.

'People had Super Saturdays and Sundays in front of the TV. They bedded down around 1 p.m. and could watch games until 8 p.m. that evening. Now they had other stuff to talk about, not just covid-related issues. Having no supporters was weird and against everything we stand for, really, but it had to be done. The lift our games gave people watching at home was worth it.'

The challenges to his leadership didn't end with the resumption of play.

At the start of October 2020, Horan woke up on Monday morning to hear radio bulletins and see social-media clips of some county championship celebrations. He didn't like what he saw. He was adamant the remaining club championships had to be shut down immediately.

This went down like a lead balloon with the membership, especially those who had outstanding domestic competitions to complete, but Horan wasn't for turning. As the country's situation worsened, it again proved to be the only course of action to take.

According to the Taoiseach, EUI data provided the government with evidence that the opening of 'wet pubs', and the county championship celebrations in certain areas, had increased case numbers.

'When I woke up that Monday morning – 5 October – and realised what had happened on the Sunday evening, I was very clear in my head that we were shutting down,' Horan says. 'The damage that would be done to communities if we were not decisive would have been huge. It was one of the biggest decisions in my time as president, but we had to do it. I got lots of phone calls about it, but we had a perfect storm at that time: the celebrations, the opening of "wet pubs" and the return of third-level students to college were all driving rising case numbers. That was the information I was getting.

'Our matches created an environment for people to go to "wet pubs" and our games were part of the problem. We had to remove the cause, and the cause was our games. It was tough, but I had no hesitation. There was pressure to stay going, and people felt it was not right to shut down, but from 9 a.m. on Monday morning I was clear in my head.'

The training breaches of four inter-county squads in March 2021 just after he left office did little to ease the scrutiny on the GAA either.

His term in office provoked thought, practicality and leadership through the global crisis. It was a presidency that got games completed, oversaw the transformation of the fixtures calendar through a split season, edged football reform closer, and showed a pathway for inclusion with the other Gaelic Games organisations.

All under intense pressure.

'Well, there was never panic. I had good, solid people around me that I could rely on, like Tom Ryan, Feargal, Shay, Cian Murphy and Alan Milton from the communications department and others. The management committee, central council and county chairmen helped steer the ship too, regularly making themselves available for meetings at short notice.'

The three years flew by, with the 2020 season so demanding that Horan must have wondered if he was president of a nation or a sporting organisation, such was the list of dilemmas and challenges before him.

He left office in springtime 2021 and reckons everyone appreciates Gaelic Games a little more now.

'Look, there is pride and satisfaction that we had the organisation set up in a robust way to look ahead to the future, knowing we could handle whatever came.'

Finding it strange, initially, not to be at the cut and thrust of the inner workings, it took time to adapt. But he is often reminded of his first day as president, when a concierge in Jury's Croke Park called him aside and asked what he should call him now.

'I've been calling you John for ages,' the concierge said earnestly, 'but what do I call you now? Do I call you Mr President?'

Horan's reply was instant. 'Yesterday you called me John and on this day in three years' time you will call me John, so just keep calling me John.'

A quick response. And practical. Much like his term at the top.

19

ROYAL FAIRY TALES

HOW THE YOUNG MEN AND WOMEN OF
MEATH LIFTED A COUNTY

At a training session in the spring of 2017, Meath ladies football coach Paul Garrigan handed each player a rock. They symbolised the size of the task ahead. They were chunky and the challenge, figuratively speaking, was to chip away at them. One piece at a time.

Meath hadn't won in any of their previous eight championship games and miracles couldn't happen overnight, Garrigan told them, but they could make progress bit by bit. The players were tasked with gradually breaking through the grit. It would be slow-going.

Vikki Wall was up for the challenge. Could it be any harder than the ones she'd faced in the past? She was only fifteen when she made her debut for the Meath senior team in 2015 and it wasn't pretty. They lost their three championship matches by a total of 77 points.

She cried in the car after most games, as her father drove home. In those days, they lost games by 20 points and upwards, and were subjected to one whipping after another. None more so than in August 2015, when Cork beat them by 40 points, 7–22 to 0–3.

On that day, for what it is worth, Wall scored all three points.

That one was an all-time low. On the eve of the game, players and interim management were still scrambling to find more players to tog. For damage limitation, they employed two sweepers to hold the imminent Cork onslaught, but it was like bundling paper into a bath plughole. They leaked everywhere. They were destroyed. To make it worse, the gruesome nature of the whole episode was captured live by the TG4 cameras.

Two months earlier, Diane O'Hora, a serial winner with Mayo during her own career, had stepped aside as Meath manager, rebuking the county board on her way for giving little backing to the women's team. She lamented the lack of the strategic plan.

They were going nowhere.

Yet even as she approached the exit door, O'Hora sensed there might be brighter days ahead, if only they got their act together. In her parting statement she suggested they might one day thrive at Croke Park.

'That seemed like a long way off,' says Wall. 'It was tough going. Always an honour to represent your county, mind, but Croke Park seemed like light years away. A distant dream.'

In this game the team, not the individual, is the ultimate champion. But with players not committing and backroom teams not sticking for long, how could harmony or stability be achieved?

Over the next two years Meath took on three more managers, slumped back to the third division in the league and made the call to slip down from senior to intermediate for the championship.

Wall never forgot that period. She looks back now and simply cannot fathom the road they have since taken.

As a kid, Eamonn Murray just wanted to play football. Growing up in Gowna, Cavan, his mornings, afternoons and evenings were spent kicking a ball.

He was only sixteen when he first encountered problems with an abscess on his leg. That hindered him. Later, he hurt his back and underwent an operation.

At twenty-three, he was told his playing days were over.

'I thought my life was finished, to be honest with you,' he says. 'A couple of years later I tried to play a fundraiser game back home, but I was done. I left my gear bag in the dressing room. That was that.'

Nowadays, sports science would have identified a route back, but in the early 1980s the diagnosis was blunt. Sport was over. Indeed, he was lucky to still be able to work. A builder based in Dublin, Murray and his wife, Claire Harman, sister of two-time All-Ireland-winning Meath legend Liam, had their first daughter, Eimear, before they decided to move to America in 1988.

'Claire had finished her nursing exams, but it was still a tough time to leave our two mothers and head off to New Jersey with a ten-month-old baby,' Murray recalls.

It turned out to be the best move they ever made. Basing themselves in Atlantic City, where Murray had a brother, cousins and an uncle who was a priest, they had a home from home.

'My back went again over there but with Claire being a nurse I only had to wait two weeks to get it operated on. There was hardly an MRI scanning machine in Ireland at the time, but there seemed to be one in every corner over there.'

They enjoyed several happy years in the US, with Sundays spent watching Claire's brother lording it in the Meath half-back line. But the call of home was powerful. Murray moved back and spent the next four years working for the Kepak Group until he left to become a self-employed tiler.

'I was working awful hours at the time, just to keep things going,' he remembers. 'Life was so busy that one evening Eimear came over, asked me to give her a lift down to the local football pitch in Boardsmill for training. I didn't even know she had joined.'

At the time, Christine O'Brien, a three-time All-Star and the heart and soul of the dominant Meath team of the late 1990s, was training several Boardsmill sides.

Once or twice, Christine heard Murray shouting encouragement to the Boardsmill players and roped him into helping. It started off with umpiring at games and quickly escalated into being a selector. Once they had him in the door, they gave him a few teams to look after. Murray obliged, but deep down he wasn't entirely sure if he was ready for a full-on managerial role.

'I was a grumpy eejit back then and I didn't like myself at that time,' he says. 'I was roaring a lot during games; I was just that way back then. I don't know where it came from, but it landed me in fierce bother with Croke Park once. It took me time to realise that I was not helping anyone. So I changed. These days if anything annoys me in games I look up at the birds, or I pick out trees that are nice and calming. That's how I deal with it.

'I used to be different. I took a suspension from Croke Park and gave them lots of it at the hearing too. I respected they had to do their job, but the likes of us were doing more in one week for ladies' football than they did in a year. They could suspend me, but I told them I would be back.'

He never really left.

Instead, he took on the mantle that Christine had assumed in the club and helped nearly every team that played, usually with one of his four daughters – Eimear, Maeve, Cliona or Aoife – to help with coaching.

Then Meath called. He managed a few underage teams and landed an All-Ireland under-14 title in 2007. Two years later they backed that success up with an under-16 crown.

'I was really into both the club and county set-ups,' he explains. 'I was with the under-21s, the minors, I think four different teams in all. One year we had 160 girls playing for us across all grades.'

All the time he was refining his job specification. Learning, listening and watching.

'I knew my exact role, which is a huge start,' he says. 'It was as a manager. I was never a coach. That's how it is to this day. I always had good coaches around me, like Eimear, Paula Cunningham, Marie Kealy, Fergal Lynch and others who were all so good to me. My job was to communicate with the players, provide a good coaching set-up and make it fun. We could go from there.'

The whole family became immersed. Eimear wore several different hats, Maeve looked after underage teams with Boardsmill, Cliona was full-back on their senior team and chairperson of the club, while Aoife, the youngest, was also locked into the game right all the way up.

'If you don't talk GAA in our house, there is little point coming in.' Murray laughs.

Out of the blue the 'big job' came.

But he didn't want it. He was grand and content where he was. He loved the underage set-up, and they were making a bit of hay too.

The county's Ladies Gaelic Football Association chairman, Fearghal Harney, rang in the spring of 2017, offering the Meath senior manager's role, but Murray shot down the notion with the rapid reflexes of a sniper.

Harney took cover for a while, but he was intent on getting his man. In true GAA fashion, he just stayed ringing. And ringing. One evening Murray answered the call and didn't say no straight away. Probably to stop the phone ringing as much as anything else.

That was enough. Harney had his man.

'The senior job didn't appeal because I just didn't need that responsibility. I knew every underage player in Meath, but I had little or no knowledge of senior players from other counties.'

That may have been true, but in Murray's phonebook there were plenty of contacts who did have that knowledge.

One of those was Paul Garrigan from Baltinglass.

Murray knew him well from the inter-county underage scene and asked him to get involved. Garrigan passed. Murray played the card that Harney had used with him – he stayed ringing.

Finally, Garrigan caved as well – he would come on board but only with Murray as manager.

The rest of the ensemble rolled together quite easily. Garrigan brought two Baltinglass clubmates with him, Paddy Dowling as goalkeeping coach and Shane Wall as defensive coach. Mark Brennan was recruited to look after the forwards. Eugene Ivers, who had worked with Jim McGuinness during his successful

Donegal reign, was later brought in as a strength and conditioning expert. Kelley Fay came aboard as sports psychologist.

These days players can sometimes drown in the ocean of information provided to them by backroom teams. Data doesn't always mean players have enough knowledge of their role, tactics or opposition style. Murray's gang, however, was different. They had a clear plan, they were highly motivated, holistic, practical and consistent. Their message sunk in quickly.

'We knew we could make some ground,' Murray said. 'But it was important to get the backroom just right. In that regard I was down at the club one evening and noticed a lady keeping score in a game and interacting with people in a lovely and happy manner.'

She was Michelle Grimes, mother of Stacey – one of the best young players in the county but who wasn't in the squad. Murray rang Michelle to ask if she would get involved with the set-up. In disbelief, she replied that she had never been involved with any team.

'I know,' Murray replied. 'But I'm looking for a new set-up, with people that were never involved with Meath before. I want you to come in as our liaison officer.'

'I know what you are up to!' Michelle laughed. 'You want me to go in just to get Stacey in.'

Murray reassured her that whatever Stacey decided to do was between the manager and the player, and nothing to do with her. He told her to go home and think about it. Michelle did just that. She decided to come on board, too.

Now to recruit more talent. Not everyone was interested in playing for the county, but Murray had most of the relevant numbers and, like a telesales operator chasing commission, he continued for weeks with the hard sell. And the odd soft one.

Stacey Grimes was duly one of the first contacted. It was tough to get her on board, he says, but they got there. 'A class act,' Murray says. 'One of the all-time greats from an early age.'

One or two that Murray called had just taken a break from soccer. They were glad to go back to Gaelic football.

Katie Noonan was contacted, but her dad reckoned she was too young to play for the Meath ladies team and felt she was more of a soccer player, in any case. Plus, he was the soccer team's manager!

Again, Murray persisted. 'We got Katie in and now I'd say she wouldn't touch a soccer ball if she saw one.' He laughs. Catriona Murray came in. Not long after she committed, she had 3–5 scored off her against Waterford but no one panicked. 'You need bigger shoulders, Katie,' Murray told her.

'I know, Eamonn, I will get them for you,' she replied.

Orla Duffy had been recuperating from an ACL injury but returned. Majella Lynch, who was Murray's captain at under-16 level, linked up too. It all came together nicely.

Before the 2017 championship a players' meeting was held at the Meath Centre of Excellence, with the new backroom team presented to the players. In hindsight, aside from Sean Boylan's coronation in 1982 as the county's senior football manager, if ever there was a transformative evening in the rich history of the county this was one.

Murray recounts: 'The coaches just arrived and made an instant impact. Paul, a class act. Paddy Dowling, everyone loved him. Shane Wall took over; he just adored it. Mark Brennan, a fine fella from Carlow, six foot plus, who had coached with

Cuala. The lads were so placid – there was never a loud voice. We each knew our jobs and roles to a tee. If even one of us didn't click, the project may not have worked.

'I trusted them all. My job is not coaching – I deal with players; I deal with their problems, and I look after them. I communicate with parents and if someone is struggling with boyfriend problems or exams, I try to help or find help. Any player who joined us would be able to close the gates and leave their problems behind. We decided we would have fun.'

At the end of the 2021 season Cora Staunton remarked that Murray should be an under-14 manager, not a senior manager, such was his outlook on the game and open, energetic style of playing. It was a lovely compliment and taken as such.

'She was right,' Murray says. 'Every week we laugh. We make a show of each other. Don't get me wrong, we are deadly serious about training, but there is room for fun too.'

Off they set to work.

At intermediate level, they organised themselves quickly enough to soon win a Leinster. In 2018, they were beaten in the Division 3 final but again got to the intermediate final where they lost to Tyrone. In 2019, they topped Division 3 and got to the intermediate final again, this time losing to Tipperary.

Failing in the 2018 final hit home the hardest. Murray cried that evening.

'I just felt I wasn't good enough,' he says. 'I questioned everything I did. It was my wife who made me go back,' he adds, his voice wavering. 'Claire knew I had to find out if I was good enough or not. And I didn't like letting the girls down.'

He looks to his kitchen window, tears in his eyes again, as his mind is cast back. 'We weren't good enough as a unit. Not fit enough either. Tyrone's strength and conditioning was a huge factor. After those finals we pledged we would have the fittest team in the country.'

They finally won the All-Ireland Intermediate title in 2020 and topped Division 2 just as the disease interrupted life. This time the players were presented with stones much smaller than the rocks that Garrigan had initially handed out. It had taken time, but gradually they had reduced in size. Just like Garrigan said they would.

The pandemic and shutdowns allowed Meath to become the fittest team in the land.

From March until mid-September 2020 they were kept apart.

'But when we got back, we were obsessed with winning,' Murray states. 'There was no denying we were going somewhere. Eugene's strength and conditioning work was masterful. The girls were in peak condition, and it meant we could play the high-pressing game we wanted.

'The players listened to Eugene's every instruction and individually trained right through Christmas, returning for the 2021 pre-season in simply amazing condition. They signalled to us that they wanted to keep going forward. I knew already, but we really knew then we had a special bunch.'

The early stages of the pandemic were tougher for the Murray family than most. In the closing stages of the 2020 club season, Eimear began struggling with chest and back pain and her participation in the county junior final against Donaghmore/Ashbourne was shrouded in doubt.

She reckoned the pain stemmed from a hiatus hernia; it had flared up during the years, so she just put her head down and played the final. But upon diving low to her right to make a save, she didn't feel great once back on her feet.

Eimear went for a scope and an ultrasound, and all was clear. Still, something wasn't right. She contracted covid and started coughing up blood. At Navan Hospital A&E they did a chest X-ray, CT scan and took other tests. When the doctor called her into one of the side rooms, Eimear became worried. They hadn't found a clot but thought she may have lymphoma.

She was admitted straight away for a biopsy and observation. As her covid test was still positive, she was admitted to the covid ward, which meant no one was allowed to be with her.

The toughest of times.

On 3 November the diagnosis of non-Hodgkin lymphoma was confirmed.

'She more or less started chemotherapy straight away,' her dad says. 'When Eimear went to get the CT scan, Aoife, who is studying to be a radiographer, knew what the outcome was, as she was watching the machine.'

Around the local pitch is a walkway with floodlights and it helps people get out and about. It was there Murray tried to get his head around the news.

'We were very worried. Eimear was on chemo full time from there. She had treatment in the Mater Hospital, and Gerry McEntee [Meath football legend and consultant surgeon] would often pop by to see how she was doing. Isn't that the lovely way of GAA people – how they look out for each other?'

Christmas Day was especially hard. Eimear, her husband and little son came to the family home for dinner but had to leave that evening as she was returning to hospital.

'That was hard going,' Murray whispers. 'But there was always support. One night at training Paul Garrigan brought the girls into a huddle to tell them the news after I gave him permission to do so. When I came in a while after, they all gathered around me,' he says, tears in his eyes. 'Those girls are like another family.'

Murray thanks the heavens that his daughter is feeling well now and reports that she is mad to get back going to matches. Having coached several of the Meath players at under-14, under-16 and minor level, Eimear also got a huge boost from seeing Meath finally win the All-Ireland intermediate final.

Little did any of them know, however, that the best was yet to come.

Eugene Ivers could sense the journey was nowhere near over. After Christmas he told Murray that the girls were ready to push on even further in 2021.

Now a senior side again, they had incredible pace and incredible fitness built up.

'People said we were mad to be running them so hard in training, but all of these girls want to turn their backs and try to tackle when they lose possession. We wanted to maintain that tactic in our games. So we needed that fitness.'

Murray maintains that the pandemic helped the side because there were no players travelling or on J1 visas. It was easier to keep momentum.

They beat Armagh in the All-Ireland senior quarter-final and faced Cork in the semi-final. With just two minutes left they trailed by 7 points. The Rebels had one foot in the final. Murray turned to Garrigan on the line and bemoaned what was happening.

'We're fucked. They are just too good for us.'

The management had prepped for everything they would face on the day, but you cannot plan for the unexpected. Something shifted in the universe. Stacey Grimes was taken down for a penalty, which she converted herself.

From the kick-out, Emma Duggan struck an equalising goal.

Duggan hit three quick-fire points in extra time to see them through.

Blitzkrieg!

'The whole thing is still a blur.' Murray smiles. 'We trained for all scenarios, to hold a lead with six backs against eight forwards and vice-versa. For when we went behind in games. Ball retention when we were winning. All of that.

'I looked up at the scoreboard and saw that we had gone from seven down to two up. That was purely down to our players sticking to the process. Doing what they trained to do. Sticking to the plan.'

After the game, as he often does, Sean Boylan, the godfather of Meath football, rang Murray. Boylan wondered if he had ever seen anything like it.

'Just to be able to talk to that man. There were times in Sean's career when he went home and cried after games, too. I know that because he shared it with me. But to hear how happy he was after that win.'

A county awoke.

Meath supporters had been denied the chance to follow this team because of restrictions but now they were souped up and ready to rock.

'We had been starved of success, and people had been starved of games for two years,' the manager notes. 'They made their feelings known to us from there.'

With the impossible dream now only one step from reality, 18,000 Meath fans purchased tickets for the final. Jack Kiernan's sports shop in Navan sold out of jerseys. They couldn't be found online either.

Murray was slightly worried about the hype but felt he couldn't dampen the romance of it either.

Vikki Wall quips that if you drew a graph representing Meath's journey in the previous ten years, it would look exactly like a 'V', so stark was the upturn.

Along with goalkeeper Monica McGuirk and captain Shauna Ennis, Wall had also played in that 40-point defeat by Cork back in 2015. That traumatic day in Thurles seemed like an eternity ago.

'Dropping down a level was the best thing we ever did,' Wall reckons. 'We went from losing every week to regrouping and finding our way back.'

She was not surprised with the sustained progression. In the 2021 pre-season there was no mistaking just how fit her team-mates were.

'A lot of us used that 2021 lockdown to drive it on again. Being part of the Meath set-up was great for me because it helped me balance my master's degree course in DCU. I was able to keep a routine and had something else to think about rather than college. Another goal to aim for.'

She elaborates: 'We didn't want fitness to be a reason for losing a game. With the blocks of work Eugene gave us, I felt like we had almost increased our intensity without knowing it.

'I actually think covid brought us closer together. When the restrictions eased, we met every week for coffee and to give out about the amount of runs we had to do.' She laughs. 'Although socially distanced, we spent a serious amount of time together and I guess that paid off.'

So, too, did her own resilience. 'It took a while to get the right people involved but, without those past losses, I wouldn't be half as motivated as I am now. I can't speak for anyone else, but I don't regret anything that happened to me along the way. Yes, we were brought to some low places, but that's part of the journey.'

Days before the final, Garrigan this time handed each player a little pebble. He told them they had chipped away at the rock so much that only a slight stone remained.

And if they cracked it, they would see what was inside.

They were geared up for a famous win. Ahead of the final with Dublin, Mark Brennan poured over five years of video footage, dissecting every move, tactic and trend that the Dubs had employed in that period. A bold game plan was devised. Meath would push right up on the champions and back their fitness levels to maintain the tempo.

'The only thing that worried me about that day,' Murray reflects, 'was the hype we encountered leaving Trim – the crowd around the hotel, selfies. I wondered, did we really need all that? The girls had not been through that before.'

Murray need not have worried. The dressing room was an oasis of calm.

'Eugene came over to me and said, "Eamonn, they are ready." He was right. They were. He had promised me at Christmas they would be ready, and they were.'

There was no roaring or shouting, nor any tables banged. Instead, before the game and at half-time, the forwards and backs split into two groups and then came back together as one.

'We went out and pushed up straight away,' Murray recalls. 'We left their midfielders alone and turned their best forwards back to chase us.'

Vikki Wall did what she always did and set the tone by tearing at the heart of the Dublin defence straight from the throw-in. It was a trademark turbo-charged run. She pierced the Dubs' armour for the first time and won a free. In just the first minute Wall showed that Dublin could be got at and demonstrated how. Stacey Grimes stepped up and converted it. They were humming.

They were intent on taking down one of the best teams of all time, a side chasing five All-Irelands in a row.

They didn't flounder once in that quest, performing not just with pace and power but with poise too, and showing remarkable game intelligence. It was a coaching masterclass. They pressed the Dublin kick-out, turned the ball over, danced in little triangles around the opposition defence, retained the ball when in possession and won frees at crucial stages.

Their tactics roller-coasted between bravery and downright lunacy. 'We pushed up so high that Dublin's top players were on their own in the middle third,' Murray acknowledges. 'When Ciara Grant got a kick-out, all she could see was green. No goalkeeper in the game could reach where the space was. It was a gamble, but we had to do something. And if we were pushing up, we were all going together.'

It's probable that only such manic and sustained intensity could have dethroned the Dubs.

'Mick Bohan had always maintained that everyone knew Dublin's system and yet didn't actually realise how difficult it was to crack until they came face to face with it.

'But we had trained five nights a week for the year, when allowed – three field sessions and two in the gym. We knew we were going to be a breath of fresh air. That system won't be good enough in 2022 and we will have to tweak it again, but it was good enough in 2021.'

They won by two points, driven on by a fierce royal roar. When the final whistle blew, Murray labelled his girls heroes forever. Back home, thousands greeted them upon their return and celebrations continued well into the week.

On the day after the game, they were gathered at the Knightsbrook Hotel watching the game when Sean Boylan rang again. The manager held his phone out for the girls to see who it was, and they answered Boylan with a tribal, collective roar.

'Sean was the one who gave us this culture,' an emotional Murray signs off. 'He gave us all something to fight for, a path for us to follow. His belief and outlook on life kept me going in my own darkest days. Always thinking there would be better days ahead.'

There were. They won the league in 2022, lost the Leinster final to Dublin, but came back to win a second TG4 All-Ireland championship on the spin, recovering from a shocking start to beat Kerry by 9 points in front of 46,000 – the majority of whom came from Meath to support their team. They kept a free-scoring Kerry side that had scored 13 goals in four games to just 1–7 in the decider.

Including the 2020 intermediate title, this was the third consecutive championship final that Meath had won at HQ. They had truly taken the world of ladies' football to a new place in terms of tactics, conditioning and counterattacking.

Indeed, in doing so they reached such a high level that other set-ups wanted their players and coaches. The Australian

Football League clubs came looking at two of their top players, Vikki Wall and Orlagh Lally. Others were scouted too. The brilliant Emma Troy, who dominated the 2022 final, was also set for a spell travelling down under. In the lead-up to the '22 final, there was also talk that members of Murray's backroom team were moving on.

Just as they hit their pomp, it looked like the team and support staff were going to break up. 'I know we could do four or five-in-a-row, but we probably won't,' Murray said after they beat Kerry. 'We had a few great years. I don't blame them for going off one bit. They don't owe Meath anything. They're an awesome bunch of players. I love them all so much.'

The team will have to rebuild again in 2023, but deep within the camp lies a steely defiance and confidence that anything can be achieved.

The rocks that Paul Garrigan gave the girls years earlier had diamonds inside. They just didn't know it at the time.

* * *

Eight days later there was another royal fairy tale.

Cathal Ó Bric always knew what his group of young Meath minors were about. From when he first trained the youngsters as under-14s in February 2018 until All-Ireland minor final day on 28 August 2021, his backroom team met the players 205 times.

'Through either contact time, face to face, or in covid times, on Zoom calls. We had eighty-eight games in those three and a half years – that's a fairly heavy load. But from the start everything would be enjoyable, we would work almost entirely with the ball and everything would be games-based.

'The ball was the focal point. Our players were getting the fitness levels raised at the same time as improving their football. Mini games in training, challenge games – that's how they learn,' he says. 'It helps them develop their own style.'

Their 2021 All-Ireland final opponents, Tyrone, sailed through Ulster. At the end of the provincial campaign, they had a combined 53 points to spare over their opponents and subsequently crushed Cork in the semi-final.

But Meath were better road-tested. A well-oiled unit. For the final, not unlike Eamonn Murray's memo for the Dubs game, Ó Bric crafted a plan to put Tyrone under pressure and force them to come from behind. It paid dividends, with a winning point from the right and off the outside of the right of Shaun Leonard's boot, deep into stoppage time, securing the county's first title since 1992.

It was a day Tyrone will want to forget – they had fourteen wides, including a close-range free missed to bring the game to extra time – but for Meath, it will never be overlooked.

The manager still finds it hard to fathom how they got through so much work – especially whilst operating online with a group of teenagers during covid.

'We had to get fairly resourceful and creative with it,' he acknowledges.

Once the country shut down, Ó Bric didn't see his players in the flesh again for fourteen months. The squad held their last physical training session on 7 March 2020; the next time they all met again was on 10 May 2021. A lifetime in the eyes of a teenager.

'Fourteen months with the lads essentially out of their programmes,' Ó Bric, school principal at St Joseph's NS, Boyerstown, says. 'In coaching terms, we were coming from the lads' under-16 year into their under-17 season, and that's a huge one. That minor year is all about narrowing the focus, refining the game plan, specifying proper kick-out strategies, working on the creation of space, tightening up our defensive structure. A critical year and it determines how successful or otherwise you are.

'Every other county was in the same boat, because we scouted around and it was clear that counties were still working hard – just in isolation and online, instead of on the training ground.'

Meath were quickly at it.

An initial fitness programme mainly consisted of 5km runs. Players downloaded the MapMyRun app, recorded their times and sent them to management. They undertook a series of skills challenges, including shooting, handling, and coordination, which they videoed and sent on for feedback.

Ó Bric then refined the programme. 'Five-kilometre runs are not really the best for games – they build stamina, but there is no real correlation to the running and twisting you do in games.'

They shortened the runs and worked more on speed, agility and quickness. This incorporated 30-metre interval running, and 50-metre, 70-metre and 90-metre runs – all to be completed within a certain timeframe. Again, all data was recorded and returned to management.

'We worked off a panel of seventy, with each coach assuming responsibility for ten players,' Ó Bric recalls. 'Through their parents, the players would send us their stats and we would deliver feedback.'

As lockdown prolonged, they changed tack again, this time bringing physiotherapist and former Navan O'Mahony's player

Stephen McGowan, also a qualified strength and conditioning instructor, on board for body weight exercises. The focus was on proper technique rather than any heavy lifting.

Soon they graduated to light weights, and kettle-bell and hand-bell weights.

'The aim was that when we did get back the players would have their physical work done, the pace and power would be there. But more so the players would have confidence that when they met opponents, they were an equal – if not better – when it came to conditioning,' the manager adds.

The Zoom sessions turned into much more than box-ticking. Every Monday, the panel split into two groups, with thirty-five in each section, and coaches would monitor six players, analysing their effort and critique.

Over a 45-minute period the advice would be minimal. A tweak on squats technique, go lower, hold the back straighter – it all served to facilitate some interaction. Establish a purpose.

At the end of 2020 they took a break. Everything had been catered for, from sleep patterns to nutrition to well-being. The plan was to rest up for a while, enjoy Christmas, keep fresh and not overdo it.

The player's parents wouldn't hear of it. They recognised the sense of belonging the involvement gave their children. There were twenty-one clubs represented on the Meath squad, spread right across the county, and those sessions were the only real outlet for some youngsters. It gave them the chance to connect and bond with each other. A chance to talk. Ó Bric soon came to realise that, for his players, the meetings were as much to do with wellness and belonging as football.

'We suggested just skipping one session but, overwhelmingly, the parents pleaded with us not to. We were enabling the players to maintain a connection with each other. They saw each other on screen, had a bit of banter, worked hard and shared a purpose.'

While other areas of their life went into freeze mode, here was something that made them accountable. The parents appreciated that.

'Anxiety, isolation – those things really hit everyone so much. We helped keep them connected while the overall goal remained in place – win a Leinster title and challenge for an All-Ireland.'

The mix was perfect.

Zoom sessions started with a playlist. From there, the slagging began. On the occasions when the coaches picked the playlist, the abuse was even worse, as country and western replaced techno and hip-hop.

Before workouts there was a 15-minute window for open chat and then it got serious for 45 minutes, when the graft started. At the end there was time for more banter before the players signed, ranking their rate of perceived exertion (RPR) on a scale of 0–10, as they logged off.

Somehow, seventy players stayed motivated and united whether through fitness runs, having a ball in hand, kicking, or handpassing a hundred times off a wall in 60 seconds, or just having a chat.

They eventually got back on a field in May 2021.

The bond was tight and there was no fumbling or fostering with the ball. They were in a good place. Covid meant exceptionally compacted championships.

Meath's 2020 minor crop beat Offaly in the Leinster final and the 2021 minors were told their provincial semi-final would be held on 14 July.

Following all the uncertainty, they finally had a focal point again.

Ó Bric knew the day would come when he would have to cull his squad. Dropping players is the roughest part of a coach's life, and when it comes to young adults it can be difficult not to tread on their dreams.

'In my four years in charge of this group of young men, reducing the numbers was the single most difficult part of the process. It was absolutely heartbreaking. We were like an extended family, but now we had to say goodbye to some. Lads we had worked with from under-14, who had done every Zoom call, skill session, sprint, every Kahoot quiz. You knew you were hurting them and their parents.'

They cut from 71 to 41. Ó Bric compiled feedback sheets for each player. The message was ninety-nine per cent positive. He identified the strong parts of their game. Next was an area to improve upon. Each document concluded with a positive reinforcement of their skills.

'And we do respect them and their families,' he says. 'So much.'

The entire management team turned up as they let the players go. Some young lads left with tears in their eyes. But they all left with dignity. Most voiced their gratitude for the chance to work at such a level.

Soon it was tunnel vision again – on the trail of a first taste of national glory at that level since 1992.

In the final seconds of the All-Ireland final, Tyrone won a close-range free to level the game and Ó Bric swivelled around to see who could be sprung from the bench pack for extra time. Tyrone's effort trailed wide, however, and the final whistle sounded seconds later. He looked to the skies.

'Relief initially,' he recalls. 'Then just unbridled joy. Happiness that all we worked for paid off. Some lads didn't make it to the end of the road, but they were all part of the journey, little pieces of the jigsaw as it started to take shape. I sincerely hope they will still have a significant role to play for Meath football.'

They may yet lock arms again. Soon after leading the side to that famous win, Ó Bric was appointed the county's 'post-minor' squad. Like Eamonn Murray and Sean Boylan, the chances are he will soon have an even more significant role to play himself in making more knockout memories for the Royals.

20

FROM PANDEMIC HOTSPOT
TO POSTER CHILD

HOW THE COUNTRY BECAME
THE ENVY OF THE WORLD

Ireland had one of Europe's longest covid clampdowns. From when the country initially closed in March 2020 to its re-opening, it endured twenty months of intense restrictions.

Unlike other countries across the continent, the government kept limitations right through, ranging from numbers allowed to gather indoors to mask-wearing and physical distancing.

Cabinet eased them somewhat in October 2021, for indoor and outdoor gatherings, but when Omicron hit that December all the usual strict measures were reintroduced, along with an 8 p.m. closing time for hospitality. It was not until February 2022 that all restrictions were fully lifted.

But throughout 2021 and those veers in and out of full lockdown, Taoiseach Micheál Martin consistently maintained that Ireland was still in a better position than most of its European neighbours because of a higher level of vaccination. Experts and professionals frequently explained how the prolific rate of vaccination in this country prevented further Level 5 lockdowns and railed against severe illness and death.

Ireland began its mass immunisation campaign on 29 December 2020 and produced one of the most successful rollouts in the world, at one point ranking number one in the European Union for percentage of adult population fully vaccinated. It was also graded number one in the EU for the number of booster vaccines administered. Meanwhile, almost seventy-four per cent of citizens had availed of the vaccination programme in the north.

Each person who received the jab was given a record card, showing the name and batch number of the vaccine they received. They returned for their second and final dose three weeks later. A further booster was delivered five months on, though this gap was reduced to three months when the Omicron variant put the country under siege. The programme to provide fourth doses started in April 2022.

By September 2021, more than seven million vaccines were administered, and nine in ten eligible adults in the Republic had been fully vaccinated. It was phenomenal. These were hailed as 'two major milestones' by the Taoiseach.

From a sporting perspective, the vaccination programme was a total game-changer and allowed administrators to plan with more confidence. It gave Croke Park officials confidence that the major disruption of the 2021 season could be avoided, despite consistent climbing numbers of infections, especially in the under-45 cohort, which included all players.

It didn't entirely stop covid from causing more anxious moments along the 2021 track, however. The country would effectively shut down again for a fourth time at the end of 2021 and right up to that point there were countless complications to contend with.

Not everyone in every squad was fully vaccinated, for a start. Some players did get the jab, some didn't, and others left it late to do so.

On the day they played Kilkenny in the championship, Dublin hurling manager Mattie Kenny lost four of his panel, including key figures, who missed out because of covid issues.

Armagh's footballers also endured disruption and, for a period during the summer of 2021, late withdrawals from team lineouts were not unexpected.

Some managers chose to confirm that the absence of certain players was down to covid-related issues, but other times no details were given.

The vaccine hadn't yet circulated widely by the time the 2021 championship started and, with older age groups catered for first, the cohort of under-30s had to wait to get their jabs. There were calls for elite sportspeople to receive the vaccine earlier than others, but inter-county players themselves pointed out they had no right to be moved up the line.

At official level, Croke Park confirmed that no action had been taken to secure vaccinations for county panels simply because it was a personal decision whether to receive the jab. Ultimately, the system was run by public health, and the association would not seek special treatment or try to enforce vaccination in any case.

The Delta variant then swept through society and targeted the fifteen to thirty-year-old age group. This put club and county teams under even more pressure, as that strain became widespread in the younger population.

With virus circulation in local communities high, the key thing was for teams to ensure they did everything to avoid being designated close contacts. Players were reminded not to travel in cars together and to minimise indoor activity as much as possible.

The association remained cautious. Hand sanitisers remained at dressing room entrances. Masks were worn everywhere, bar the showers. Gyms operated to similar guidelines. Water breaks continued until the end of 2021. County finals saw captains lift trophies on their own, and cups had to stay in the presentation area after speeches.

As summer progressed, however, the vaccine became more widely available and fewer cases among panels were reported. Finally, it looked like a straight stretch of road beckoned for the association.

But from the start this virus held the edge and kept everyone guessing.

And little did the GAA realise that one of the trickiest bends of their pandemic journey was just around the corner.

21

RED HAND TRIBULATIONS AND TRIUMPHS

TYRONE OVERCAME COVID DISRUPTION TO TAKE THE TITLE

In mid-June in Killarney, the 2021 Allianz football league semi-final ended with Kerry hitting Tyrone for six goals. It was a hammering at Fitzgerald Stadium.

The home side plundered goals left, right and centre, and that well-worn joke of the two-metre social-distancing rule being taken literally, this time by the Tyrone defence, was thrown out again.

It was a tough trip down south. Darragh Canavan, blessed with a footballing lineage so rich that it's almost not fair, is one of the brightest players in the game, but he was taken off injured after just three minutes. It wasn't a simple injury either, and one of the team's physios, Paul O'Neill, rushed onto the pitch to attend to him.

O'Neill was a fine footballer himself. He played a key role for his club, Donaghmore, and won a Sigerson Cup with Queen's University Belfast in 1990, landing player of the year in that tournament. He played alongside Feargal Logan in the Tyrone under-21 teams of 1988–89 and with the county senior side too. He sustained serious injuries on a number of occasions, including damaging his cruciate ligament, and had back and shoulder operations on top of that. These days he helps look after the Tyrone players' bodies and well-being.

'We were brought straight to Tralee General Hospital by Dr John Rice, a consultant who also helps the Kerry team,' O'Neill says. 'And by the time we got back, the final whistle had sounded. We knew the result. We were almost relieved to have missed the game.'

The hope was that the weekend in Killarney would be a good starting point for the road that lay ahead, and the trek south was a while in planning. Logistics culminated with fifty-eight rapid lateral flow coronavirus tests for the players and backroom members before they made the 430-kilometre trip.

'I remember the relief when the last test came back and everyone was clear to go,' Feargal Logan, the team's joint manager with Brian Dooher, recalls. 'It was an important gathering for us. Bonding trips were obviously not something you could countenance in covid times, but the trip, the game and the overnight stay were welcome, for we felt it would bring us all closer together. It was June, we had only been a month or two together and, as it was our first year in charge, this trip was a good chance to get to know the players.'

They leaked five goals in the first half alone, though, and it could have been worse. David Clifford fisted wide when a goal was on, while his brother, Paudie, and teammates Seanie O'Shea and Stephen O'Brien also had goal chances. Kerry poured forward at every opportunity.

'I'll be honest,' Logan adds, 'I was fearing they might hit us for ten. And if they did, then that was it for me and Dooher. We were up the road.'

Both literally and metaphorically.

As things stood, it put the new joint-management team under pressure. Not that either man had much to prove, mind.

Dooher, with three senior All-Irelands from his playing days, also held a key role in the county's under-21 All-Ireland success of 2015, and holds iconic status in the county. Away from Gaelic football, he is also at the top of his game, serving as Deputy Chief Veterinary Officer for the Department of Agriculture in Northern Ireland, a key position in the NI Executive. He is frequently called upon at all hours by his office, especially with the complexities of Brexit, and facilitating the trade of meat produce is a significant part of his remit.

Logan is just as busy and prolific. A partner at Logan & Corry solicitors, alongside Eamonn Corry in Omagh and Coalisland, County Tyrone, he has been immersed in private practice for over twenty-five years in areas of litigation, mediation, arbitration and dispute resolution. A Tyrone blueblood, he has been synonymous with football in the county since the mid-1980s. He was a midfield stalwart of the 1995 All-Ireland-final team that narrowly lost to Dublin, before managing the county under-21s to 2015 All-Ireland glory. In 2005, he was player-manager of his club, Stewartstown Harps, who reached the All-Ireland junior final only to lose to Eamon Fitzmaurice and Paul Galvin's Finuge side at Portlaoise.

Two extremely successful men with little spare time to give, they decided to join forces and became automatic choices to replace Mickey Harte as senior team managers.

'Maybe having two of us is a help, but we do double up all the time; we always want to be talking and working out decisions, and it is still very busy,' Logan says. 'But if that's the trek you make, you have to get on with it.'

Absolute trust is vital in such a dynamic.

'Well, both of them are honest,' Paul O'Neill chips in. 'They are as you see them.'

Logan adds: 'It's not that Brian and I go back that far, or that we were "buddy-buddy" for years or anything. We were together with that under-21 crop, along with Peter Canavan, but Peter had to stand back from further management roles because his bloodline is so strong. [Canavan has two sons and several other family members who have featured or could play on various Tyrone teams up through the ranks.]

'So it's not as if we plotted and planned. If anything, it would be Paul who knows all my back catalogue because he lived it with me. Call it part coincidence or part fate, I don't know. What I will say is in the overall backroom team everyone has equal standing. All through 2021, I told the county board that I didn't know how far we would go, but I did know that we had twenty people who were genuine, sincere Tyrone people who would empty themselves for the team. It is all about the group and I just felt that they wouldn't be found wanting for anything.'

O'Neill says that autonomy worked a treat. 'The backroom team managed their own departments,' he adds. 'Everyone is happy when they are in control. We were given our space and there was no "this is the way you do it".'

Logan quips that both Dooher and he were simply too busy to helicopter in and out. 'We might not have a perfect management formula, but we appreciate all the expertise of the backroom team and the fact they were prepared to just get on with things,' he says.

'Firstly, we have damn good footballers. Then Joe [McMahon] and Holmsey [Colin Holmes] and Peter Donnelly [strength and conditioning, and performance] are all top-class and take the coaching. Part of that was us recognising their expertise, being happy to trust them and realising that we are under huge time pressure. I go back to that famous line: "Why buy a dog and bark yourself?"'

Coming together in a year dominated by the coronavirus and subsequent attempts to curb surges at various points of 2021, Logan recounts how the senior squad didn't meet collectively as a camp until the middle of April.

'The players just wanted to train by then.'

The camp was hearing of other counties reported to be training up to three times a week. Logan says that Tyrone stuck to public-health guidance as comprehensively as they could through 2021 and points out that, as a solicitor and a Department of Agriculture official, and with a lot of frontline officials throughout the backroom and among the players, neither he nor Dooher were in a position to break any training restrictions.

He makes an interesting point on the work they had undertaken up to then, however.

'The players did all their fitness and conditioning work themselves, but we also have the bank of theory on GAA matters, tactics and strategies. Through lockdown we held Zoom meetings on all aspects of performance, how to play the half-back role, how to cover space, restarts and counter-attacking. From January to March, we got through so much work. The Zoom meetings would break out into smaller workshops and there would be reports back, data given, presentations made.

The learnings were massive. It was homework for the players but with the data software out there it was accessible and important.'

Martin McGirr of Fr. Rocks Cookstown and Logan's own clubman, Daragh Burns, were central to this performance analysis.

Looking back, he is convinced that the month after the Kerry hammering was when the team found its way.

'The coaches went full steam ahead, the players emptied themselves and from mid-June to mid-July, that's when we got going. I was nervous before the championship opener with Cavan. They were the Ulster champions and a good side. I was worried we wouldn't win, and I fretted. When we did get through that one, I felt that no matter what else happened we could stand over a championship win as Tyrone managers. That was another fear erased. It came thick and fast from there. Beating Donegal was special because they'd had a hold over us for much of the last ten years. Very quickly we navigated our way into an Ulster final.'

Yet the thread of an already strange year only got quirkier.

In the week leading up to the Ulster final against Monaghan, which was fixed for Croke Park on 31 July, Logan's phone hopped with texts from players complaining of no sense of smell or taste. He felt a bit off himself and eventually tested positive for the virus – along with five Tyrone players, including big hitters like Tiernan McCann, Rory Brennan and Frank Burns.

Logan looks back in time and describes it as a 'horror week'.

'My wife, Eileen, is immunosuppressed and was shielding throughout covid. She had it and, as I was obviously a close contact, public-health officials confirmed that I was to restrict until midnight of the day of the final. I couldn't leave the house, never mind go to a game. I then ended up succumbing to the virus myself, so I was in restrictions for longer. It was mayhem. As a panel, we had done all we could in sticking to the regulations. Maybe in their own spare time some of the lads had socialised and fraternised with each other after the Donegal game, but as a squad we did all we could to restrict movements. On every single occasion we genuinely honoured every regulation we could. In training, everything was done outdoors at Garvaghey and only at matches did we use dressing rooms. On Ulster final day we used the dressing rooms in Croke Park.'

And then to be left watching that game from his living room?

'Ah, it wasn't nice. Everything was going on. I had to try and get some energy then to look into work stuff at night because we were so busy in the office. It was horrendous with that alone, never mind being in an Ulster final, having covid issues in the camp and then not being able to attend the final either.'

He watched the game on TV and stayed connected to Joe McMahon via WhatsApp. There was a twenty-second delay between their calls and the TV pictures that bounced into his living room. In a Gaelic football match, twenty seconds can mean the difference between a cup raised and a head lowered.

'Well, the one thing it showed to me is how little difference you actually make.' He laughs. 'I was a hundred miles up the road and everything was tickety-boo without me.'

Tyrone played the Ulster final with a depleted team, and short one manager. It was a day that the joust between two wandering wardens of the goalmouth took centre stage. At one juncture Niall Morgan pressed so high on a Monaghan kick-out, he almost bore down on Rory Beggan's goal. Tyrone prevailed by a point.

Next up were Kerry again.

That would be a whole new ball game.

After the Ulster final, the drama heightened.

'Whether it was the situation from the week before the final regressing further, whether it was us being together in the dressing rooms at Croke Park, or whatever, I don't know, but the following week the whole covid thing just blew up altogether,' Logan remembers.

'Naively, I had hoped that our experience with it might have been capped with losing the five players who missed out against Monaghan and that we could proceed from there.'

Instead, the week after that Ulster final win saw the virus spread like bad news through the camp.

'It was like a torch being lit,' the joint manager adds. 'And it was an absolute head-wrecker. By the Tuesday after that game, five or so of our finishing forwards from Ulster final day were wiped out with covid.

'From that Tuesday to Thursday, we were reeling. Our numbers at training went through the floor. Some boys, I suspect, were trying to train through, but we tested everyone and ended up sending so many home.'

On 9 August, Tyrone requested a postponement for their scheduled All-Ireland semi-final with Kerry and they got it. The match was pushed back six days to 21 August.

However, Tyrone had sought a two-week deferral and county chairman Michael Kerr stated that management would not take any decision on the postponed contest until they decided whether they would be capable of fulfilling the fixture.

'At that stage, in fairness to Croke Park, they gave us a week and we felt comforted by it. But we needed another week,' Logan says. 'Boys were just finishing up their isolation period and were only getting back. We couldn't have men getting out of bed during the week of the Kerry game.'

On 12 August, Tyrone told Croke Park officials that they were in big trouble.

'We contacted public health and they came out to test us as a group at Garvaghey,' Logan continues. 'They set up a station and by that night we had data that there were seventeen covid cases among players, fourteen of whom had played in the Ulster championship. In addition, positive cases were detected among five or six members of the backroom.'

On 14 August, Tyrone GAA released a statement saying that its management committee had decided it was not able to field its senior football team in the rescheduled All-Ireland semi-final. The statement said the county had received 'expert medical opinion on the existing and future health and welfare of the players who contracted the covid-19 virus during the period of the last two weeks'.

Logan paints a bleak enough picture of that time.

'We were testing everyone and sending them home,' he says. 'The physios really put themselves at risk. There is a playpark in Garvaghey and the lads had four tables pitched out there because the weather was so great, and we tried to function that way. But we were in serious bother. The truth is that I had three of the worst weeks of my life around that time. The week before the Ulster final and the two weeks after it.'

The expert medical opinion Tyrone had received was from Paddy Mallon, Professor of Microbial Diseases in the UCD School of Medicine and a consultant in infectious diseases in

St Vincent's University Hospital in Dublin. Professor Mallon's findings were crucial in the camp, uniting behind the decision to look for an extra week.

'Paddy requested dates and lists of symptoms for each player and backroom member, and asked for rankings of the degree of severity that they had experienced. The results there were varying – some lads had hardly any symptoms at all, whereas one player was hospitalised for two nights at Craigavon hospital,' Logan explains.

Paul O'Neill leans forward to make a point. 'That same lad who was hospitalised came back to us four days later, looking to play,' he says. 'There was a huge amount of attention placed on us during that time, but this is what I always come back to – our players always wanted to play, but they were simply not able to. Guys who would be household names for their stamina and engines were down on their knees after one run. Some guys couldn't make it up a flight of stairs. It was up to us to protect them.'

Professor Mallon's report listed every player's status, included the latest updated data, and included the virologist's report that, in his opinion, it was unsafe to play on 21 August. It also stated that, in his professional opinion, it would be significantly safer to play one week later.

'With that we went to GAA management and said we needed more time,' Logan recalls.

The approach wasn't immediately unanimous.

'Some of the lads were like, "Let's play the bloody game on the 21st." On the Saturday before we were due to play, there was a meeting of everyone involved in the middle of the football pitch that we were training on at Garvaghey and the discussion invited everyone to give their opinion. Lots of players naturally wanted to play. On the other hand, one or two players felt that if [Professor Mallon] had felt it was not right to play, then they shouldn't.'

Logan states that they considered every possible stipulation and scenario but ultimately it came down to this: they couldn't put their players through an All-Ireland semi-final on 21 August with so many just having had one week to fully overcome contraction of the virus.

After the players' meeting, Logan and Dooher spoke to the county board and reported that the group decision was that they would not be able to fulfil the fixture on 21 August, as they wouldn't do themselves proper justice.

They needed another week.

The management committee agreed.

On 14 August, the Tyrone board issued a statement outlining that it was not in a position to field its senior football team in the rescheduled All-Ireland semi-final. It was a landmark moment, not just in the 2021 championship but in the association's history.

It has that proud history of completing championships despite wars, civil wars, pandemics and outbreaks. However, having proceeded through the minefields that 2020 laid, it now seemed like the 2021 series would have an asterix beside it.

From a financial perspective, the GAA could have done with the game proceeding too, especially with 2020 being the worst year in its fiscal history. With the All-Ireland semi-final potentially not taking place and at least €1 million in gate receipts lost due to its cancellation, the 2021 season would be greatly damaged.

The needs of Kerry, Mayo and Dublin also had to be considered. While Sligo's withdrawal from the 2020 championship – due to an outbreak there – had been less than pleasant, there was no time for rescheduling at that juncture. But losing serious contenders like Tyrone at the business end of the championship threw everything up in the air.

Kerry certainly felt that way. They didn't want to reach an All-Ireland final without having earned the right and wanted the game to go ahead. On 15 August, they put on record their frustration at the situation, but said it was their 'overarching wish . . . to ensure that the All-Ireland semi-final against Tyrone was played at the earliest possible opportunity'.

Confusion reigned and frustration hung in the air.

On RTÉ's live show on 14 August, former Kerry player Tomás Ó Sé said that Tyrone did not 'box off' the threat of covid. The five-time All-Ireland winner reckoned Tyrone had questions to answer and that it would dilute the championship completely if they didn't play.

'There's a lot in me that would be angry with why this is here,' he said. 'Tyrone landed into the Ulster final, and they had a situation. How that wasn't boxed off . . . a lot of teams have had that similar situation, but they boxed it off and they nailed it and it's after getting worse in Tyrone.'

Others felt a further extension was appropriate.

'Feargal Logan and Brian Dooher are honourable men,' Ó Sé's fellow pundit Colm O'Rourke said. 'If they are saying that they're not able to play, and their medical staff are saying they're not able to play, I think the GAA should give them the extra week.

'It's an amateur game, I don't care how they got [covid]; people were saying, "Ah, they were all out socialising." I don't believe that for a minute. I think they should be given the benefit of at least an extra week.'

Much of the anger aimed at Tyrone centred on the suggestion that the outbreak may have been related to post-match celebrations from the Ulster final. Tyrone, however, always insisted it was 'a community-based issue'.

There was much to back up that theory, too. In August 2021, the Delta variant of the virus began sweeping through society. Over the next four months there were 70,000 cases of it identified in the North alone, according to public-health records.

It hardly mattered at that stage how the virus had infiltrated the Tyrone camp. Croke Park bosses knew they just needed to act swiftly.

On 14 August, Mayo defeated Dublin in their All-Ireland semi-final. Croke Park contacted Mayo to sound out if they would agree to another week being given to Tyrone. They said they were happy to have the final pushed out by a week.

Croke Park contacted Kerry again, who, after consultation with players, management and board officials, agreed in principle to the Tyrone and Kerry semi-final going ahead on 28 August.

On 15 August, HQ confirmed that the second All-Ireland SFC semi-final, involving Kerry and Tyrone, would take place on Saturday, 28 August.

The winners would proceed to a final meeting with Mayo two weeks later on 11 September.

The decision had been made with the integrity of the championship in mind and to ensure that Kerry were not denied a semi-final outing.

Croke Park's Feargal McGill is practical about how that matter played out.

'Tyrone requested a postponement of their All-Ireland semi-final, and we gave them a week, consistent with our rules.

Tyrone were disappointed they only got a week and they made that very clear to us. But a lot of people, and not just Tyrone people, lost sight that this was not just about one team or game. A postponement affected Kerry; Mayo had yet to play Dublin in the other semi-final, and any postponement could have affected them too. There were four teams still involved at that stage and granting any more than a one-week extension would have had a knock-on effect for the other three counties and club players in those counties who had waited patiently for their domestic games to commence.

'We gave Tyrone our view and we knew that a one-week extension would see all players being available from the Tuesday before the designated fixture date and we hoped it would be sufficient.

'Tyrone issued a statement saying they didn't feel they would be able to fulfil the fixture. That was on a Saturday. Over the weekend Dublin exited the championship [14 August]. Kerry looked at the situation and said they didn't want to be in an All-Ireland final without playing a semi-final – that it would affect the integrity of the championship. Kerry contacted us on the Sunday morning, said they would consult their players and gave the view that they would wait the extra week to play Tyrone. Mayo were happy for that to happen and for the All-Ireland to go back to the first weekend in September. So over the course of that weekend, Kerry were happy, Mayo were happy and Tyrone were happy. Once we had the three counties aligned, it was possible for us to take that decision [to give Tyrone a two-week extension rather than one]. A week before, they were not aligned,' McGill added. 'And we were obliged to follow our rules until all three counties were happy. There was a lot of outside noise, but we got on with the job.'

Logan says it is important to give credit to all involved in the process.

'We have gratitude towards Kerry,' he says. 'It was very important that the extension was given but, in the end, it showed that the general fairness of our association prevailed. I know that there are people who had a go at us over what happened, but people take bites at everyone in the GAA at some stage, especially those on a higher platform, and all I can say is that the overall spirit and fairness of the GAA can never be forgotten here.

'I know people will feel hard done by and it is easy to feel grateful when you win but to the people who let us get on with playing when we were at our most vulnerable, I would commend them on their fairness.'

Logan's turbulent times hadn't come to an end yet, though.

In an extensive interview with journalist and author Declan Bogue on 16 August, one of the takeaways from the piece was a comment the joint Tyrone bosses made about the vaccinations rollout from January to March of that year. He referred to the availability of the vaccine and the age of cohorts eligible to get it at that specific time.

Logan stressed there were several players in the Tyrone panel who were vaccinated but said it was a personal choice and that management hadn't made it mandatory. He said that they had been aware of timings of vaccinations for the different age groups, with his players not coming into the frame for their jabs until late May and June. Due to the compressed nature of the league and championship, there was an anxiety that if players were vaccinated, they might feel ill for a period, as in some cases the vaccine had laid people low.

'Vaccination has been a conundrum,' Logan told Bogue. 'We didn't make it mandatory across the board. There are some players vaccinated for a variety of reasons, be it because they work on the front line or in healthcare. It's one of those things – even with the vaccination, people are still getting it and, with first-hand experience of that, it lays you low.'

A storm followed.

With the virus enjoying a swift upsurge, newspaper columns and airtime minutes were devoted to Logan's comments. Some deemed them to be unsatisfactory and irresponsible. Much of the public sympathy that had been with the county's footballers because of their plight diminished.

The shrapnel flew fast and hard. Logan was firmly in the line of fire.

'I did the article with Declan and the words I used were that the vaccine was a conundrum,' he recalls. 'Straightaway I started getting texts. "You are a bluffer, Logan." "Tyrone are bluffers." I was getting all this stuff, as if I was an anti-vaxxer.

'I tried to keep away from it. I didn't read social media because it would only feed the paranoia, but you would want to see what my own friends were sending me, thinking they were putting me in the picture! I was absolutely slated.

'I want to clarify now what I meant. By using the word conundrum, I didn't mean the vaccine itself was a conundrum. I was talking about the roll-out of it, the timing of it, the availability of it in the early stages and how the roll-out might affect our players with games coming so soon after. I meant that managing the logistics and flow of the vaccine roll-out for us as a squad was a conundrum. The process was the conundrum, not the vaccine, particularly in the early stages when the whole world was getting to terms with it. My comments centred on what was happening during January, February, March and April, when the vaccine was only available to certain age groups and cohorts of people. The number of infections were falling in spring 2021 and it wasn't until the new variant arrived in late July and early August that matters became very difficult again, and the importance of the vaccine, which was by then more readily available, was most relevant.

'I was talking about the scenario earlier in the year when vaccination was available only to certain critical groups in society. Our medical team had kept everyone appraised of the availability of the vaccination, as and when it arose, throughout the year.

'But there was debate everywhere. As well as being an anti-vaxxer, I was then heralded as someone who potentially felt that football was so important that it came before public health.

'Is that what I meant? Of course not. Does it get to you? Of course, it does. There were a couple of serious libels as well. I came across them, even though I stopped reading and looking at my phone. You couldn't avoid it; people were just sending me this stuff.'

Going into that Ulster final with virus concerns, Logan missing the game himself after being struck down, seeing an outbreak decimate the squad, the entire postponement and extension process, the accusations that the camp hadn't dealt well with the spread of the virus, and then the theory that vaccines weren't a high priority within – distractions were everywhere.

Tyrone were never ones to look far for a cause and if they wanted another one it was right in front of them now.

'I don't think we took on the cause,' Logan says, 'but I will put it this way: sometimes out of adversity comes opportunity.'

On 28 August, that opportunity finally knocked against Kerry, and, in extra time, Tyrone kicked the door down.

Kerry came into the game, having facilitated their opponents, without a game in five weeks. Before that they had cruised through Munster, with the windows down, the car in third gear and the music blaring.

It didn't help them at all. They were caught cold on the day.

And yet the victory had all the hallmarks of a great Tyrone performance, too. For instance, Conor Meyler didn't give player of the year contender Paudie Clifford a look-in. All three members of the Tyrone full-back line had scored before half-time. Cathal McShane came off the bench and scored 1–3. And Darragh Canavan came on and set up a goal.

After the game, however, there were some testy exchanges with the press corps.

'Suffice to say it was an interesting press conference,' Logan quips.

He was asked if they felt sheepish, having stated how bad things were, looking for a two-week extension, and then winning the game.

'The truth is that of course we felt sheepish,' he responds. 'But it wasn't as if we had made it up. There was sickness in my household, along with other households. I felt vulnerable, the lads felt vulnerable, and we simply could not have put in a performance had the game gone ahead on the 21st. It was ultimately a player safety matter.

'Our goals won that Kerry game for us. I was stressing beforehand that they would strike early and in just their third attack they went for the jugular. They had been scoring goals for fun in the league and I was worried we wouldn't have the juice in our legs to stay with them.'

Paul O'Neill saw the players at close hand in training and was similarly concerned. 'We used the water breaks the best we could,' he says. 'I was with Ronan McNamee for one of them and he was asking to be taken off, that he couldn't go any more. But he did. And all the lads did. Fergal is right – the goals bailed us out. But the boys put in some shift, too.

'The players' stats were well down on what they would normally be, but what impressed us in the backroom most was their resilience to keep going at it. I think the previous few weeks had galvanised them even more.'

If eyebrows were raised at the recovery of Tyrone's players for that Kerry game, scarcely a word was uttered after their clinical dismantling of Mayo in the final, which saw them lift Sam Maguire for the fourth time in a ruthlessly economical way.

It was a day when Mayo's forwards didn't click, they squandered four goal opportunities and missed a penalty. Tyrone, in contrast, received just two sights of goal but each time they struck with precision.

On the day they were efficient and well-drilled; they got their match-ups spot on and they delivered a performance of ruthless excellence.

Sixteen years after he captained the county to 2005 All-Ireland success, Dooher joined Dublin icon Kevin Heffernan, another Dub, Tony Hanahoe, Cork's Billy Morgan and Kerry's Páidí Ó Sé in having both skippered and managed their county to All-Ireland glory.

And after leaking six goals to Kerry in the league, Tyrone had conceded just one in the entire championship. They achieved one of the most dramatic All-Ireland wins of all time.

Logan looks back now and acknowledges that all was well because they managed to win. But he does make the point that the varying restrictions, rollouts, lockdowns and general scenarios north and south of the border made life extremely complicated during 2021.

'It led to big issues, two sets of regulations,' he says. 'When things were improving up north, they were deteriorating in the south, and vice-versa. It was ultimately a comment during one such scenario that got me publicly flailed. But there were many waves and peaks within the virus's spread.'

He is relieved that it's all behind him now, that the cup was won. The 2022 season proved to be much more complex with the team losing several players and never finding full form, losing to Derry in Ulster and crashing out to Armagh in the qualifiers. But when Logan looks back on 2021 he feels gratitude for Kerry's grace and huge pride in his own players' resilience.

'We had serious footballers on a mission. Great footballers who challenge themselves every night of the week to play in a massive club structure; players who are inherently ambitious. And that's the bottom line. Everyone was talking about Mayo, but our guys had been pushing hard for years too. On All-Ireland final day, they were waiting to push the walls down.'

22

LIFTING THE TREATY

HOW LIMERICK'S HISTORY-MAKING HURLERS TRANSFORMED THE GAME

With the Delta variant running riot, it was the end of November 2021 when Limerick eventually got to enjoy their own official celebration for the previous two championship wins. On that night, Kyle Hayes was presented with eleven medals at the county's back-to-back All-Ireland medal ceremony at the Strand Hotel.

Hayes was only twenty-three but went home with more honours than a decorated military sergeant. A month later he claimed a third All-Star award alongside a record eleven other teammates. They had swept the boards.

His haul was one that most players could only daydream of. Two Celtic Crosses from the 2020 and 2021 All-Ireland senior final wins over Cork and Waterford respectively. Three Munster medals, from 2019, 2020 and 2021, and Division 1 league silverware for 2019 and 2020. The team also received trophies for their 2019 Munster hurling league win, the Super 11s Fenway Hurling Classic victory in Boston in November 2018, whilst Munster and All-Ireland minor runners-up medals from 2016 were handed out, too.

That golden catch, enriched by further Munster and All-Ireland titles, their third in a row, in 2022, reflected the county's current dominance of hurling's shores, light years away from the empty trawls that returned to Shannonside after decades of fruitless excursions.

Their success has transcended sport too.

'Those lads have changed a lot of things for Limerick people,' says former player Niall Moran, who made forty-six championship appearances in the green and white. 'For years the county struggled with our identity away from playing fields. Limerick had a bad reputation and we had to play down a lot of what was made of us. The labels that stuck, like "Stab City" or "Crime Capital of Europe". Those were very unfair, and we had to deal with them.

'Back, then, onto the playing field and, prior to 2017, we had this reputation as being an almost dysfunctional county in GAA circles, riddled with stories of ill-discipline and a drinking culture. No different to the accusations about being a crime capital, those labels were totally unfounded.

'But since 2018 we have been held up as a shining example of what the GAA should be and how the modern game should be played. And that has had a huge impact on the morale and sense of self of Limerick people.

'Morale is high outside the field, too. The regeneration of the city and county has been strong. Industrial estates like Raheen have gone from strength to strength. Businesses are coming to Limerick and setting up here, and our sense of identity has really improved and strengthened. A decade ago, a Limerick hurler could walk unrecognised down the street, whereas a Munster rugby player would be chased. Now kids are going around wearing Limerick gear and the players are instantly recognisable. People are so proud of them for what they have done for us over the last few years.'

Moran makes no bones about the comfort the team gave Limerick folk during the public-health crisis.

'In some rural places there are two social outlets – Mass and a match at the weekend. Masses were taken away from people for a long time during covid, and all people had to look forward to were matches on TV and dissecting them. And look what the Limerick team has done for these people.'

Slowly, deep scars from times past are healing, wounds that were often self-inflicted or at times down to a lack of organisation and quality coming through the ranks.

From 1973 to 2018, the county won no All-Ireland senior title and, when they did manage to sketch out the rough skeleton of a road map, the transition to the top flight was gridlocked by a series of obstacles. As the years passed, the pursuit of happiness lingered painfully, prompting local author and hurling devotee Henry Martin to write a book depicting the hurt – a book fittingly called *Unlimited Heartbreak*. They did have phases of joy here and there, but those were as fleeting as a shooting star.

Between 2000 and 2002 the county, with Dave Keane at the helm, won three All-Ireland under-21 titles in a row. Those kids were Limerick's class of '92. But unlike at Old Trafford, there was no domination at top-flight level. A number of those underage stars did feature at the highest grade but some only in spurts. Managers came and went like buses in a depot. There were five between 2000 and 2006 – including Eamon Cregan, Dave Keane, Pad Joe Whelahan, Joe McKenna and Richie

Bennis. It didn't help. There was no continuity.

They scarcely featured again at under-21 level for another eight years. A low point was the record 17-point hammering to Clare in the 2006 All-Ireland qualifiers. Another was the 2009 drubbing by Tipperary in the All-Ireland semi-final.

That hammering was something of a eureka moment. Afterwards, concerned citizens such as Shane Fitzgibbon, Eibhear O'Dea and Joe McKenna knew it was time for action. They staged something of an intervention in the underage ranks.

* * *

Striving to rejuvenate the county's fortunes, work began at the bottom and soared upwards. A hurling development plan was drawn up in 2011. It focused on basics.

By now Munster rugby was a powerful force, having contested four European cup finals, winning two. Such was the power of the oval ball revolution that Munster GAA employed a dedicated hurling coach in Limerick to improve penetration. That was a big addition.

The next landmark was coercing the juvenile divisions of the Limerick board to gel within an academy-type system. A sub-committee was set up, driven by Fitzgibbon, O'Dea and Cregan, the iconic former player and manager.

O'Dea and his workgroup were warned that the boards would never unite and that there were simply not enough quality coaches to help. A deaf ear was turned to that narrative. After much persuasion the divisional boards came together and a range of top-quality coaches were indeed appointed. At last, there was a flightpath ahead.

They may have lost the 2022 All-Ireland under-20 final to Kilkenny, but there is no doubt the cogs are turning.

'You could soon see the lads start to come through the system,' Aoife Sheehan, the former Limerick camogie player, says. 'Be it at schools level or with underage teams. No one could have known what lay ahead, but there was excitement around the place from a long way out. There were green shoots.'

Cregan, a man who had battled longer and harder than most for Limerick hurling, took the under-14s. Fitzgibbon himself looked after the under-15s. Ger Hegarty took control of the 16s, Anthony Carmody the 17s and the likes of Brian Finn, Ger Cunningham, Frankie Carroll and Mike Galligan all played roles, too.

Jerry Wallace was installed as the director of hurling for the underage academy. Dr Áine MacNamara was introduced to facilitate a culture of high performance. One evening she brought every Limerick manager into a meeting – from senior boss at the time, John Allen, all the way down to the under-14 coaches. When she asked if the primary goal for those managers was for their teams to win, almost every hand went up in agreement.

Dr McNamara had a different slant. She reckoned only John Allen's hand should be raised. The others should be principally focused on developing their hurlers for long-term good.

And so the focus turned to preparing young hurlers for the big stage, rather than prioritising success at a stage in players' careers when they should only be taking off. Conditioning was a big focus. Despite the concerns of traditionalists who felt that bulky bodies did little for one's hurling skills, Andy Murphy was brought in as strength and conditioning coach. Those who followed in this role maintained a high bar. A database of players' fitness statistics was created and is still in use today, as Limerick's hurling terminators rule the roost.

Those early academy players started off lifting no weights, only focusing on technique. A new Limerick strategic plan recognised that fifty-seven per cent of primary school children in the city were now playing Gaelic Games. Five years earlier that figure had been just eight per cent. Work on the ground had paid off big time.

Saturday mornings at UL became an institution for the coaching and games development department. Between 9 a.m. and 1 p.m. the minor team, followed by the under-16s, 15s and 14s, trained on Astro pitches there. They worked in cycles of six weeks, meaning that no schedule, goal or target was too overwhelming.

In 2014, their under-15 side, managed by Leo O'Connor, won a Croke Park-organised tournament. The following year, under Joe Quaid, they won All-Ireland plates at under-15 and an All-Ireland 'A' title. A settled foundation had been put in and blocks were being added all the time.

Players such as Seán Finn, Cian Lynch and Aaron Gillane were part of a squad that won the All-Ireland under-16 title with Quaid and they became a showcase for the Academy 'system'. Gillane is an example of what hard work and proper coaching can achieve. He featured on 'B' teams in his early years but stands now as one of the leading hurlers in the land.

A rising tide lifts all boats. Brian Ryan's Munster minor-winning teams of 2013 and 2014 drove the project on, too. There were under-21 provincial crowns in 2015 and 2017.

Just beneath the coalface, Limerick were quietly humming.

All the while John Kiely was forging his own path too, graduating from under-21 selector to under-21 manager to county intermediate boss before assuming the top role.

Everything and everyone seemed to be in place. The right man in charge of the senior squad, the players hardened in body and mind, prepared in the right way, the correct structures yielding dividends and serious resources in place. Limerick had managed to build something magnificent under our very eyes.

At senior level, it took them two years to refine a style that few could cope with. But during the covid years they only reinforced their mighty grip on the game.

In May 2021, they lost to Galway in a league game. Before that they were unbeaten in fourteen. From there, they went through the 2021 championship undefeated. At the end of the season, Kiely had masterminded three All-Ireland titles, and a fourth triumph would follow in 2022 when they beat Galway in a thrilling semi-final and dispatched of Kilkenny after a titanic tussle in the decider. Not bad for a county that had spent forty-five years in the wilderness.

Tom Condon retired in the middle of that run, having won Celtic Crosses in 2018 and 2020. He says there is very little out there that could ever upset the camp, simply because it is so focused.

'The covid experience wasn't pleasant for anyone, but because the foundations are so solid that didn't faze our lads either. We stayed in contact through Snapchat and WhatsApp; the matches behind closed doors were eerie but they did go to plan, so we just got on with it.'

Disrupted by injury, Condon went from being a first-team player to fighting for his place in 2020 and often missing out on the official twenty-six-man match-day panel and having to watch championship games from his own sitting room. He took all of that on the chin.

'If I saw something on the field, I'd go over to the lads on the full-back line at the break and check if they had noticed it too. Just try to help. That was the beauty of it. Not everyone was going to make the twenty-six on match days, but we all trusted each other. I always smiled going to training, no matter what. While it was tough not making the squad for games, you put your head down and worked through the next session. Fellas were disappointed on the Friday night before the match if they didn't make the cut, but the good of the squad had to come first.

'It is one big family. And mighty craic to have been a part of. I wanted to stay there for as long as I could.'

On the weekends where he didn't make the squad, Condon and the other non-matchday panel members trained on a Sunday morning of a game with strength and conditioning coach Mikey Kiely. John Kiely himself was in attendance whenever he could make it, too, despite having a championship game to manage hours later.

They trained in venues such as Effin. But during the pandemic, with only a set number of players allowed inside the stadium, that was the extent of their involvement with the team. A tough championship day experience for anyone.

'You would go off then and watch the game at home with your family,' Condon says. 'It certainly got me ready for retirement and gave me a taste of what was to come. You would be dying to be there in the stadium with your teammates. It was tough.

'For the 2020 All-Ireland semi-final against Waterford, we travelled up to Dublin with the team but stayed behind in the hotel. The team and management went to Croke Park to play while the rest of us watched on TV until they came back. For the final, we were allowed in the stand but not in the dressing room. I will always remember after the game being ushered from beneath the stand in the stadium to another place and it was just the strangest feeling. A venue of 82,000 people and no one in it. Back, then, to Limerick. Nothing happening anywhere and no one in the streets. So, from that point of view, it was tough.

'But there was never any hassle about it. Those lads are absolute gents, and we have such a good relationship that you would still meet them regularly. The thing is we pushed them hard. There were times when the "B" team beat the "A" team in training, and we left John scratching his head! They will be caught some day again because that is life, but it's hard to see them stopping anytime soon.'

* * *

With a strong pulse rediscovered, heartbreak now belonged to others.

Limerick turned the game of hurling on its head and totally transformed its dynamic. Steely, working through the lines, power runners all over the field, space in front of a lethal full forward line and quite often playing on the line – and sometimes over it – the opposition never captivated them unduly. Whether the seas were calm or raged around them, they would paddle their own canoe regardless. Their standards and targets are set internally, and they don't accept evaluation from external sources.

It won't last forever, naturally, but for now the chasing pack dawdles in the distance.

'Hmmm . . .' The former midfielder Paul Browne smiles. 'These plaudits coming from outside the county make me worry.' Browne retired through injury with an All-Ireland medal in his back pocket from 2018 but remains heavily involved in the harnessing of the game in the county. Haunting memories of the past, he reckons, still fuel the pursuit of future glories.

'Look, it's all great to hear the tributes, but the truth is that everyone on the ground here worries that we could lose what we have. It's difficult to fully grasp the mood of the county if you are from outside Limerick. The external view focuses on our success and excellent performances in big games, but I just think the most impressive thing is the people in the county have taken a sense of great pride in these lads, in what they are doing and in that sense of excellence they are achieving.

'There may be a few bandwagon fans, but I genuinely don't get the sense that Limerick people are arrogant or in your face about the success. We know where we came from and that it could all disappear very quickly.'

As Niall Moran suggests, the city itself worked hard to shed itself of past image issues and continues to attract new business, development and investment. It is a vibrant, inclusive and progressive place to be.

The county's hurlers seem to epitomise this vigour. There is a new breed of confident young talent streaming through, players like Cathal O'Neill and Adam English. They learn to develop a strong mentality and perform in an environment where structures, facilities and resources are as good as anywhere else in the country.

Having spent long enough at the back of the hall, there is a ferocious desire for Limerick to retain that hard-fought spot at the head of the top table.

'I'd imagine they all want to make hay,' Moran adds. 'To take a leaf out of the great Kilkenny team's book, where Brian Cody was a totem and the players took his lead. It's the same in Limerick. John Kiely is very sensible, level-headed and affable. You sense that all his qualities have transferred to the players. I think on the bus back home in 2018 he pre-empted a lot of temptations and challenges that lay ahead and delivered a great speech highlighting those. It seemed to have struck a chord. Maybe John would have been aware of previous failings of teams. The players listened. They have grown enormously on the field and are growing off it, too. Don't get me wrong, they won't all be without flaws; they are lads in their twenties, but in the main they have been impeccable in how they represent themselves. They want to keep this going and Limerick people do, too.'

Browne is one of those in the engine room, driving future generations on, setting the tempo and ensuring a healthy rhythm for Limerick hurling in the years to come. He works as games development administrator for the northside and is also head of coaching in the Limerick academy, working alongside overall academy leader Pat Donnelly, head of strength and conditioning Darragh Droog, and Patrick Jones, who oversees the sports psychology department.

JP McManus (who has been backing Limerick for a long time) and his brother, Gerry, rowed in behind to offer support in terms of resources. This contributes to ensuring proper practice for their upcoming elite in areas such as skills, conditioning, nutrition, hydration and mental preparation. At senior level, the results are there for all to see. In the academy, they are looking four to five years down the line.

'This golden age won't last forever,' Browne cautions. 'But we would love to be like Tyrone, for example, who reach Ulster finals every couple of years and always seem to be there or thereabouts at the business end of the All-Ireland series.

'We don't want to go back to the days of winning a Munster title once every ten years – don't forget, we went from 1996 to 2013 without winning one. Right now, the senior team is driving it on and I'm just in awe of the hard work and the culture in the group, how they have sustained everything throughout the past few years.

'Bringing others into the fold now is the goal and, so far, it's working. I see young fellas going into that group and, within two or three months, they are physically different; they are so confident and yet they stay humble.

'I think you could do a PhD study on it, on the culture of a group, how a shared mindset, physical preparation and values can help integrate new talent into a tried-and-trusted system. Young lads are being drafted in here, their bodies are quickly adapting, and soon they are all on the same hymn sheet. No one is missing a beat.'

* * *

The covid years altered Browne's professional plans to drive underage hurling. He began his new role just weeks before the pandemic started. A blank canvas awaited, but with rules, restrictions and guidelines fluctuating it was hard to outline any clear picture of what could be done.

Instead, 2020 was a grand compilation of online interactions, from Zoom meetings and quizzes to virtual cookery classes and workouts. The academy coaches tried every trick to keep youngsters from under-14 to under-20 in some way connected, as the virus spread and regressed.

It was a novelty at first, but it soon wore off. By the time 2021 arrived, the young players were fed up looking at each other on screens and were like locked-up bulls raring for a green field.

'You start a new job and you're trying to make an impression.' He laughs. 'Then the virus lands and you're wondering what is next. I actually ended up taking everything week by week, looking no further than that.'

Ardscoil Rís teacher Moran reckons the past couple of years had a big effect on his profession and on his students, too.

'I found it very difficult to teach the curriculum like I usually would. But most of us would look at their role as teachers as being a pastoral one. Every day involves getting to know students, their lives, problems, and a lot of times you would be acting as counsel when maybe they didn't have any other outlet.

'I found it hard not to have that engagement and I would say they really missed that interaction with teachers too. School life is fundamentally having a syllabus, but school life is also about meeting pals, going to matches, concerts, going to debs, and I think a chunk of all these kids' lives were removed.'

Moran's former teammate Shane Dowling empathises with the strangeness and hollowness that the pandemic brought. Just months after he too had been forced to prematurely call time on his career through injury, Dowling found himself working for RTÉ at the behind-closed-doors 2020 All-Ireland senior final.

'I was only retired six months, just out the door, when I was sent to that final,' he says. 'It was so weird. I drove up to Croke Park and parked outside the Hogan Stand – when could you ever do that for a big game? I went into the hotel across the road, did a Zoom call for the *Up for the Match* TV show and then ambled across to the stadium. There was pretty much no one else around.'

For possibly the first time ever, Dowling didn't feel comfortable at Croke Park.

'Knowing the players and their families, knowing the work everyone had put in over the years, I felt almost like a fraud being there, to be honest.

'On that evening of the 2020 final, I was like, "Why should I be here with the media when parents of the players are not here?" Maybe it's just me – I do admit that, on one hand, I was delighted to have had the privilege of being there – but a part of me still felt it wasn't right.'

Like Dowling, Aoife Sheehan spends much of her time working as a media analyst with RTÉ and other outlets. She is less concerned with the prospect of the good days slipping away.

'The lads have won a lot, but they have held it together well,' she says. 'Maybe covid helped that. For two years, the country was shut down, which meant that they weren't pulled and dragged for public appearances all over the place. That would have been a help. I'm not so sure the lads would be into that anyway.

'Instead, they managed to celebrate quietly with their families, partners and friends. They had a team holiday and one with their partners, and even from the little bits they shared on Instagram and other platforms it was all nice and low-key. I don't know if their culture or make-up would really see them going mad with what they have won. Societal changes mean that young people really look after their health and bodies. The lads on this team are opening coffee shops. Years ago, it would have been pubs. This is a different era and even if the country had been fully open, I'm not sure if the lads would have been too distracted. They are good fellas.'

Just as well. In Limerick hurling circles, the prospect of standing still is nearly seen as a form of regression. It's not countenanced – a slight on their aspirations, almost.

* * *

When Limerick landed those record twelve All-Stars in 2021, it reflected their absolute supremacy. Their displays through 2020, 2021 and 2022 were clinical, with the '21 final a case study in how to execute an elite sport game-plan on the biggest day of all, and the '22 decider a classic example of showing resilience under fire and finding a way to win.

'Just their ball execution, their handling, they always seem to know what is best on the field,' Sheehan says. 'One thing I noticed, too, was the guys who didn't even make the official squad gave non-stop support and encouragement to their team-mates. It was unreal. Universal support.'

Paul Browne heartily echoes that sentiment. 'At the top, the culture you see comes from John Kiely and it seeps downwards,' he states. 'It has happened in the past where one or two fellas might lose the run of themselves and that is only human nature. Their wings would have been clipped fairly quickly: they might end up getting a bit of special treatment at training, they could be kept on the bench, or they may be called aside – he has ways of doing it.

'But the thing that keeps the lads humble is the goals they set for themselves, the targets they set every week and the standards they hold.

'They don't look past the end of a season, they just go game to game, picking out the stats that need attention each time and striving to hit the next target.

'Humility comes from that. If they fail to meet one goal, they just try harder the next time. If there is a perception of failure, it's only within the group and they themselves set the definition of failure. It's all intrinsic.'

The team's consistency is what impresses Dowling the most. He sighs at the mention of the word 'hunger' when people question if Limerick can retain their drive.

'That's a word that is stupidly thrown around,' he says. 'Most of these lads are in their mid- to late twenties, and just look at the buzz they get out of it. They have a brilliant management team in John and Paul Kinnerk and the other coaches, and they all know the system inside out. The set-up has been in place quite a while now and you see the joy in their faces. They understand Limerick do not have a bucket load of All-Ireland titles and they want to make hay while the sun shines.

'They have ways of keeping it fresh. A couple of new lads were added to the panel each year. They are always evolving.'

The clinical 2021 All-Ireland dismantling of Waterford, that record haul of All-Stars, and that magical Munster-final comeback against Tipperary in 2021, from 10 points down in searing heat to absolutely torching their opponents in the second half, and their sustained brilliance in 2022 – all are key indicators of a team near its peak.

Browne says the academy plan is simply to keep county standard hurlers from under-14 to under-20 connected to the new culture for as long as possible.

What an environment to be part of.

23

FOG LIFTS FROM OVER
THE FAITHFUL

A PROUD COUNTY BACK IN DREAMLAND
AFTER DECADES OF HURT

Offaly, sick of nostalgia's stale taste, are deep in their own rebuilding project.

Cocooned near Clonmacnoise, Seán Lowry, the county's three-time All-Ireland senior football winner, was glad to watch phases of it unfold.

Aside from the three lockdowns the country experienced, Offaly also had a regional shutdown alongside Kildare and Laois early in the virus's spread because of higher incidence rates than other counties.

Lowry has a passion for beekeeping and holds a strong interest in woodwork, which led him to renovate a cottage two miles away. Those hobbies kept him busy during the intense restrictions. Weekends were spent watching his nephew, Shane, play golf and taking in wall-to-wall Gaelic Games coverage on RTÉ and TG4.

'The world changed quickly,' Seán says. 'I turned seventy early in 2022, so I was at that age where you were minding yourself.

We were vulnerable. I have a daughter, Sarah, who lives beside us and has a lung complaint. I didn't want to bring anything back to her. We kept to ourselves, and I know that thousands of people were on the front line helping us, and I know of others who struggled too. But I felt so sorry for younger people, teenagers and those in their twenties. I have two teenage grandchildren and they missed out on school, the teenage discos, sport and socialising. They have enough to be worried about at that age without all that ongoing and it took its toll on young people all over Ireland. Especially those stressing about exams and that.

'Having said all of that, I tried to enjoy the lockdowns as best I could. There was nowhere to go, I didn't have to be anywhere. There were no funerals, weddings, matches – I actually enjoyed coming home from work on the cottage, relaxing in the evenings, knowing that you could throw on the pyjamas, light the fire, read a book and you'd be grand. Suddenly, all the urgency was gone. Some people need others, but I am happy in my own company.'

Offaly is a tight-knit place and the forty-one clubs there established a community response forum in the first lockdown.

The board had its own issues through the crisis, with those four shutdowns wreaking havoc with their games' programme, finances and just about everything else in its remit. It meant their 2020 championships had to be held over until 2021, and four separate domestic schedules compiled by fixture-makers in response.

That was far from ideal and put underage Offaly teams and managers under massive pressure to get games and competitions played, possibly contributing to some serious injuries that players sustained later in the year.

About a year into the pandemic, though, a spark lit within and caught a hearty, roaring fire. God knows it was welcome, for their hopes had been doused long enough.

Once gloriously successful and irreverent in their own likeable way, they waned alarmingly as the years passed. Certainly, as a hurling force. They slipped to Division 2 of the league and fell to hurling's third tier, the Christy Ring series. At underage level, in both codes, they were beaten by counties they would traditionally have dealt with. There were plenty of off-the-field distractions, too, with issues challenging their executive over the years.

The county wasn't united.

A glorious rise met with a sad decline.

'People around twenty-five years of age would never have seen Offaly in Croke Park,' Lowry says. 'Whereas in my playing days, kids grew up watching us go there a lot. We contested thirteen All-Ireland finals in hurling and football between 1960 and 2000, and won seven, four hurling and three football. That was serious now, especially for a county with a small population. I don't think another county of a similar sized population [circa eighty thousand] has really done what we did since. But we encountered hard times after that,' he says.

'Looking back, we had a honey pot of footballers in my time and then in the 1980s a group of young hurlers came up through the schools and enjoyed great success in the 1990s. But then production lines ceased, and we suffered, especially in hurling.'

In December 2019, a group led by former two-time All-Ireland-winning hurler Michael Duignan challenged for several positions on the county executive. Duignan was duly elected board chairman, Dervill Dolan became treasurer, while Colm Cummins took the role as secretary a year later. Quickly the new-look administration adjusted structures, development plans and the general outlook of the county. They wanted positivity as quickly as possible, to immediately plough new ground in the hope that one day the soil would be fertile again, which would encourage more growth.

Whether Duignan is something of a lucky general or a born leader, within a short period of time he was able to oversee a remarkable turnaround in their fortunes. The senior hurlers, on former manager Mick Fennelly's watch, stopped the rot and restored some pride by winning the Christy Ring Cup and then pushing hard in the Joe McDonagh Cup, all the time climbing back up the ladder. Meanwhile, John Maughan's senior footballers gained promotion to Division 2, their highest league placing since 2006.

Their fundraising caught life, too. A joint venture between the county board and its clubs saw a 5-kilometre walk along Tullamore's Grand Canal surpass the €200,000 mark. More than seven thousand people were involved in that fundraiser, nearly ten per cent of the county's population.

'We really sensed people were coming behind us again,' says Brendan Minnock, who served as public-relations officer in 2020 and 2021. 'The walk was a simple project; indeed, it had taken place previously, but this time Michael decided the clubs would get a 50–50 split of the proceeds and the whole thing just took off. There was almost a countdown to see what the final figure would be. Everyone would have been delighted with €100,000, but we got double that. Offaly people were only waiting to support us. The sense of solidarity was huge. Things just kind of went from there.'

In January 2021, there were three people on the county's

coaching staff. By January 2022, Duignan wanted eleven coaches employed. He got his wish. The executive prioritised the areas of club development – coaching and games, and financial stability – and a drive began in all those areas.

They took on two more coaches, a games development administrator and a games promotion officer (GPO), while another eight clubs applied to bring coaches in.

Because of covid issues and closed-door stadiums, gate receipts in the county dropped from €359,000 in 2019 to €89,000 in 2020. Alarm bells rang loud and clear on that front.

In April, a partnership with Shane Lowry to develop financial support and pay a particular focus on underage development was announced.

'Just to see someone like Shane coming in and backing us was massive,' Minnock says. 'Like, it lifted everyone. That man is so humble. One weekend he could be playing with Tiger Woods, the next he'd be in the stands at O'Connor Park and not a bother on him. Obviously, his stock is of the highest regard in terms of Offaly GAA, but the people here really do love him. He came in with a vision, but even from chatting to our various teams about high-performance, never mind the fundraising side of things, could you have a better role model?'

Lowry's brief centres on helping to support the board's commercial and fundraising arm, improving the county's underage coaching programmes and the development of educational bursaries.

His family is one of the great Gaelic football clans. His father, Brendan, and uncles, Seán and Mick, won All-Ireland medals with the county in 1982. That famous Offaly side stopped Kerry from completing the five-in-a-row, and Brendan scored 0–3 in that final, the highlight of twelve years spent representing the county's senior footballers. That display crowned an All-Star award at left corner-forward for him.

'It's great from a family perspective that out of five brothers, three of us won All-Irelands, and Shane is so involved now,' Seán says. 'I think it's Shane's humility and ability to relate to people that sets him apart, to be honest. He's never changed, and if winning the British Open – the one they all wanted – didn't change him, I can't see it happening now. That was another lovely boost for us all to have during those times, to see Shane in the thick of it.'

He had helped previously. When Offaly established their training facility, the Faithful Fields, a golf classic was held to raise funds. 'Shane was involved in that, with Michael Duignan, and Kieran Keenaghan and his dad Brendan, and €160,000 was raised, so that was a big effort in itself and the link had been there previously,' Seán points out.

For all the profile and PR attention the official alliance between Lowry and Offaly created in 2021, it was the work of men of the quiet fields, like Martin Cashin, who in 2021 completed a five-year term as coaching officer, and games manager Liam O'Reilly, who helped ensure there was a stream of underage talent starting to flow freely again.

The vision of Tom Moloney, as operations manager, had also set Offaly on the right road again before he retired in 2021.

So when Duignan and his crew came to the top table, they found green shoots were visible. Amid the undeniable onfield decline of the previous decade, efforts had been taken by previous administrators to try and stem the regression. The appointments of Cashin, O'Reilly and Moloney were proof of that.

But the new team had lofty targets – they wanted the player to be the epicentre of everything in Offaly – from nursery, club, school, college, underage to those who play elite. A pathway all the way up.

Offaly had already started to develop talent at underage again, and reached both hurling and football Leinster minor finals in 2020. Two years later, the minor hurlers ended a twenty-two-year wait for a provincial minor title by beating Laois in front of a huge crowd of 12,500.

Undoubtedly, though, it was the All-Ireland success of the under-20 footballers in 2021 that caught the eye, not just for the quality of young men on show but also for their style of play.

One of those who stood out like a beacon was Cormac Egan from Tullamore. He lit up the Gaelic football world with his dynamic, turbo-charged approach to the game. His grounded interview after beating Dublin in the Leinster final, where he displayed an acute sense of place, pedigree and passion, was one of the reasons the public latched onto this team.

'It is what Offaly football is all about, what it was built on in the 1970s, the 1980s, all the way up,' Egan said. 'Boys' grandads and even older would have played in them great Offaly teams; we thought we would have to reinstall that back into this team.'

It was like a rallying cry. If Duignan and his crew felt a warm ember glowing because of the progressive projects throughout the shutdowns, their under-20 footballers simply set the place ablaze.

It was an odyssey that started in modest fashion: a one-point win over Wexford, a two-point win over Westmeath. Those games could have gone either way. Next was a win over the Dubs, before another fine day out against a vibrant Cork in the All-Ireland semi-final.

A crowd of 20,000 watched them take on Roscommon in the All-Ireland final at Croke Park, with around 13,000 from Offaly. Such was the demand for tickets in the county that the Ticketmaster website crashed with the high volume of traffic.

With the game in the melting pot, Minnock looked up to the giant TV screen at Croke Park, wondering what fate had in store for his team. At that exact moment the TV cameras captured Shane Lowry sitting high in the stands cheering the team on.

'It was like when Munster rugby were playing the Heineken Cup final, and the TV cameras shot back to Limerick to show a huge crowd supporting the team in O'Connell Street. That straightaway energised the Munster crowd in Cardiff stadium; the team then fed off the crowd and they got over the line.

'The whole thing was just a release for us. Young people who had heard stories of Offaly winning in the past were finally able to see it in the flesh.'

The board was taken aback by the numbers who attended the game and wondered how they could retain such levels of support going forward. Even if that fan base each contributed an average of €20 a year to the county, imagine the help it would provide to their development.

That's the commercial aspect. From a purely emotional point of view, it was a rare day in their history, just like the heady times of yore. Grown men and women were crying afterwards. Following years spent with head bowed, ambling through the abyss, they were walking on air again.

While crowds were allowed back into the grounds, mass

outdoor gatherings like homecomings were not yet permitted at that point, so the players retreated to their clubs for a low-key salute. They were soon back out with their underage club sides, helping to coach and encourage them. A fair crowd of the youngsters were out again on Christmas morning 2021 for a charity event with the Tullamore Harriers Athletic Club to raise funds for the Offaly Hospice. A measure of the values those young chaps hold.

'The fog lifted with these boys,' Seán Lowry adds. 'The fact that the success came out of the blue was brilliant because it was not really signalled. I think we found a lot of "big day" players along the way, and the final was such an emotional occasion – it was amazing how we outnumbered Roscommon spectators so much, because both counties are similar in size. We had new supporters and diehards there.

'What really delighted me was families going, bringing young boys and girls who had never got to see their county play in Croke Park.

'And wow, the style of football they played! These days Gaelic football is about cutting down on space and swarming opponents. Our lads are athletes, but they play with style, find space and break through lines by kicking or direct running. They lifted the mood here, and so did Duignan and others. A new broom does that anyway, but Duignan is kind of infectious. He has your phone number and that's it – when it rings no one says no to him. He got an extra push on from people when he came in.'

What is sustainable now?

'We must maintain the momentum and stay driving it on,' Minnock says. 'A few bad results here and there, which is always possible when you have small resources and a small population, and that energy may wane a bit, but we do have progressive plans.

'The Faithful Fields training facility is one example of the good work that was done over the years by different people in this county before 2020 and 2021– the trick now is to drive it on further. That's what Michael and his committee are working on. They are upbeat and tapping into our pride and history. It does look bright again.'

Seán Lowry agrees. 'The foundation is there now to build further. We have fine teams in production, the players seem to have no egos. They are humble, too – ask them to do a job and they do it.'

As 2022 began, a new sponsorship package with local company Glenisk, believed to be worth around €750,000 over five years, was announced. More good news.

Despite the success of their brilliant minor hurling team who won a Leinster title and reached the All-Ireland final (which they lost in dramatic, heartbreaking fashion to Tipperary), the 2022 season didn't progress like they would have wished. The footballers lost their first game in the championship to Division 4 side Wexford and fell to the second tier, the Tailteann Cup where they bowed out at the semi-final stages. They were relegated from Division 2 too, although their fate wasn't sealed until the final seconds of the final game.

Their under-20 footballers lost to Kildare and their minor colleagues found it tough-going in Leinster. They didn't make the Joe McDonagh Cup final in senior hurling, losing out on scoring difference only. It serves as a reminder of the lengthy path still ahead, one that Shane Lowry flagged in late April 2021 at the launch of his backing for the county.

'I think there's a long road ahead for Offaly GAA, but hopefully this is the start of great things,' the golf champion said. 'We're probably not going to see any reward over the next few years, but in ten or twenty years, if I could somehow see an Offaly man walk up the steps in Croke Park I'd probably die a happy man. That's what this is all about for me.'

That's the target. Offaly folk are dreaming big again.

24

EASTERN PROMISE

BREAKING NEW GROUND IN TROUBLED TIMES

One summer's evening in August 2020, as they returned from a training session at Henry Jones Playing Fields in Castlereagh, the East Belfast Gaelic footballers were told that suspect devices had been found under their cars.

The club, established in a non-GAA heartland, was founded not long after the pandemic began and had only been in existence a few months. Already, though, it was renowned for its cross-community inclusion of both unionists and nationalists.

An anonymous call to police claimed that explosive devices had been left under cars parked at the council-owned pitches, although nothing unusual was discovered upon a police search. The following day, however, there were two further security alerts in East and West Belfast after the Police Service of Northern Ireland (PSNI) urged people connected with the club to check underneath their vehicles.

Suspect devices were found after that session at the Henry Jones grounds, and a man was arrested on suspicion of possessing and making explosives connected with the incidents.

'We just got on with it,' club co-founder David McGreevy says. 'It didn't deter anyone. The players all came back the next night. We are in our third year now and still training away. That investigation is ongoing, but everyone in the area saw that what happened was completely wrong. Someone putting pipe bombs under young people's cars?' he adds, incredulously. 'I'm not sure what else there is to say.'

The club actively promotes friendship and cooperation between both sides of the political divide. It is the first GAA outfit in East Belfast since St Colmcille's was formed in the 1950s.

McGreevy and Richard Maguire established roots in May 2020. A Down native, he gave a decade lining out for the London footballers. Maguire is part of East Belfast Regeneration projects, where he ran courses for people with gambling and drug addiction and mental-health problems. Between them they saw a gap in the market for a club in the area and, with the virus pressing pause on life, both felt it was the right time to get the project off the ground.

On 31 May they put out a tweet gauging the interest in starting a club in the East Belfast area. Expectations were modest. They might get enough numbers for an underage team. Maybe two. Within 24 hours, the reaction was so overwhelming that neither man could turn back. They pushed ahead with their plans, opened membership two months later, and quickly attracted a thousand members, with four hundred players coming from all parts of East Belfast and others who had never engaged in the sport before.

They landed on a neutral crest. It displays the Red Hand of Ulster (in black) and the yellow Sampson and Goliath cranes of Harland & Wolff, with its motto 'Together' in English, Irish and Ulster-Scots.

It was hectic from the start. They affiliated with the Down leagues and installed Linda Ervine as club president. What an inspired move that was. Ervine has a strong loyalist, unionist and Protestant background; her former brother-in-law, the late David Ervine, was a former member of the UVF and leader of the Progressive Unionist Party, who helped broker the Good Friday Agreement.

In 2021, she was awarded an MBE for services to the Irish language and currently runs an Irish language project in the city. Ervine was a perfect fit for East Belfast.

With early activity greatly restricted due to covid measures, training sessions were held when and where possible. The bomb alert that followed didn't halt progress or enthusiasm. Nor did another alert from the PSNI that suspicious objects had been discovered on two cars linked to the club just before it played its first senior hurling game against Warrenpoint.

And though they lost 2–17 to 1–14 it hardly mattered. Something bigger was at play.

The initial goal was to set up an under-12 team and take them up right through. See what would happen at adult level. Instead, they had such a rapid lift-off that by 2022 they had 450 paying members and eleven adult teams. The level of activity was so high that they were forking out £2,000 each week just for pitch hire.

'Along the way I learned that there is a difference between members and paid-up members.' McGreevy laughs. 'And being honest, we would have way more teams if we had more coaches. That's the truth. The interest has been massive. Going forward, we just need to get our own pitch now.'

Another key addition to the backroom team was founding member Ciara Boake. Not long into the club's existence, Boake established a partnership with the 'Home Plus Charity' organisation on University Street in Belfast to open East Belfast to Sudanese, Nigerian and Syrian immigrants.

Children were invited to the club each weekend, taught the basic skills of the game and told to go make friends. Soon, their parents started to come along, often armed with dishes of food, made from recipes of their native lands. Summer camps were held. Boake arranged for buses to transport the children from their centres, which were spread across Belfast, to the training pitch. She also arranged for an Arabic translator for newly arrived Syrian families.

'Ciara came to us with her idea and we just said, "This is what we are all about, get cracking,"' McGreevy recalls. 'When kids are kicking a football, they don't need to speak the same language. They communicate through playing.'

Each Saturday morning saw new 'bus friendships' made, with conversations flowing between children from all different backgrounds. It was heartening to see.

'Everywhere I looked around the club, I found perspective,' McGreevy says. 'People just seemed to be enjoying themselves. I had given my whole playing career trying to win, but I wonder if I had the right idea at all. For our first football game, some players had never taken part in a match before. We lost by 40 points, but they came off the field buzzing. Enjoyment and craic. They'd just dabbled their toes in the sport and loved it. There I was for twenty years obsessively trying to win. That night I sat back and took stock of what I was about.'

The paperwork, however, was a colossal pain in the ass.

Accessing a dual signatory bank account proved to be a nightmare, McGreevy says, as it was a facility that not every bank offered. Without a bank account, the club could accept no membership or donations. In fact, they could do little or nothing. Opening one became a priority. A stressful one, at that.

'There was one occasion when we were so close when at the last second it didn't work out,' McGreevy remembers. 'When we eventually got that sorted, it was a massive weight off our shoulders. Up until that point there were a handful of us who had paid for the pitches, footballs, cones, poles, hurls, sliotars – everything you can imagine for a four-code club – in a five-month period. The figure at that stage was well over £10,000.

'In the end, I would say a hundred-plus people didn't pay their membership fees, including some who had trained and played games for us. It was only because of the hundreds who did pay that we were able to function.'

They found themselves in the headlines, too. Clubs in Ireland had periods where they were temporarily shut down as the virus took hold. 'Inevitably, we had our own few days closed because of covid, but unlike most other clubs in Ireland we made the local 6 p.m. news!' the co-founder exclaims. 'What should have been just an internal club WhatsApp message, for some reason, was blown into a main news bulletin. It must have been a slow news day.'

It demonstrated the scrutiny that the club would face.

'Yeah, the attention was there,' he admits. 'Some guy also decided to send me photos of people wearing East Belfast gear who weren't socially distancing,' McGreevy elaborates. 'This went on for a few months. I didn't know any of these people in the photographs, none of them were members, they were obviously people who liked what the club stood for and bought our gear. I never replied to this guy's almost daily emails. I learned very early days not to engage with people like this; it only gives them oxygen, and I was too busy anyway.'

Aware of that spotlight, the hype that their establishment had caused, and conscious of what they stood for, they remained determined to do things right.

'At our first board meeting, apart from myself and Richard, none of the other six people knew each other. We met at a bunscoil up in North Belfast. Illy [Waterford native Irial Ó Ceallaigh, one of TG4's team of weather presenters] organised this. I didn't have a clue who Illy was. I had done my due diligence on all the others apart from him. A quick Google search and I realised he was quite famous, a great singer and weatherman. At least I knew then I wasn't entering a nest of vipers or something.' He laughs.

'Good governance was the most important thing to us and keeping an eye on the different skill sets people had. I had this massive Excel spreadsheet that was password-protected on my computer, which I definitely wasn't going to share with anyone.

'Meeting everyone face to face for the first time was weird. I had to introduce myself and then everyone else to each other. We set an agenda for the following four weeks and looked no further. David Doherty finished off the first meeting by saying, "This is probably the first GAA club foundation in the history of Ireland that didn't involve pints."'

It was soon time to up the ante and prepare for the different codes. In the first few weeks, McGreevy took all the men's and ladies football sessions by himself. It wasn't long before he was exhausted.

Help arrived from Lee Costello and Shea Curran, and it was needed. Half of the ladies' team had never played football before and were just familiar with the sport from TV snippets. There was a lot of coaching to be done. The mentors worked through basic skills and drills, refining them from foundation level upwards. Whilst taxing, it was never wearisome on the soul. Just exciting.

'My home is in the middle of the Down countryside and our kitchen window has a fine view of nearby fields,' McGreevy explains. 'I often see my mum looking out in springtime at all the new lambs, calves and foals roaming in the open space, and she would always remark how that sight was good for the heart. After we came back from restrictions, it felt like I was looking out the window at home again. We got to know each other on open pitches, and it felt that good to be at training. It was a nice moment, girls making friendships with others they never had the opportunity to meet before.'

Whilst there are some sections of the community in the north, minorities, who it seems may never accept alternative viewpoints or backgrounds, this club gave different communities the chance to gel, find common ground, form friendships and benefit from good physical and mental health.

With no set home, however, they continue to train and play wherever they can find a field, a lot of the time using public parks and fields across Belfast, but often travelling to West Belfast to get venues. That's not ideal for a team named East Belfast.

'It has stalled us a wee bit in outreach,' he admits. 'People are joining and then having to go across the city to Falls Park to play games. We have a pitch committee that operates with military precision, but it's the massive thing holding us back. We are big enough as is, but if we want to appeal to more people, we need to find a home in the years to come.'

With 150 children in their underage set-up, a new culture is fast-forming. The club is diverse in its thoughts and remains progressive.

'We don't do "can't",' McGreevy states. '"Let's just get that done" is the motto.'

Despite the massive numbers, they also struggled to attract female members for some time.

'There seemed to be some sort of narrative that ladies' football or camogie wouldn't be a priority. But when that was shown to be nonsense, when we insisted that the ladies' codes would have equal ownership, and that the club would not just revolve around men's teams, that was a game-changer. We had a huge take-up then.'

They haven't stopped reaching out – to everyone.

As the war in Ukraine raged in 2022, they were again to the fore, offering to bring isolated children into their club. Ciara Boake was once more the driving force in helping to identify young families, either native or new to the area, in need of support. With one in four children in the north living in poverty, and a refugee crisis across the globe, the club felt compelled to act.

'Covid restrictions have been lifted, but it's clear that isolation has had a negative impact on our children,' Boake said. 'And as we started getting back to normal, many children remained isolated, both economically and socially. A child is a child, no matter where they come from or how they got there. And they deserve the support to thrive.'

In this regard the club implemented several practical support strategies, including helping pay for club memberships, organise transport and provide kits and equipment for children.

A 'club buddy' system was also organised to further integrate families into the community, with multicultural events celebrating traditions from all communities encouraged and an inclusive summer camp held.

Welcoming refugee and migrant families and helping them integrate into the community through sport is high on their list.

'The devastating invasion of Ukraine led to 1.5 million people fleeing their homes in just ten days,' Boake adds. 'There has been much talk of selective empathy, where some people have seen more similarities with the Ukrainian families seeking refuge than others. It is sad to think of families who have lived through similar conflict and are now living isolated amongst us.

'All people forced to flee their homes have the right for asylum, refuge and safety. And at East Belfast we welcome all. The GAA manifesto states "Where we all belong". That's our goal.'

They truly do live by that creed.

25

MORE THAN A GAME

HOW THE COUNTRY'S LEADER LOOKED TO THE GAA DURING THE PANDEMIC

In April 2022, Taoiseach Micheál Martin rated as the most popular leader in the country.

A survey for the *Irish Times* showed that Martin was ahead of Eamon Ryan, Leo Varadkar and Mary Lou McDonald in the popularity polls. His party had seen a steady rise in its approval since its lowest point a year earlier. It had been a tough start for him as Taoiseach, but on a quiet Monday morning in Government Buildings, just weeks after that poll, the leader of the country was totally relaxed and in flying form.

In his office at the Department of the Taoiseach there are portraits of three of the country's most influential political figures: Eamon De Valera, Michael Collins and Harry Boland. With great enthusiasm, he gives some historical context behind the paintings. Quite clearly, such is the passion in his voice when he speaks of the three men, it is not a vantage point that he takes for granted.

Leader of the Fianna Fáil party since 2011, the Cork man was elected to front a three-party coalition consisting of Fianna

Fáil, Fine Gael and the Green Party in June 2020. It was the first time in history that former Civil War rivals Fianna Fáil and Fine Gael governed together, and the immediate focus was the social, economic and cultural recovery from coronavirus before the office of Taoiseach handed back to Fine Gael at the end of 2022.

Martin is grounded and has a love of sport that is deeply embedded in his family's roots. He holds much personal perspective from restrictions, too. The virus prevented his wife, Mary, and their children from travelling to Dublin's National Convention Centre to celebrate his election as Taoiseach. That was a huge blow to the army of supporters who have backed him since his first election to Cork Corporation in the mid-1980s and seen him climb the political ladder.

Twice he missed out on the traditional St Patrick's Day summit between the Taoiseach of the day and the US president. In 2021, the White House's strict covid protocols meant that the meeting between the two leaders was held online. In 2022, the Taoiseach tested positive for the virus just hours before he was due to meet President Joe Biden in Washington DC.

Aside from the personal side of it, he had to chart a course for the country through one of the greatest public-health crises in a century. He saw dark days, new dawns and felt the great uncertainty that knocked us off our tracks. It was a period punctuated by 'state of the nation' addresses, which either confirmed new lockdowns, re-established restrictions or unveiled road maps to recovery and eventual freedom.

At the tail end of it all, the Taoiseach was able to stand over that outstanding vaccination programme, which he felt offered the country a way out of the crisis.

He was also highly instrumental in ensuring that the 2020 and 2021 All-Ireland championships were played and completed. And in making sure people had something to look forward to in testing times.

'It was important to play them,' he stresses. 'To me, the All-Irelands would stand as a symbol of resilience against the pandemic. The nation was bowed down because of the virus and we needed to lift people's spirits,' he says.

'Even though they couldn't go, they could watch games on TV. I didn't want 2020 to go down as the year we had no championships or All-Irelands. History would show that was the year there was no final and I didn't want that.

'I knew we could do it. It would not be an ordinary championship, but it would be something. I knew we could get there, and the GAA felt we could too.

'And I don't say this lightly for one second. Having the games, especially in the dark winter of 2020, they were a life saver. They were a life saver for some people. I mean that.'

The Martin family have a deep connection with Gaelic Games. The Taoiseach's son, Micheál Áodh, is the current Cork senior goalkeeper and younger brother Killian is emerging nicely at club level, where he plays as intermediate netminder for their club, Nemo Rangers. The boys' uncle, Sean, a well-known Cork City councillor, played between the sticks for the county in the 1976 All-Ireland minor final.

And with an encyclopaedic knowledge, the Fianna Fáil leader easily rattles off Cork teams of yore and old statistics and recounts classic games. Ultimately, the love of sport and Gaelic Games streams back to Turners Cross in 1969, when he was born to parents Paddy Martin and Lana Corbett.

His father was known as 'The Champ'. A bus driver and inspector with Córas Iompair Éireann, Paddy was among the founders of the National Bus Workers' Union and a gifted amateur boxer who represented Ireland thirteen times, often headlining events at City Hall in the 1940s and 1950s.

In 1951, Paddy took on Joe Bygraves, who later won the British Commonwealth title and in defence of it beat Henry Cooper. But in the partisan surrounds of Cork, Bygrave fell to Paddy Martin, the young man from the Glen in the city's northside. That fight would be talked about for years.

'My father boxed and played Gaelic football in tandem,' the Taoiseach says. 'He played football with St Nicks [sister club of Glen Rovers] and lost four county finals with them. He boxed parallel to that with Ireland and internationally. It would be boxing on a Saturday night and back down to play football with St Nicks on Sunday.

'Nicks had a great rivalry with the likes of the army, the gardai and Clonakilty at that point, and Dad played with luminaries like Christy Ring and Jack Lynch and some of the all-time greats that the clubs produced in hurling and football.

'He played soccer, too, with Freebooters, and later with Frank O'Farrell, who went on to manage Manchester United.'

The Turners Cross area where the Taoiseach was born boasts an array of sporting organisations such as Cork Celtic FC, Nemo Rangers, and the school teams at Colaiste Chríost Rí, which effectively served as an academy for Cork hurling and football teams.

'By the time he got married, my father was fully with the GAA. He played his last soccer game in a Munster senior league final under the name Paddy Morton because of the ban [GAA players were not allowed to play soccer at the time], re-joined St Nicks the following day, and played Gaelic from there.

'That was an example of the multi-code system in Cork, and we loved it. That was what we grew up with. For example, Dinny Allen and Dave Barry were obviously fine footballers and great soccer players, too. Dinny Allen won an FAI Cup medal with Cork City in 1973 and had to wait until 1989 to win an All-Ireland with Cork. Mad. It is just a mad sporting city all round, though. I grew up in that environment.'

After his primary education in Chríost Rí, just around the corner from O'Connell Avenue, the future leader of the Irish Republic progressed to secondary school. With his brothers Paudie and Sean, he joined Nemo Rangers as a kid.

'There was one small hut on Patrick's Street which served as a games room, and then the club would bring us out to play games at the Tramore Road. It had galvanised sheds where we could change, and we walked out to play there,' the Taoiseach recalls.

'I think we were very lucky to grow up at a time when Nemo was really taking off. Chríost Rí were in several finals, Nemo were going well, Cork were going well – we would make paper hats as kids, go to the games to support, and it quickly became a cultural thing.

'We had a teacher called Br Colm, who was from Donegal. He trained teams at the school for decades and won fifty Munster titles for the school across all codes and levels. He was my history teacher too, and I developed a passion for the subject from him. When we entered secondary school in 1973, he spent the first month strategising how Cork could win the upcoming

All-Ireland final against Galway. He would stand at the blackboard and go through the team layout. He reckoned the team had a strong spine – with the likes of Humphrey Kelleher, John Coleman and Denis Coughlan – and that would be enough.

'We played Gaelic all the way up along,' he says. 'My twin brother Paudie was better than me, and Sean, who is two years older, was a goalkeeper and played in the 1976 Munster and All-Ireland Cork minor team. He was understudy to the legendary Billy Morgan at senior level, but was deputy so long that when Billy was going to America, Sean didn't believe Billy would go. He was getting married at the time and so packed it up.

'As teenagers, we got to see Nemo win its first county senior title and that was quite something. We also got to see Cork win All-Ireland titles, and saw our local hero, Billy, the personification of Cork football, give incredible victory speeches. We had the culture from Chríost Rí too. My father would bring us to football matches in Killarney when we were even too small to see what was happening, and we would go on the train to Thurles for the hurling matches. Ever since then those are games you just have to go to.

'That was the upbringing, really. That's the culture. That's our DNA.'

Both he and Paudie focused hard on driving the underage set-up at Nemo. They were Bord na nÓg administrators at seventeen, organising the juvenile section, and were coaching by the age of twenty.

'Our Saturday nights were spent at meetings,' he chuckles. 'How exciting were we? I remember taking a team from thirteen right through to minor, where we lost a final, and after we lost the final I think people thought I was too young to be a manager. But we made the best of friends, and that connection is there forever.'

* * *

From the outset of the pandemic, the Taoiseach says there was a huge focus placed on mental health.

'The early phase, those first three or four months, for people who were unaffected by the virus, was almost something of a novelty in a sense.

'We didn't know what we were dealing with, and we had to be cautious, hence the lockdowns. We were very conscious of people's mental health and the impact that restrictions would have on young people. Spring and summer are times for young people to be out there on pitches or whatever they like to do.

'We were restricting all of that and it was a big concern for us. The elderly were confined to 2km and 5km limits too, and they were nervous. But I still reflect that young people had it worse in a way. I have a twenty-year-old at home [Cillian] who is in third year in college and I know what they missed out on.'

With the target of helping to give people a lift, the government met with Croke Park officials in August 2020 to discuss the prospect of games being played that year.

'We were impressed with them,' the Taoiseach says. 'They needed financial help and we gave them €15 million in 2020 and €20 million in 2021. We helped other sports, too. Like with enterprise, we didn't want shells at the end of the pandemic. We had to keep businesses intact, and we wanted to keep sporting organisations intact too. The FAI had a horrendous time pre-covid, with all that happened in their association, and we were anxious to give them a fair wind as well.

'What impressed us was that the GAA knew what was realistic in terms of the 2020 championship, what was possible and what was not. Overall, we didn't have difficulties in saying we would fund sport. We knew that clubs of all codes up and down the country were the heartbeat of the land.'

Martin admires how the association held firm when huge pressure came on at different junctures to open club premises to locals, as young people especially struggled with the lack of an outlet.

'They shielded the government well, put it that way,' he says. 'They said, "We'll look after our operations – but we need X, Y and Z."'

The GAA were obviously not the only ones taking heat for not opening their facilities. Most of that shrapnel flew in the Taoiseach's direction. He didn't have too far to travel to face it either.

'I was getting advice everywhere. My two lads at home were giving me lots of counsel, for a start. They were watching the science all along, in fairness. Initially they were all up for having a zero-covid policy in the country, before changing their minds on that later.

'Cillian was telling me that the training pods were a stupid idea, that no one was obeying them. I was saying, "I don't want to hear this!" Everyone was telling us what we could do. Advice was there, left, right and centre, but, look, that's understandable.'

As he reflects, he is in no doubt where and when momentum shifted in the country's fight against the disease. And in the ability of sporting organisations to be able to resume games, with crowds back in large attendance.

'The vaccination programme was the game-changer,' he states without hesitation. 'The big concern was that the virus was very transmissible in a congregated setting and that made it hard for sport to make quick progress. But public-health officials were conscious of the benefits of sport too, so we were all of one frame of mind.

'The vaccinations changed everything. It meant we could phase back towards normality.

'Another important decision was our move to deem GAA an elite sport, even though it is not professional. It was important to include the GAA players in the category that was going to be allowed to return to sport during Level 5 restrictions. It was important for the players, and I think the county needed sport – even if just on TV – to lift themselves.

'And it did lift people. And with the split season, you can see that legacies have come out of the whole thing.'

Trying times for the organisation have already been outlined, including that tentative period when they lost that elite status. But the over-zealous county final celebrations, training breaches and invite to Dr Glynn to present the empirical evidence which led to the association curtailing its activities and crowd limits were very high-profile matters. The Taoiseach is sanguine about most of those and has his own insight into one of those episodes.

'We opened pubs in September 2020 and club finals were held around that time,' he says. 'Following one weekend's celebrations which were well publicised, John Horan rang me to say, "Taoiseach, we are cutting out all county finals now. They are gone."

'Now, Nemo were due to play Castlehaven the following Sunday in the Cork senior football final.' The Taoiseach laughs again. 'So, there was pure silence on my end for a good few seconds and then a few more again,' he says. 'I was thinking of the calls I would have to make to Cork that night and in my mind I was like, "Are ye sure about this?"'

When he went home, his son, who had been diligently preparing for the big game, was all out looking for answers.

'I got desperate flak at home from Micheál Áodh.' He laughs. 'I said, 'Hang on, we didn't ask them to do it."

'Although I must say the headline "Taoiseach intervenes to save Cork football final" did enter my head for a minute,' he jokes. 'That was before I decided "Taoiseach stays shut up about Cork final" was probably a safer bet. At the end of the day, you were right in the middle of it and none of it could be helped. I would imagine the GAA were very anxious about the negative publicity that the final celebrations would gain.

'One of those cases was with the Rockies [Blackrock]. But in fairness to them, they had planned for all the celebrations to be curtailed and limited to their own premises until some fella tweeted that the team were walking down Church Road – and half the village then went out and walked the other way to meet them,' he says.

'Look, I don't get hot about it. A lot of that was human nature.'

Regarding Croke Park officials asking Ronan Glynn to explain why bigger crowds couldn't be allowed to attend games, the Taoiseach says Dr Glynn dealt with the issue in an admirable way.

'Public health personnel, including the Chief Medical Officer Tony Holohan and Ronan, took a lot of heat. People were wondering, "Why is this happening?" Everyone can be an expert.

'In general, we worked with the sporting alliance group of the GAA, IRFU and FAI very well. Lessons can be learned from that – all bodies working with government in a sensible way to ensure the phased and gradual return of sport.

'That earns trust. We were confident in their capacity to do what they said.

'With the GAA and the celebrations and mask-wearing, people have to be realistic about human behaviours, too. The whole two years was a massive human behavioural experiment. We got the public to hold tough and the extraordinary thing was they held tough for so long.

'The phased returns, the controls, the constant messaging on health and safety, it did work. And in getting back to play games, the GAA adopted a similar policy.'

* * *

The Taoiseach was in his back office when Mark Keane scored late in the 2020 Munster semi-final to give Cork a dramatic, late win against raging favourites Kerry. He let out a whoop of celebration and immediately hit the phones to chat to friends he would normally be at the game with or might share a pint with afterwards.

In 2021, he was in the stands watching Micheál Áodh take punishment from the same opposition, as they lost the Munster final. It can't be easy watching your son compete at the highest level – especially in the most testing position of the lot.

'I'm becoming more philosophical about it.' He laughs.

'As he's a goalkeeper, its murder watching – the pressure is on. Micheál Áodh himself would say that Stephen Cluxton raised the bar and changed the role of modern goalkeeping. He came up to Croke Park to watch him closely and look at that famous kickout he had, where he would find half-forwards in space.

'But, on the whole, it is extraordinarily enjoyable to watch them play. He started out playing in goals in soccer and as a half-forward with Nemo. They lost nearly every game underage with Nemo because the club doesn't really worry about those things, only from under-16 upwards.

'He played soccer with College Corinthians and got great goalkeeping coaching at FAI level from Steve Birmingham.'

On that Corinthians team – among others – were Eoghan O'Connell, who later signed for Celtic, and Brian Lenihan, who played for Hull City.

'They were a great team, and lucky that they all came together at the one time. I've followed his teams since he was ten or eleven, though I knew he would get serious with Nemo at around sixteen, when there was no real future with soccer. The Nemo lads quickly put him in goal and he pulled off some brilliant saves in an under-16 match against Douglas, who had Tony Davis in charge. Tony recommended him for the Cork under-16 development squad. He has been playing for Cork teams since. He has great application through all the ups and downs. He learns all the time and stays at it.

'We got great joy when he won a county title with Nemo because my father had lost four, and when Micheál Aodh won one we felt like it ended a taboo in our house, although Sean had won county medals.

'He has found his own way and got great coaching along the way too, from the likes of Steve, Hauley O'Neill, Ger Kealy and his current coach, Paddy O'Shea.

'As I mentioned, Cillian is a goalkeeper too. We just get so much joy out of watching them play. Cillian's Feile team reached the All-Ireland final but lost to Naas.'

The Taoiseach's face clearly lights up when he speaks of those moments and what those sporting memories have done for his family.

'You can resonate with other parents and it's great to be part of that community. So, it's total joy and it has helped us through all our difficulties and traumas in life.'

Does the son take any advice from the father?

'Not a bit,' the Taoiseach replies.

'Mary is mad as a hatter at games, so I have to try to keep her cool,' he jokes. 'That's about my role in the whole thing. When he was eleven, College Corinthians asked Micheál Áodh and a few others to present medals to under-8s and at the same time the Nemo under-13s were playing. He wanted to go to the medal presentation, but I told him he couldn't let down his other team.

'That evening he asked Mary, "Does Dad think he is going to dictate the rest of my life?"

'He was only eleven.' The Taoiseach smiles. 'But message received and fair point, too. It was a great lesson for me. Back off – he has a life to lead. Fathers make a mistake at times; they can put too much pressure on kids.

'He is religious about telling me nothing that is going on in the Cork squad and I have to keep at arm's length anyway, so it suits me. I never even find out who is injured. I was at Cork's 96FM and C103 Sport Star awards in April of 2022 and I was talking to Brian Hayes. He was chatting about a challenge match Cork had played and I hadn't a clue what he was talking about.

'"Sure, Micheál was playing?" Hayes continued.

'He simply will not tell you anything and I won't ask either. I will text him "Best of luck tomorrow" before a game and after that it can wait until afterwards. I also know when he doesn't want to talk at all because that is self-evident,' he says, laughing again.

With his tenure as Taoiseach set to complete at the end of 2022, the Corkman is glad that sport helped people through such a turbulent time.

And the legacy of it all?

'I mentioned the split season. But how well the sporting organisations came across when they all worked together was impressive. It was very important that there was strength in unity and an alignment between the organisations. They behaved professionally and sensibly instead of shouting and roaring and throwing brickbats. They showed the spirit of what they were about, and it does augur well for sport here going forward. You can see Stephen Kenny's Irish soccer team, from what they put into it, that every player wants to be there. Hopefully there are great days ahead there also. I look at Chiedozie Ogbene, who played with Nemo, and see how happy he is to wear the Irish shirt. What a footballer he was. His biggest strength was that he knew how to tackle without fouling. His speed, too. Micheál Áodh was always ringing him, but eventually soccer came calling. He still goes out to Nemo to train when he comes home after the soccer season, and we all get a kick from watching him.

'And female sport, too. I have to mention the progress that has been made. Jack Chambers met the camogie and Ladies Gaelic Football Association bodies in the early stages of the pandemic. They put their hands up for funding, said, "Hey, we are here too," and we ensured they received funding. That was so important. Female sport is growing across all codes and the five-year strategic plan is centred on equality and integration.

'I see it in Nemo. We were slow initially to get the ladies' game going there, but it has totally changed our club. There is a more collegial approach, and we are bringing more people in. It's great.

'Equality of treatment must be a key legacy from this pandemic. Funding must go across all sports. The Gaelic Players Association and Women's Gaelic Players Association joining up is very significant too.'

Fundamentally, the Taoiseach feels that what covid illustrated is the centrality of sport in our lives and from a mental health and physical health perspective.

'Completing the 2020 championship is something I was very determined to make happen. In my heart I was saying, "These games must go ahead." It was almost as if we had caved into this thing if we couldn't have an All-Ireland. The championships had to happen. It's who we are.'

26

GONE BUT NOT FORGOTTEN

LEGENDS LEFT US WITH LEGACIES COMPLETE

The Colonel

Carl Walsh will never forget the hurt in his father's eyes.

It was a July Sunday in 1979. Earlier in the afternoon, the Kerry footballers had come to Miltown Malbay for the Munster semi-final and left just as quickly, having inflicted a 9–21 to 1–9 trouncing.

That was the nadir for Clare football. Indeed, so bad was the drubbing that the scoreboard operator was on his honkers praying that ruthless Kerry wouldn't raise another green flag because his board couldn't facilitate double-digit goals.

Later that year, with the people of Clare still scarred from the hammering, Kerry landed yet another All-Ireland title. The drubbing they gave the Banner was scarcely a footnote of reference.

But they never forgot it in the towns and villages around West Clare. They spoke of it, but briefly and in hushed tones only. It became known as the 'Miltown massacre'.

The destruction was a turning point for Noel Walsh, a Gandalf-type figure for the fellowship of Clare football, a life-long crusader for fairness, one who raged against injustice and imbalances in the GAA.

Just like that day in 1979.

'I will always remember how sad and defeated he was at home that night,' Carl says. 'It took an awful lot out of him. But he was strong. He gathered himself and vowed to get the resources needed to improve football in the county. He wasn't going to accept that massacre.'

As the decade turned, Clare's displays slowly improved, with Walsh and others endeavouring to ensure greater organisation, coaching expertise and the development of young talent from within.

Help was needed on the outside, too. They couldn't continue treading up mountains if they wanted to make any headway; there had to be some attempt at a level playing field.

For the previous twenty-five years, the championship's seeded structure meant that Cork and Kerry contested every single provincial final. They held a duopoly on the Munster football market. The others were just minority shareholders, there to keep the marketplace going.

'Dad saw from a mile off that the Munster championship format was unjust,' Carl continues. 'He wanted to provide an even playing field for all counties. He made submissions, wrote documents, attended meetings and chaired countless debates on the road to ensure fair play for all counties. It was all to break the Cork and Kerry dominance of the championship.'

Some didn't want to hear Walsh's counsel – they were happy enough to have the top two dominate the province – but he campaigned relentlessly; he couldn't be shushed. And it was his constant lobbying that eventually led to a breakthrough in 1991, when the Munster Council finally relented and dramatically restructured their senior football championship.

Now the marketplace was open. Everything – in the lead-up to the final, at least – was there to be played for.

'I was amazed at his patience, chasing down what seemed to be a lost cause,' Carl says. 'He just kept playing the issue, not the man. In the end, he was successful.'

The open draw was born. And history would soon be made.

In 1992, Walsh's beloved home county kicked the door down and won the Munster title. As recently as 2020 the effect of Walsh's bravery was still evident when Tipperary ended that eighty-five-year wait for a senior title. What a legacy to leave.

Noel passed away in Ennis Hospital at the end of April 2020 due to pneumonia caused by covid-19. He was eighty-five.

'What I miss most,' Carl, now living in Australia, says, 'is the chats on a Sunday night. An hour long, every Sunday evening, and I couldn't get a word in edgeways.' He laughs. 'It was a monologue. All things Clare, all things GAA. That's what I miss most.

'He used to write to me, too. Dad wasn't one for email. Once a month I would get a letter in a big A4 envelope, with all the cuttings from the *Irish Examiner*, *Clare Champion* and the *Irish Independent*. I'd take that envelope out at night and read the contents before going to sleep. You would miss that, too.'

Carl and his dad were joined at the hip. As a youngster he looked on as Noel went about his business, managing Clare on three separate occasions and never venturing too far away from the set-up at any stage in between. They went to countless training sessions, matches and meetings together.

'It was a wonderful, winding and enlightening journey. We went to everything from junior "B" matches in West Clare to loads of All-Ireland finals together. Our first one was in 1974. We travelled the length and breadth of Ireland with the senior football team. They had lots of talent, but we saw several teams in action who never made the big breakthrough that they deserved. But, thanks to Dad, my geography was second to none. I knew every inch of Ireland.'

Noel was a former army colonel and a visionary. He may not have been manager when they made that historic title break-through in 1992, their first in seventy-five years, but he was the main reason they got the chance to compete for the cup.

His love affair with the county's football scene was passionate and genuine. He won two Clare senior football championships with Miltown and served as club secretary and chairman. As a player he also represented Clare at minor and junior level. Aside from his three terms as Clare football manager, he had twenty years as a selector.

And apart from several decades of work on the field, he was also their chief strategist and administrator. It was he who brought John Maughan on board as manager for that famous '92 campaign, during which Walsh served on the backroom team with Carl as sub-goalie.

'Noel knew better than anyone what the team needed at that point,' says his friend, fellow Clare man, Gaelic Games patron and enthusiast Martin Donnelly. 'And that was someone organised and into discipline. Noel went back to his army experience and got John, another army man, in. The rest is history.'

Though hailing from football stock, Walsh also harboured a deep love for hurling and, as chair of the Munster Council from

1995 to 1998, he sat proudly in office whilst the Clare hurlers marched to two All-Ireland victories.

As chairman of the provincial council, he had the honour of presenting the Munster hurling championship trophy in 1995 to his county's iconic captain, Anthony Daly.

He also chaired the influential Football Development Committee whose work paved the way for the introduction of the All-Ireland qualifiers in 2000, another seismic shift in the GAA's history.

'That was the most exciting time of his administrative career,' Carl says. 'On that committee were kindred spirits, like Eugene McGee, Colm O'Rourke and others. I think they got him, and he got them. They pushed hard for major change; they didn't get exactly what they wanted, but it led to the qualifiers and that was progressive enough at the time.'

After three years as Munster Council chair, he ran for the GAA presidency, fought hard to revive the Railway Cup and was hugely influential in the spread of floodlights to grounds throughout the country.

He was one of the most prominent campaigners for the abolition of Rule 42 in 2005, calling for the temporary opening of Croke Park to stage soccer and rugby games during the rejuvenation of Lansdowne Road.

Following that motion, he then campaigned for all county grounds to be opened to other sports. His work in this area later provided a foundation for the GAA's relaxing of the rule to allow the Liam Miller tribute match to go ahead at Páirc Uí Chaoimh.

After four decades of service with the Defence Forces, he retired at the rank of lieutenant colonel.

His passing was tough on all those who knew him and worked with him in GAA affairs, but for his wife Ursula, son Carl, daughters Lisa and Noelle, and his grandchildren, losing a figure like him was exceptionally difficult to deal with.

'Being in Australia really felt like a million miles away at that time,' Carl reflects. 'It was tough for a long time, but the hurt was eased by the fact that Dad didn't suffer, he passed away quickly. He had his life lived. That helped us too, the fact that he had made an impression on this life. And you think of people who helped him in his final day, the likes of Nurse Eilis Cleary from Miltown Malbay, who held Dad's hand in his final moments and comforted him as he slipped peacefully away. Eilis is a wonderful person from a great family. It was fitting that she was there. She is truly one of our frontline heroines.'

Martin Donnelly thinks about him most days still.

'You'd miss him as a friend. All he did was fight for Clare football, fight against imbalances and injustices, and you couldn't have enough people like that in this world.

'You'd miss him on Munster final days. And when the future of the football championship came up for discussion at Special Congress in October 2021 and Congress 2022, I was thinking about him again. Proposal B and the Green Plan – both advocating the league-championship model – would have been right up Noel's alley. He would have taken to the floor and fought for balance to be restored.

'But you know what? His legacy is alive. The work he undertook helped the likes of Clare, Tipperary and Cavan win provincial titles. Carl is in Australia and in the lead-up to that Special Congress he was also getting his point across on social media forums that it was time to embrace Proposal B, time to change the structures.

'Noel was one of most honourable people I met in my life, and he would have looked down from above, proud of Carl for continuing the fight.

'The thing I loved most about him was that he would always make his point in a very reasonable way, he would never shout you down. Coming from his defence forces background, he could have taken positions that were authoritarian, but he was never like that. He was rational and respectful.'

Both men grew up in West Clare, Walsh in Miltown Malbay, and Donnelly in Cooraclare. The first real working contact they had was in 1992, when they were each invested in the county's rise.

'He would have made a great president. Social media wasn't a thing back then, but he used the national media as a platform, and such was his respect that he found plenty of column inches devoted to his wishes. He kept the plight of the underdog in the headlines and used the media to get his points across.

'He was so fair and balanced. Maybe the hierarchy of those times didn't always appreciate his views because he was so vocal when he saw something that needed to be changed.'

Walsh's contribution to the GAA was again recognised in 2000, when he was elected a trustee of the association. When Carl attended Special Congress of 2021 virtually, as an Australasian delegate, he wore a watch the GAA had presented his father with during his time as trustee.

'He was there with me on the day, and it was nice to continue that tradition. I often think about how he went for president on those two occasions, but I am not really sure if it would have been for him. He wouldn't have been a man for the circuit a president has to undertake.'

Carl's memories of his dad will never fade, such is the splendour of the magical journey they shared together.

'I only saw him cry twice. Once when I won the Sigerson Cup with UCC. I looked over and saw him bolting to me with tears in his eyes. The other occasion was when a neighbour of ours died in an accident. Those were the only times I saw him cry. He was a strong man, an army man, and a fair man.

'From a sporting point of view, '92 was the one for him. That was no fluke. We worked hard for that – everyone involved. We reached the National League semi-final at Croke Park in 1993 and we were the first Clare football team to play in Division 1. This was no accident. The work put in by Dad, John Maughan, the selectors, the players and the backroom team was unprecedented. Until the day he died, he gained immense happiness and satisfaction from that golden era.'

Just another memory from the chock-full vault that Noel Walsh left.

A life truly lived.

The Master

Jim Ryan remembers reading the local paper on the day after his brother, Eamonn, had passed away. It was the start of January 2021 and followed an illness bravely fought.

Owing to public-health guidelines at the time, the removal and Requiem Mass were for family members only. Had the country been free of restrictions at the time, one can only imagine the crowd that would have turned up to pay their respects.

'I was reading the *Echo* and the headline bade farewell to a wonderful teacher, manager and family man,' Jim says. 'Isn't that a wonderful legacy to leave behind?'

As 2021 ended, the Ryan family and friends prepared for an edition of *Laochra Gael*, the brilliant TG4 documentary series that shines a universal light on the lives of GAA icons. In researching for the series, Jim and a pal estimated that Eamonn had been at the hub of 144 title wins.

'No tournament games there either.' Jim laughs. 'All championships, from Cumann na mBunscol right up to senior All-Irelands. Imagine the effect that had on people, how many players were helped along the way. And you know what? Eamonn wouldn't have wanted any fuss over that at all. Still, is it any wonder we called him "the Master"?'

Education was a constant theme of Eamonn's life and his affiliation with UCC was exceptionally strong too. He won two Sigerson Cups there and played for the college in the 1967 Cork senior county final when they lost to Beara. He graduated with a BA in 1966, a HDip in Education in 1967 and later returned to the college as development officer, assisting with Gaelic football and hurling teams there. He also coached their camogie team to Ashbourne Cup success.

At UCC, Eamonn was also a GAA tutor for the sports studies department, until illness prevented him from attending his much beloved Mardyke for classes. He also served as a tutor with the department of modern Irish from 2011.

Following his graduation as a student, he held the position of school principal of Watergrasshill NS.

'He taught me in national school,' Jim chuckles. 'I was outside in the corridor most of the time. Later in life he would joke that he didn't have me out in the corridor half enough.'

He had previously served as manager of the Cork men's senior football team in the early 1980s, but it was his seminal tenure as Cork senior ladies football manager that defined him. There was no road of flowers leading to glory, but Ryan planted seeds, nurtured a fantastic culture and led the team to ten All-Irelands, ten Munster championships and nine national league titles.

Following his tenure with the Cork ladies in late 2015, he once again linked up with the men's senior set-up, taking up a backroom role in Peadar Healy's management. When he passed in 2021, there was an outpouring of grief.

'There were messages from everyone and everywhere,' Jim says. 'From President Michael D. Higgins to Taoiseach Micheál Martin. He had met them all. But messages were put together by players, teams and people he worked with across the years too, and I know they meant a huge amount to Eamonn's wife, Pat, their children and grandchildren.'

Cork Ladies Gaelic Football Association described him as 'a legend in his own lifetime'. They were right. And he would have been a legend in any lifetime.

From late 2003, Ryan simply transformed the face of ladies' football. His car, an unfussy white 2000 Daihatsu Cuore, was nicknamed the 'Butter Box' by his players, and on the hour-long trek from Cork city to training, Ryan would lose himself in music, all the time preparing for training that lay ahead.

Before he got the job as manager, he had applied for a position as coach. That application was typically modest. He sent in an A4 sheet outlining his credentials – that he was a retired headmaster, had all relevant coaching qualifications. When Mary Collins got the job as manager, she brought him on board as coach.

In 2004, he took the main job and challenged the players to raise their standards and create a new bond from within. At his first meeting with them, he talked for just three minutes, but the players knew they had someone special on his hands. He was sixty-two at the time, well versed in the rambling highs and lows of life and sport. The girls liked him from the start, but they soon grew to adore him. The feeling was mutual.

In 2004, Ryan battled prostate cancer, but not even intense treatment could stop him from paving new ground with his team. They would play 151 league and championship games under his watch. They lost just twenty-three.

In 2005, they landed an All-Ireland title and from there something special grew.

'Something happened at that time,' Jim says. 'A great team was formed. TG4 started showing all the games, there was huge interest around their journey, and the profile of the ladies game has only grown since then.'

Eamonn was to the manor born.

'Sure, how could we miss it?' Jim asks. 'My father came from Charleville and was a good rugby player and a handballer, and Mam was dragged to every match, even though she had no interest. Eamonn played for Cork and won two Munster senior football titles. Mick, another older brother, was a priest and he played Cork minors and intermediates.

'My sister Kathleen played camogie with both Cork and Kilkenny. She reared six kids and some of them have played camogie and hurling for Kilkenny.

'As a nine-year-old boy, I had three heroes in the house with me. Everyone else was talking about Mick O'Connell, Eusebio or Pelé, but sure I didn't even have to leave home for heroes. I had no way out – I had to be interested in sport and it was the same for Eamonn and the rest of them.'

In retirement, Jim spent much of his time travelling across the world attending sporting events. 'I just kind of followed on from our childhood,' he says. 'There was one time when, as kids, we were in Dublin five weekends on the trot for matches. Now, at the time that was like going to a European city. You wouldn't sleep the night before with excitement.

'Eamonn gave me lots of trips to attend. He continued that sporting tradition in the family. I went to nearly all his matches and I don't think success changed him one bit. He wouldn't take anything for coaching a team; I'd say Pat is still finding vouchers from clubs after what he did for them. Eamonn only took positions because he wanted to, and he didn't look for, or take anything, for doing them.

'No matter what the sport, Eamonn's philosophy was simple. Get the basics right, put the player first, stick with them, give them belief and leave no stone unturned.'

Humble as it was, that outlook worked wonders. Before Ryan immersed himself in Cork ladies football, they hadn't even won a Munster senior title in the championship's thirty-three-year history. An All-Ireland title wasn't on their radar. Instead, they had to endure hammerings at the hands of Kerry and Waterford in the 1980s and 1990s.

He brought in a new ethos, first as coach and then manager. They went on to claim twenty-nine titles out of a possible thirty-six throughout his reign.

In 2014, they were named RTÉ Sports Team of the Year after claiming their ninth All-Ireland title in ten years, beating off stiff competition from the likes of the Dundalk soccer team, the

Cork camogie team and, of course, the Irish men's rugby team. The great joy for the team was that the vote for the award was a public one. They landed close to 25,000 votes. Jim reckons the Irish rugby side were next on 19,000.

'I'd say that was the occasion that really meant the most to Eamonn. The fact that the girls had been recognised in such circles, with other great teams competing. I have a picture of them all posing together in the hallway, and he is smiling from ear to ear! That was the pinnacle, that they were acknowledged by the people. He was chuffed.

'It had become fashionable to watch ladies' football and that was down to this team. At the start, crowds were not big, and I was at a few games by myself on a few occasions. I noticed a shift, though. One day I rang a few friends to tell them to watch a cracking game that was being broadcast by TG4, but when I rang, they were already watching it. I knew then something was happening.'

The historic road they travelled was documented in *Relentless*, a fine book on their legacy authored by Mary White. Towards the end of that book Ryan recalled the journey they had all been on together.

'They did their best, I did my best, and we all had a great time.'

Typical modesty. It was one of the greatest journeys the GAA has ever seen. Undertaken by a fine team. Navigated by one of the best coaches of all time.

The Innovator

Fr Tom Scully passed away a month before his ninetieth birthday after complications arising from covid. Once again, at any regular juncture, there would have been a massive turnout to bid farewell, such was his influence on this life. Instead, at the dawn of April in 2020, no one from the outside world was permitted to carry his coffin, drape jerseys over it, or accompany him to his final resting place with a guard of honour.

There was no one from his GAA family allowed to speak warmly of him as he departed. And that is one of the most saddening consequences of the pandemic.

Had eulogies been allowed, it would have been difficult to keep any oration under 30 minutes.

'Offaly's Jack Charlton' was how one newspaper described Fr Tom, and the label was not handed out lightly. Anyone who played under his watch adored him.

When he oversaw the Offaly team, he would give the footballers a loan of his car, especially if there were special occasions looming. Once he threw them the keys to attend the wedding of teammate Mick Ryan. The players collected the car, headed to Athlone, had a great night out, brought the car back to Fr Tom's house the next day and he duly dropped them back into Tullamore town for a few more pints. He had no problem treating his players like adults because he knew they were totally committed and would do anything for him.

When he passed away on 7 April at St James' Hospital in Dublin, his death left a huge gap in the hearts of those men.

'News of Tom's passing was a blow in itself for anyone who knew him, and what made it more upsetting was that the lads on the Offaly team he brought to the 1969 All-Ireland final couldn't go to his funeral because of restrictions,' says former Offaly interim football manager and Professor of History at UCD Paul Rouse. 'They were so upset by that.'

A native of Aharney, near Tullamore, Fr Tom studied philosophy at UCD, followed by theology at the Oblate Scholasticate in Co. Kilkenny, where he was ordained as a priest on 15 September 1955. The following year he was assigned to Belcamp College in Dublin, where he would teach mathematics for the next thirteen years.

'Fr Tom was always thinking outside the box,' Rouse continues. 'People talk today about the likes of Niall Morgan and Rory Beggan leaving their goal and coming out to operate as a sweeper or even a third midfielder, but Fr Tom employed that tactic as far back as the mid-1960s when he trained the school team. They won three Leinster Colleges championships, beating storied teams like St Mel's along the way. There was one game when they were close to bowing out of a championship, six points down into the second half. Tom told their goalkeeper to leave his position and veer up towards centre forward. That move worked. It turned that 6-point deficit into a win.'

It was an outrageous tactic for its time, a roving ramble that was still turning heads when Morgan and others leaned heavily on it from 2020 onwards.

'Fr Tom was an innovator,' Rouse says. 'Simple as that.'

Those ground-breaking tactics and his motivational skills were greatly appreciated. From an early stage, he lived his coaching life sticking close to the 'Three Gs' principles: get the ball, give it, and go make space to receive a pass.

'On top of that there was his personal connection,' Rouse says. 'I don't know what you would call it, an aura maybe, but he had a gravitas. He was intelligent, had a mathematical brain, but clicked so well with people. There was steel, too. One of his fundamentals as a coach was to train his players super-hard.

Once they'd built up that conditioning, he could go anywhere with them.'

Fr Tom wasn't into criticising players. Instead, he acclaimed them, encouraged them and pointed out alternative ways to do their business on the field, if the need presented itself.

Rouse remembers his own childhood days back in Tullamore with huge warmth. He recalls evenings spent at home with his grandparents and parents and locals for card games.

'Endless noise. Happy noise. My mind always goes back to a time around the early 1980s,' Rouse adds, his mind drifting back. 'My father and mother are playing 25. Grandad and Nana, too. Our next-door neighbour, Tom Ravenhill, a serious card player, is playing. And Fr Tom Scully is there.'

Only eleven at the time, Rouse also secured a place at the table. Special dispensation was granted to stay up and join the deal. The fire was roaring, the card game was underway and the craic was mighty. Fr Tom was back home from England and right in the heart of the craic.

'Anytime you saw Fr Tom was a good time. Charisma, energy and positivity, he had the lot. But half the time in our house his only concern was winding up my granddad, Dick "the Boiler" Conroy.'

The pair had a lifelong friendship. 'The Boiler' was one of Fr Tom's selectors on Offaly's crusade to the 1969 All-Ireland. And Fr Tom knew exactly how to get The Boiler to blow.

'Tom went on a rant about how he didn't rate certain players, including an All-Star who was deemed by the Boiler as one of the greats. Granddad knew he was being wound up and tried to keep focused on the deck of cards in front of him. But he lost it. Eventually the lid came off and the whole room cracked up.

They are the memories I have. See, I never really thought of Fr Tom as a priest. He was just a family friend.'

Before Rouse was born, Offaly had been threatening to emerge as a force in Gaelic football. They won the O'Byrne Cup for the first time in 1955 and subsequently built on that by claiming Leinster senior football titles in 1960 and 1961. A new generation was storming through with notions that they could win a first All-Ireland senior title. Young men like Willie Bryan, Martin Furlong and Tony McTague formed the core of a super team that beat Cork to win the 1964 All-Ireland minor crown.

The challenge was to build a senior team around them and mould the emerging talent with those remaining from the senior side that had lost by a point to Down in the 1961 All-Ireland final.

At the start of 1969, Fr Tom was deemed the man for the job. It had been eight years since their first final appearance and momentum was waning. Managers came and went at a furious rate and the proportional system of picking players meant that large bands of selectors wielded way too much power, often stunting progress.

Undeterred, when he arrived to take the team for the first session, he couldn't help but cop that morale was on the floor. Players were talking about emigrating. They were totally disorganised. As he made his way over to the group of players a county board official told him that he was wasting his time.

'But Fr Tom never wasted anyone's time,' Rouse says. 'Least of all his own.'

He went back to basics. Clicked with the players, saw what motivated them. They, in turn, liked his approach and strove to do well for him.

Fr Tom saw hope. Just like he did with Belcamp.

Springtime of 1969 was prosperous, with signs of growth. Fr Tom guided Offaly to the national league final for the first time in history and, though they were hammered by Kerry 3–11 to 0–8, their journey was only beginning.

'They powered their way through the Leinster championship and no team got within five points of them,' Rouse recalls. 'It was momentous because it was only the third time ever that we won the Leinster championship.'

Cavan held them to a replay in the All-Ireland semi-final, but in the replay they prevailed and made the final for a rematch with Kerry.

'Fr Tom thought they would win that game, such were the strides they had made. But it wasn't to be. They played poorly enough on the day – the consensus is they left a bit behind them and yet they only lost by three points: 0–10 to 0–7.'

He didn't realise it at the time, but it was to be his last match as Offaly manager.

A one-year teaching appointment at St Benedict's College, Johannesburg, from 1969 to 1970, followed. He didn't stay there long, the injustice of apartheid proving too much to live with, and instead moved to take up a role as Irish emigrant chaplain in England, first in Manchester (1970–71), and then as director at Catholic Housing Aid Society, Birmingham (1971–75). His next appointment was as pastor at St Peter's Parish, Leigh-on-Sea (1975–81).

Surprisingly, his services as Offaly manager were effectively dispensed with after the '69 campaign. It is believed that his naturally affable way and his close relationship with the players didn't go down well with some members of the county board.

In 1971, Offaly finally won their first All-Ireland senior title – without Fr Tom at the helm but no doubt benefitting from the foundations he laid.

'I don't think missing that weighed heavily on him through his life,' Rouse says. 'He had far more important things and affairs to attend to. He felt the team didn't perform to their max on the All-Ireland final day of 1969, that maybe not everyone fully believed Offaly could win, and he would be animated when discussing that, but it didn't burden him for life or anything like that. Again, he had other far more significant affairs to attend to.'

In Manchester and London, where he served as director of the Irish Centre in Camden in the 1980s, he found himself at the epicentre of a crisis. It was a time of crippling recession in Ireland and people flocked in their droves to London, Manchester, Birmingham and other places.

'Up to recently, statistics showed that one in six people in Coventry were born in Ireland,' Rouse says. 'That shows the amount who flocked to England. It was a desperately hard time, and the Irish went to find work as navvies and cleaners but the work he did, following on from the work by Bishop Eamonn Casey in looking out for Irish emigrants, was way more important than any football matter.

'The loneliness was something that always struck him. The sense of isolation that the newly located Irish found, especially those of an older age who had been decades in the UK at this stage but still hadn't found their way.

'Neglect and abandonment, that's what the Irish faced, and Fr Tom looked for practical ways to fight that. He set up day-care facilities and provided lunches and recreational facilities, not just for Irish people but English, Poles, anyone who wanted to come. At any given time, the day centre in the Irish Centre could cater for 150 older people. He and other priests would provide food and a place to chat and play cards and even take classes.

'Fr Tom always said that loneliness knew no nationality or boundary. He was no narrow nationalist. Any facility that he worked at was opened to the public. Predominantly, it was Irish people, but all were welcome. He wanted everyone to see how other cultures worked and fared.'

Waves of Irish emigrants filled London's streets but always found a soft landing at Fr Tom's door.

It was no surprise. Back in 1966 he had also founded the Catholic Housing Aid Society after the collapse of a tenement building in Dublin in which elderly residents were killed. In 1967, Dublin Corporation allowed the society to develop a large site at the top of Gardiner Street and so a block of forty-five senior citizens' flats was built three years later. Short appointments followed in Edinburgh before he moved back to Ireland and worked at Inchicore, where he lived in retirement.

It was because of his work in Dublin and the UK that he was chosen as the Offaly Person of the Year in 1989. This is a distinction held in the highest esteem by the people of a proud county. It has also been bestowed on luminaries like ex-Taoiseach Brian Cowen, Open champion and Ryder Cup golfer Shane Lowry, champion jockey Pat Smullen and iconic stars Brian Whelahan and Matt Connor.

Fr Tom was less than a week in hospital, only pulled down by the virus just shy of his ninetieth birthday, and was still on the phone, checking and caring for others until his final days, when he passed.

'Our family will be forever linked to him,' Rouse reflects. 'He married my parents and one of my brothers. He said Mass to bless our own house when we moved in.

'He was ministering until near the very end. I went to see him in the centre where he resided and they all loved him there.'

When Rouse took over as Offaly senior football interim manager in the summer of 2018, Fr Tom rang to wish him luck. He reminded Rouse that his grandfather had been a selector with Offaly, so too had his father, and now it was his turn. He added that The Boiler would have been very proud of him.

'It was a very emotional thing to hear. He was in touch again to congratulate us when we beat Antrim. He always knew what to say. Mind you, when he called to the house later that year, he fairly wanted to know why we had lost to Clare!

'You meet someone like him in life and you never forget it. When you did meet him, it was an event. He is bound in my memory for his friendship with my grandparents, and in the lore of Offaly football he is bound there forever. The number of lives he influenced all over the world is unreal – through football, through his work dealing with Irish emigrants, his humanity and understanding in helping our exiles cope with that loneliness and isolation. It is absolute Christianity.'

Those who served with him at the Oblates also have a trove of powerful memories to summon. One young priest who worked with Fr Tom in the late 1970s recalled his team philosophy in the Latin phrase *Age quod agis*. It means 'do well, whatever you do'.

Another Oblate who served in the UK with him told how Fr Tom was the first man to encourage him to go home for Christmas, for which he was grateful.

In retirement, Tom worked tirelessly on the lawns and gardens at the Oblates, designing and scoping out flower beds, making sure the colours blended perfectly.

When former Belcamp student, Kilkenny hurling legend and three-time All-Ireland-winner Frank Cummins was inducted into the GAA Hall of Fame at Croke Park in 2017, he invited Fr Tom to join him for the event, citing him as one of the biggest influences on his career.

Friends say it was the highlight of Fr Tom's later years.

'He would have been in his element that day,' Rouse says. 'It just shows what Frank thought of him. Fr Tom tended to have that effect on people. An inspiring man.'

He leaves an eternal flame.

EPILOGUE

Even after the harshest of tempests the sun will shine again.

Saying goodbye to loved ones during this crisis, seeing others fall ill or lose a way of life are all milestone events people will never forget. But people tried their best to move on. They wanted to. And the flicker of light that suddenly cracked through on 21 January 2022 illuminated the country.

On each previous occasion that Micheál Martin had spoken publicly to the nation in those televised addresses, he had stood outside Government Buildings and delivered solemn and sombre messages. This time he was smiling.

'I have stood here and spoken to you on some very dark days. But today is a good day. Humans are social beings and we Irish are more social than most. As we look forward to this spring, we need to see each other again, we need to see each other smile, we need to sing again. Spring is coming. And I don't know if I have ever looked forward to one as much as I am looking forward to this one.'

And with that we were moving on. Quickly, too. Indeed, after being in a dark place for so long, the speed at which all restrictions were lifted took everyone by surprise.

After four lockdowns and five waves, the National Public Health Emergency team was stood down in February. Live press briefings and daily case reports ceased. Masks were optional. Full crowds were allowed back to GAA stadiums. People returned to their desks and picked up on the humdrum of regular duties.

The Omicron variant, which had cut through the country early in the year, preceded two sub-variants of the highly trans-missible BA.2 strain and fuelled another surge. After that came the BA.4 variant in early summer. It looks like the virus is not going anywhere too quickly.

But we had done our time, most of us were well protected and boosted, and life had to go on. The moment the Omicron surge peaked the Taoiseach announced that Ireland was finally free of all constraints.

Fourth doses of the vaccine were rolled out and, with the fire in retreat, one of the longest and strictest sets of coronavirus restrictions in Europe came to an end. The country re-opened in a hurry.

One of the first acts the Taoiseach took in the days after was to unveil a new portrait of Professor Mary Horgan, the first female President of the Royal College of Physicians of Ireland, at the college.

It was only the third female portrait to hang there in its 368-year history, joining Dr Kathleen Lynn, who was Chief Medical Officer during the Easter Rising in 1916, and the late Laura Brennan, the powerful patient advocate and ardent promoter of the HPV vaccine, who died of cervical cancer aged twenty-six in 2019.

Professor Horgan received the distinction for her work with Nphet and leading the expert advisory group on rapid testing, a tool everyone became quickly familiar with to help protect each other. Her contribution to ensuring a safe return to sport for children and adults, through her work with the GAA, including the re-opening of the Cúl Camps, was monumental. It allowed thousands of children to experience some normality during the pandemic.

Around the same time as the portrait was unveiled, GAA president Larry McCarthy called for a standing ovation for John Horan at Congress 2022. It was the first full in-person gathering of GAA officials since 2020. Acclaiming the man who had gone before him and who had steered the association through one of the biggest crises it had ever encountered, McCarthy's salute to Horan was met with a thunderous response from the floor.

Loughmore-Castleiney were awarded Munster GAA's 2021 club of the year; Marianne Walsh went back to work as Mooncoin hung on the scent of further honours.

Domhnall Nugent graced Croke Park once more with Antrim in the 2022 Joe MacDonagh Cup final win and linked up with charity organisation Inspire to work on the importance of talking about mental health. He also set up his own organisation, Let's Face It, to share real-life experiences of the dangers associated with drug and alcohol abuse, and offer perspective on dealing with trauma, stress and depression.

East Belfast GAA continued to show the way forward for cross-community harmony in the north, attracting even more members and maintaining support for impoverished children and inclusion for all.

Crowds couldn't get enough of big games. For the 2022 Munster hurling final between Limerick and Clare, 11,000 terrace tickets sold out in eleven minutes. The Ulster football final saw Donegal sell a record number of tickets ahead of their meeting with Derry. Both provincial finals were complete sell-outs.

David Brady's call requests are not as demanding these days but he's never far away from a phone charger at the same time. By ringing around, spreading a bit of cheer and chatting about Gaelic football, Brady compiled a colourful catalogue of Irish life. 'I think I got more out of those calls than anyone I rang,' he insists.

'Here's one last story. I was onto a man from Charlestown late in 2021 just to see how he was keeping, but he never really answered that question! He took off telling me about how much Mayo football meant to him and the whole family.

'The lot of them loved Mayo. So much so that his daughter – who had married a Roscommon man and moved there – actually moved back to Mayo before their first child arrived because she couldn't handle the child being born in Roscommon.' Brady laughs heartily. 'Jaysus, how could you not love that?'

Normal business resumed in Croke Park.

Peter McKenna set about repositioning the stadium as a major live venue and announced seven concerts for 2022, featuring two Ed Sheeran and five Garth Brooks gigs. More than 160,000 turned out for the Sheeran concerts alone, whilst the whole country seemed to have bought tickets for the Brooks events.

Feargal McGill and the administration turned their attention to domestic matters again. The agenda was as busy as ever. The restructuring of the football championship, the introduction of the Tailteann Cup in 2022, driving integration with camogie and ladies' football, and agreeing a players' charter with the GPA until 2023 were all priorities.

Sponsorships were retained and new deals announced. A new broadcast rights deal from 2023 onwards was blueprinted shortly after a five-year strategic plan was unveiled by the association.

Despite huge losses of €33 million for 2021 and a €34 million deficit for 2020, the GAA was off the ropes. There were several knock-on effects, including e-ticketing, which not everyone is over the moon about, split seasons, direct communication between Croke Park and clubs, and working from home – a trend that should significantly boost rural clubs.

Expectations of further winds of the virus are never too far away but will hopefully only amount to a thunder that roars in the distant background.

Ultimately, though, perspective is what Feargal McGill feels the whole experience delivered.

'Chasing county and All-Ireland titles is a fantastic thing and it captivates our people,' he says. 'But it is not life or death. And we need to remember that. It's fantastic to be involved in the pursuit of development, but there is no point in taking someone's head off either. Maybe we had lost our way a little bit in that regard.'

The storm had passed, the great upheaval was behind us and there was calm again.

The skies looked clear. And when we look up now, maybe we see things a little differently.

ACKNOWLEDGEMENTS

I would like to thank everyone who helped me write this book.

To Professor Paul Rouse for his continuous help, expertise and encouragement.

To my friends and colleagues Pat Nolan, Mike Finnerty, Garry Doyle and Damien O'Meara for their offers of help and encouragement along the way. To Paul Clarkson, Government Press Secretary, for his assistance. Thanks as always to Siobhán Brady for her continued support.

Everyone at Black & White Publishing approached this project with their usual enthusiasm and professionalism. Thanks to you all.

Thanks to Declan McBennett, head of RTÉ Sport, for his support.

So many people shared their stories and experiences of dealing with life in a pandemic and you can read their personal insights here. Without them, their recollections, co-operation and trust, this publication would have gone no further than just forming the seed for another idea.

Writing a book is never easy and only for so many of the GAA community being so helpful and courteous, this one certainly would never have seen the light of day.

Ultimately, I felt it was important to tell the story of the GAA in covid times. I covered every detail of the association's plight and recovery during the pandemic for RTÉ and that's where this book originated from. It was a remarkable time and shook many of us upside down. Hopefully, the personal and human stories, the tales of resilience in the face of what was experienced, shine through.

I was lucky enough to have grown up with the GAA, mainly through my late father, John, who passed away in 2019. Dad was a low-key stalwart, mentor and administrator, who worked behind the scenes all of his life for Nenagh, Kilruane MacDonaghs and Tipperary. My mother, Mary, and my siblings, Sean, David and Collette (it would have been no different for our late baby sister, Elizabeth!) all accepted that the family home in Lisgarode was like a temporary GAA office at the best of times with jerseys on the line, tickets in the hallstand, managers, selectors, players and chairmen coming in and out. Water bottles in the boot of the car, substitution slips – mainly for myself – in my father's pocket. Sure, it was an ideal upbringing.

Now my own family in Naas – my wife, Ruth, and our three lovely children, Jamie, Chloe and Aaron – also find our days revolving around hurling, football, camogie and ladies' football. Each of the kids has thrived with their own involvement in the GAA and when covid hit we were again reminded in our house just how important the association was. No different all around the country, I am sure.

ABOUT THE AUTHOR

Damian Lawlor is a bestselling author and sports broadcaster with RTÉ. He comes from Kilruane in County Tipperary and lives with his family in Naas, County Kildare. This is his eighth book.

ALSO BY DAMIAN LAWLOR

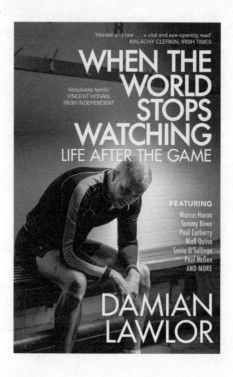

'Honest and raw . . . a vital and eye-opening read'
MALACHY CLERKIN, IRISH TIMES

'Absolutely terrific'
VINCENT HOGAN, IRISH INDEPENDENT

'A captivating insight into the struggles faced
when Irish sports stars retire'
EDDIE O'SULLIVAN